Marx and the Common

Historical Materialism Book Series

The Historical Materialism Book Series is a major publishing initiative of the radical left. The capitalist crisis of the twenty-first century has been met by a resurgence of interest in critical Marxist theory. At the same time, the publishing institutions committed to Marxism have contracted markedly since the high point of the 1970s. The Historical Materialism Book Series is dedicated to addressing this situation by making available important works of Marxist theory. The aim of the series is to publish important theoretical contributions as the basis for vigorous intellectual debate and exchange on the left.

The peer-reviewed series publishes original monographs, translated texts, and reprints of classics across the bounds of academic disciplinary agendas and across the divisions of the left. The series is particularly concerned to encourage the internationalization of Marxist debate and aims to translate significant studies from beyond the English-speaking world.

For a full list of titles in the Historical Materialism Book Series available in paperback from Haymarket Books, visit:
www.haymarketbooks.org/category/hm-series

Marx and the Common

From Capital *to the Late Writings*

Luca Basso

Translated by David Broder

Haymarket Books
Chicago, IL

First published in 2015 by Brill Academic Publishers, The Netherlands
© 2015 Koninklijke Brill NV, Leiden, The Netherlands

Published in paperback in 2016 by
Haymarket Books
P.O. Box 180165
Chicago, IL 60618
773-583-7884
www.haymarketbooks.org

ISBN: 978-1-60846-695-5

Trade distribution:
In the US, Consortium Book Sales, www.cbsd.com
In Canada, Publishers Group Canada, www.pgcbooks.ca
In the UK, Turnaround Publisher Services, www.turnaround-uk.com
In all other countries, Publishers Group Worldwide, www.pgw.com

Cover design by Jamie Kerry of Belle Étoile Studios and Ragina Johnson.

This book was published with the generous support of Lannan Foundation
and the Wallace Action Fund.

Printed in Canada by union labor.

10 9 8 7 6 5 4 3 2 1

Library of Congress Cataloging-in-Publication data is available.

MIX
Paper from
responsible sources
FSC   FSC® C103567
www.fsc.org

Contents

Introduction

[According to Le Chapelier, giving the decree of 14 June 1791 in France] the workers must not be allowed to come to any understanding about their own interests, nor to act in common and thereby lessen their 'absolute dependence, which is almost that of slavery'.

Capital, Volume 1

• • •

Now, since the state is merely a transitional institution of which use is made in the struggle, in the revolution, to keep down one's enemies by force, it is utter nonsense to speak of a free people's state; so long as the proletariat still *makes use* of the state, it makes use of it, not for the purpose of freedom, but of keeping down its enemies and, as soon as there can be any question of freedom, the state as such ceases to exist. We would therefore suggest that *Gemeinwesen* ['commonalty'] be universally substituted for *state*; it is a good old German word that can very well do service for the French 'Commune'.

FRIEDRICH ENGELS to August Bebel, 18–28 March 1875

∵

Recent years have seen a renewed interest in Marx, not least on account of the world economic crisis. This followed the years of *damnatio memoriae* that resulted from the failure of 'actually-existing socialism' and the uncritical acceptance of capitalist domination as the only possible future. Certainly, rethinking the problems that Marx posed does require casting off the old orthodoxies, but it is important that we do so without giving up on the destructive power of his thought. A rigorous historical and theoretical analysis of Marx's texts does not necessarily mean signing up to a 'depoliticised' vision of Marx, the 'classic philosopher'. Nor does consciousness of the crisis in the Marxism–workers' movement–communist party plexus necessarily lead to some Manichean counterposition between Marx and Marxism, holding the man himself in high esteem while seeing Marxism from Engels onward as a mere mystification of some supposed original 'message'. To appreciate Marx has always meant taking a non-neutral, non-equidistant position, and thus the Marxisms with the most vitality have always sought to 'rerun' Marx's reflection on the basis of the historical and political conjuncture that they themselves faced. Moreover, the perspective that Marx set out is intrinsically political, as the afterword to the second edition of *Capital* makes clear: 'In so far as Political Economy remains within that horizon, in so far, i.e., as the capitalist regime is looked upon as the absolutely final form of social production, instead of as a passing historical phase of its evolution, Political Economy can remain a science only so long as the class struggle is latent or manifests itself only in isolated and sporadic phenomena'. Marx's text 'admits' to setting out from the point of view of the proletariat, which cannot just be grafted on to the bourgeois standpoint. It envisages a material transformation of the present situation, on the basis of a continual exchange between the analysis and the breaking-apart of the real.

However, no recognition of the 'class' character of Marx's reflection and its drive to revolutionise existing assumptions should neglect the overall theoretical plane on which his critique of political economy is based. His evaluation of the working class's political role does not stand in isolation from the conceptual structure of his critique of political economy: working-class subjectivity cannot be articulated and practised without a full exploration of the 'spectral objectivity' of the capitalist mode of production. As such, in conceiving the theory-praxis relationship, it is necessary to take account not only of the connection between these dimensions, but also of the fact that they do not directly match: neither dimension can be deduced from the other. In this sense, we ought also to bear in mind the possible separation of theory from politics. The difficulty inherent within this question derives from the fact that even though Marx's critique of political economy is of political significance, we cannot immediately deduce politics from the critique of political economy. Two perspectives that both forcefully pose the problem of the relation between theory and practice – though they are different, or even irreconcilable – are the perspectives of Louis Althusser (and his school) and of Italian *operaismo*. Moreover, not only do we face the possibility of a 'split' between these elements, but we also need to understand that the real is not immediately visible and transparent, since the capitalist mode of production presents an opaque character – as becomes clear in Marx's analysis of fetishism, in his polemic with classical political economy.

It is based on these coordinates that this book, set out in four chapters, examines the relationship between the individual and communal dimensions, and thus the intersection of the individual, class, society, and community, as discussed by Marx from the 1860s onward. Though a fully freestanding work, from the chronological point of view it picks up from *Marx and Singularity*,[1] which revolved around Marx's journey from his first texts to the *Grundrisse*. Indeed, the object of the present book is both *Capital* and Marx's late historical-political writings, attributing particular importance to his reflection on the state and the political activity of the working class, with reference to events like the Paris Commune and to organisations like the First International. From these emerged a 'Marxist' politics that not only had its own internal difficulties, but proved clearly irreconcilable with either Bakuninite anarchism or Lassallean statism. I then consider – as well as numerous texts linked to specific conjunctures, among them particularly telling ones revolving around his analysis of Russia – his extracts on the natural sciences, *in primis* the so-called *Ethnological Notebooks*. In this sense, the question of anthropology does not only play an abstractly philosophical role, but rather resonates with its constant encounter with politics *sans phrases* as well as with the natural and social sciences of the time. Furthermore, these writings are useful in studying the question of the forms of 'the common', on the basis of an articulated vision of the historical scenario, which is not reducible to Western-European experiences. In the book's subtitle, I have used the expression 'the late Marx' to denote the period we are here addressing, though the 1860s are also part of our object of analysis, and not only the final years of his output. I have preferred to use this terminology in order to avoid falling into a static (and, in some regards, sterile) counterposition between the 'young' and the 'mature' Marx, since I am convinced that there is a substantial continuity throughout Marx's trajectory, even if it is not linear and unproblematic.

Following the complex relationship between theory and politics, we will seek to examine the relation between the individual and the community, as it concretely appears with its determinate characteristics within the capitalist mode of production – that is, in its specific difference with regard to the forms of production that preceded it. If these latter were distinguished by the unity of man and the community, the capitalist system is, instead, founded on a structural element of separation: a division that concerns not only the relation between individuals and the means of production, but also the relation between each individual and their own capacity to labour. The question of class plays a crucial function in this terrain, a role that cannot be hypostatised at either the ontological or the sociological level, since it poses itself in intrinsically political terms. Moreover, capitalism is the first mode of production in which antagonism (which is often latent, and not *in actu*) is not

---

1   Basso 2012.

just an effect of its dynamic, but its very condition: society is based on a division into two, an irreconcilable 'contradiction in process' between capital and labour. Within this situation, there emerges a potentially expansive declination of living labour, insofar as the use-value of labour power is not only directed toward the valorisation of capital, but can also constitute a disruptive opposition to capital, 'breaking' its 'dead mechanism'. Of course, labour power is not a possession, but rather is sold as the temporal availability of a subject – the worker. The worker is thus left deprived of the means of production: the capitalist buys something that only exists as a possibility, which is, however, inseparable from the living personality of the *Arbeiter*. There is, then, an element that can never be 'cashed in', since the worker's body can never be fully 'captured'.

References to communism continuously traverse this horizon, even though Marx rarely described it in any detail and even though there are a number of ambiguities in this regard. Essentially, there are two ways in which he articulated this question. The first – to use the formulation given in the *German Ideology* – sees communism as 'the real movement which abolishes the present state of things', that is, it pulls apart the *status quo*, on the basis of a continual political 'investment' in the moments of working-class subjectivation. The second poses communism as organisation, an institution capable of giving rise to a communal government that allows these practices to 'sediment', rather than dispersing irrecoverably. Insofar as 'social individuals' cannot be considered able to act in a purely spontaneous manner, communism refers also to the existence of a plan by which they can control social production. Taking this approach, it is necessary firstly to grasp the anticipatory character of struggles that take place within capitalism but which are communist in tendency, and, on the other hand, to be fully aware of communism's discontinuity with regard to capitalism.

What we are attempting to do, here, is to articulate the 'acting in common', the *Gemeinsam handeln* (to use an expression cited at the top of this introduction, from Marx's chapter on accumulation) of working-class singularities, in their differentiation, in their non-seriality and antithesis, when faced with wage labour and the state form in which individuals are subsumed to the 'social power' of money. We should be aware that in the present situation there is no unique and universal subject, and thus the question of subjectivity is an extremely complex and articulated one, irreducible to any immediate solution or the easy identification of a 'way out'. Moreover, in this context, we also ought to register the global dimension of struggles, rejecting any type of communalism that is either functional to the state dynamic or else purely reactive to it. For Marx, communism was not posed as an ahistorical end, but rather as part of history: and for this reason, 'being in common' [*Gemeinwesen*] could not be determined once and for all, but rather had to be recalibrated for each particular situation, and constantly open to rectification. In any case, the tendency towards the realisation of working-class singularities does not imply a sort of 'ethics' of labour, but on the contrary a radical challenge to such a logic, adequate to a potentially ever more all-pervasive dominion of capital:

> If we may take an example from outside the sphere of production of material objects, a schoolmaster is a productive labourer when, in addition to belabouring the heads of his scholars, he works like a horse to enrich the school proprietor. That the latter has laid out his capital in a teaching factory, instead of in a sausage factory, does not alter the relation ... To be a productive labourer is, therefore, not a piece of luck, but a misfortune.[2]

---

2   *MECW*, Vol. 35, p. 510.

Fetishism and Subjects: Between Reality and Mystification

At a different level of reality, Marxism seemed to me to proceed in the same way as geology and psycho-analysis ... All three showed that ... true reality is never the most obvious of realities, and that its nature is already apparent in the care which it takes to evade our detection.

CLAUDE LÉVI-STRAUSS, *A World on the Wane*

•
• •

The 'Enigma' of the Commodity

Throughout all of Marx's *oeuvre* he was attentive to the individual dimension, from his first texts up until *Capital*. His outlook on this question was based on a constitutive ambivalence in the capitalist mode of production: on the one hand, the individual is configured as a *novum* with respect to the previous productive forms, in which man was linked to his own community as if by an 'umbilical cord'; yet on the other hand, there now appeared the other 'face' of social power, materialised in money. As such, the development of the individual and his subsumption under capital represent two sides of the same coin. Moreover, the concept of individuality itself has a dual register. It not only represents the polemical reference point of Marx's discourse, but also connotes the perspective that he is himself articulating. After all, far from posing communism in organicist terms, throughout each phase of Marx's itinerary he understood it to mean individuals' full realisation – or, to use a terminology drawn from contemporary French philosophy, the full realisation of the 'singularities' as they 'act in common'. We see this from his delineation of 'individuals as individuals' in the *German Ideology* to the 'social individuals' to which he

---

1 Repeated long visits to the Berlin *Staatsbibliothek* were fundamental to the realisation of this book. I would also particularly like to thank – for their attentive reading and insightful discussion of this text – Michele Basso, Ferruccio Gambino, Cristina Marras, Fabio Raimondi and Maurizio Ricciardi.

refers in the *Grundrisse*.[2] He further elaborated his conception of individuality in *Capital*, in continuity with his previous reflection but also by adding new elements. A study of fetishism – in its both economic and juridical manifestations – is of no little use for the purposes of understanding this. Such an analysis will bring to light a significant aspect of Marx's reasoning, namely the crucial importance of the dimension of opacity, based on the interlinking of reality and mystification.

A section of the very first chapter of *Capital* Volume I is devoted to the question of fetishism, 'The fetishism of commodities and the secret thereof'. In his *Afterword to the second German edition*, Marx emphasises that he had made important changes to the pages in question: 'A commodity appears, at first sight, a very trivial thing, and easily understood. Its analysis shows that it is, in reality, a very queer thing, abounding in metaphysical subtleties and theological niceties ... The mystical character of commodities does not originate, therefore, in their use value. Just as little does it proceed from the nature of the determining factors of value'.[3] Its enigmatic character derives from the form of the commodity itself.

> ... A commodity is therefore a mysterious thing, simply because in it the social character of men's labour appears to them as an objective character stamped upon the product of that labour; because the relation of the producers to the sum total of their own labour is presented to them as a natural social relation [*gesellschaftliche Natureigenschaften*] ... between the products of their labour. This is the reason why the products of labour become commodities, social things whose qualities are at the same time perceptible and imperceptible by the senses.[4]

Before delving into a specific analysis of fetishism, it is worth examining the commodity, which plays a crucially important role within the logic of Marx's discourse. Indeed, *Capital* begins by representing the capitalist mode of production as an 'immense accumulation of commodities'; and the single commodity constitutes the 'elementary form' of this mode of production.

> The wealth of those societies in which the capitalist mode of production prevails, presents itself as 'an immense accumulation of commodities'

---

2   See Basso 2001, 2008a/2012.

3   *MECW*, Vol. 35, p. 82.

4   *MECW*, Vol. 35, pp. 82–3.

[*eine ungeheure Warensammlung*], its unit being a single commodity. Our investigation must therefore begin with the analysis of a commodity.

A commodity is, in the first place, an object outside us, a thing that by its properties satisfies human wants of some sort or another. The nature of such wants, whether, for instance, they spring from the stomach or from fancy, makes no difference. Neither are we here concerned to know how the object satisfies these wants, whether directly as means of subsistence, or indirectly as means of production.[5]

Here we might ask why Marx's discussion begins by addressing the commodity. Marx himself provides one first answer to this question, in his 1867 *Preface to the first German edition* of Volume I:

Every beginning is difficult, holds in all sciences. To understand the first chapter, especially the section that contains the analysis of commodities, will, therefore, present the greatest difficulty ... In the analysis of economic forms, moreover, neither microscopes nor chemical reagents are of use. The force of abstraction must replace both. But in bourgeois society, the commodity-form of the product of labour – or value-form of the commodity – is the economic cell-form.[6]

Two themes in particular emerge from this passage: Marx's use of a method based on abstraction, and his recognition of the 'cell' character of the commodity.

As concerns the first of these themes, it is worth remembering that Marx's method was based on advancing from the abstract to the concrete: for example, in the 1857 *Einleitung* he stressed that 'The concrete is concrete because it is a synthesis of many determinations, thus a unity of the diverse. In thinking, it therefore appears as a process of summing-up, as a result, not as the starting point, ... the method of advancing from the abstract to the concrete is simply the way in which thinking assimilates the concrete and reproduces it as a mental concrete'.[7] He thus delineates a form of logic that allows us to arrive at the concrete by taking the most abstract category as our starting point. Marx's

---

5 *MECW*, Vol. 35, p. 45.

6 *MECW*, Vol. 35, p. 7.

7 *MECW*, Vol. 28, p. 38. On the importance of the 1857 *Einleitung* for understanding Marx's method, see the various interpretations in Della Volpe 1964, Althusser 1969, Rovatti 1973, Negri 1991, and Jánoska (ed.) 1994. On the relation between abstract and concrete in *Capital*, see Ilyenkov 1982.

exposition is not identified with a determinate historical trend and is not of a phenomenal character, but, instead, indicates the conceptual development of the commodity. In this regard, it is worth drawing a distinction between exposition and inquiry: to cite the *Afterword to the second German edition*: 'the method of presentation must differ in form from that of inquiry. The latter has to appropriate the material in detail, to analyse its different forms of development, to trace out their inner connection. Only after this work is done, can the actual movement be adequately described'.[8]

Marx had for years engaged in research into the existing documentation and the facts to which it attested, and in so doing he followed down paths which do not appear in his results, since his object of inquiry was the capitalist mode of production itself. The paths in question do appear, in part, in his notes and references. Such research could begin from the 'concrete', since it had 'to appropriate the material in detail'. In *Capital*, however, Marx sought to explicate the internal logic of the process of his discoveries, by way of demonstration: his analysis began from the abstract. If he had instead immediately begun from the 'real and concrete' then we would find ourselves confronted with a confused, indistinct picture of reality. But categories reproduce – ideally – the relations of the really concrete.[9] As will soon become clear, this approach is far from any sort of 'logicism' impermeable to history and politics:[10] to recognise the pertinence of abstraction for the purposes of understanding Marx's method does not imply that we are dealing with an ahistorical conception.[11] To return

---

8   MECW, Vol, 35, p. 19. On the question of presentation – which is not to be understood in 'composite' terms – see Macherey 1965.

9   See Schwarz 1978.

10   The so-called 'logic' school in Germany (in particular Backhaus and Reichelt) has insisted on the logical structure of Marx's reflection, on the fact that he does not start out from empirically tangible data. In particular see Backhaus 1997, Reichelt 1970, and Reichelt 2008. Heinrich (for example 2004, 2008), though using a different method and arriving at partially different results, also sets the theory of value at the basis of his reflection on *Capital*, examining the (successful or otherwise) overcoming of Ricardian economic theory. While necessarily some differences do exist, this approach interacts with the Anglo-Saxon neo-dialectical framework: see in particular Arthur 2002. For a critique of Hegelian readings of Marxism, see Micocci 2009. The perspective developed in this chapter is not in harmony with the 'logicist' approach, which though aptly bringing to light some of the distinctive characteristics of Marx's reasoning, such as the link between value and money, provides a 'theoreticist' interpretation of *Capital* at the expense of its real political significance.

11   See Michaud 1960, which rightly insists on the significance of the historical dimension of *Capital*, in a polemic against any 'theoreticist' interpretation: 'after discovering the funda-

to the question of the commodity *qua* elementary form, the unit of use-value and exchange-value, it is worth making clear that:

> Use values become a reality only by use or consumption: they also constitute the substance of all wealth, whatever may be the social form of that wealth. In the form of society we are about to consider, they are, in addition, the material depositories of exchange value.
>
> Exchange value, at first sight, presents itself as a quantitative relation, as the proportion in which values in use of one sort are exchanged for those of another sort ...[12]

What is new in Marx is not the fact that he expresses such ideas,[13] but rather the specific way in which he structures his reasoning. The commodity, use-value and exchange-value, or better, use-value and value, constitute the element that more than any other allows us to think 'material content' together with 'social form'. Besides, in his *Notes on Adolph Wagner* Marx points out that 'Mr. Wagner also forgets that for me neither "value" nor "exchange-value" are subjects, but *the commodity*'.[14] But we must note another aspect on top of this one – a consideration present in a previously cited passage – where Marx states that the commodity is the 'elementary form' of the capitalist mode of production.

From the perspective of the totality – the capitalist mode of production – the commodity is a 'cell', which is thus still incomplete and must undergo transformations in order to attain full development.[15] To grasp what capitalism is, we need to understand that the commodity functions as its genetic material. After all, in the first chapter of Volume I – the object of our analysis – the commodity is defined as 'the most general and most embryonic form of bourgeois production'.[16] In the *Grundrisse*, Marx stated that 'The first category in which bourgeois wealth makes its appearance is that of the commodity',[17] and in the *Einleitung* he said that 'It would ... be inexpedient and wrong to present the economic categories successively in the order in which they have played the dominant

---

mental traits of capitalism it was necessary for his exposition to draw a close connection between history and theory' (p. 199). See also Vilar 1978, particularly pp. 88–90.

12   *MECW*, Vol. 35, p. 46.

13   We should remember that it was not Marx who first adopted the concepts of use- and exchange-value: see Smith 1976.

14   *MECW*, Vol. 24, p. 534.

15   See Vygotsky 1965.

16   *MECW*, Vol. 35, p. 93.

17   *MECW*, Vol. 29, p. 252.

role in history. Their order of succession is determined rather by their mutual relation [*Beziehung*] in modern bourgeois society, and this is quite the reverse of what appears to be their natural relation or corresponds to the sequence of historical development'.[18]

Here we see Marx's awareness of a 'gap' (which does not necessarily imply an inversion in the proper sense, as the passage we just quoted may seem to suggest) between the real object and the object of knowledge, thus challenging the 'ideological' myth of an immediate mutual correspondence between the two planes.[19] In this sense, the order of the concepts here presented is not directly related to the order in which they appeared historically. The starting point of Marx's exposition is the essential determinations of capitalism, which are also its most simple and abstract (commodity, value) determinations. In his *Theories of Surplus-Value* Marx maintains that this genetical presentation is a re-elaboration of the results provided by his analysis, which is 'the necessary prerequisite of genetical presentation, and of the understanding of the real, formative process in its different phases'.[20] As such, the relation between logic and history is no simple question: exchange-value is constituted, on the plane of logical validation, in the sphere of production, but genetically it originates in the sphere of circulation, through the connection that communities establish with the outside world. There is a complex relationship between genesis and logical validation, not a straightforward one.[21] In terms of historical development, it is land ownership that precedes capital; but at the level of systemic immanence, capital is preceded by value.

In this regard, it is necessary to proceed from our previous considerations concerning the structure of the commodity *qua* 'elementary form': it is simple, but also embryonic of the total development of capitalist society, following a logical-genetic modality. As Marx makes clear at the beginning of *Capital*, this situation is realised within the capitalist mode of production. He is thus referring specifically to this mode of production, since although commodities did also exist in precapitalist orders, only with capitalism did the commodity become the dominant structure. The starting point to *Capital* is to be found not in the concept of the commodity, but in the forms that the various different objects that play the role of commodities within capitalism take. As we can see from Marx's *Notes on Adolph Wagner*, his analysis of these elements compels him to seek out the practical conditions of possibility of commodity exchange:

---

18   *MECW*, Vol. 28, p. 44.
19   See Althusser 1970.
20   *MECW*, Vol. 32, p. 500.
21   See Krahl 1971.

> I do not proceed from 'concepts', hence neither from the 'concept of value', and am therefore in no way concerned to 'divide' it. What I proceed from is the simplest social form in which the product of labour presents itself in contemporary society, and this is the '*commodity*' ... my *analytic* method, which does not proceed from *man* but from a given economic period of society, has nothing in common with the German-professorial association-of-concepts method ...[22]

His starting point is thus the commodity in *Konkretum*, not the commodity as a concept. In *Capital*, the commodity is conceived as a unit of use-value, material content; and of value, social form. The division of labour is not, however, a sufficient condition for commodity production: the producers must be autonomous and independent, each of them the owner of what they produce. The commodity is, in the first place, a product to be exchanged: the result of the labouring process creates a use-value not for those who have realised it, but for others: social use-value. The commodity is a commodity only if it is consumed by others, meaning, if it is exchanged. Only thanks to the mediation of exchange does the product become a commodity: if the product remains in the hands of the seller, it does not become a commodity. A further clarification is necessary, in this regard:

> So far as it is a value in use, there is nothing mysterious about [the commodity] ... It is as clear as noon-day, that man, by his industry, changes the forms of the materials furnished by Nature, in such a way as to make them useful to him ... The mystical character of commodities does not originate, therefore, in their use value. Just as little does it proceed from the nature of the determining factors of value.[23]

In order to understand the 'mystery' of the commodity, which does not derive from its 'content' but its 'form', it is thus worth further examining the category of value. In the first chapter of *Capital*, Marx establishes a clear distinction between value and exchange-value: indeed, he states that the two concepts should not be considered identical. Exchange-value is a quantitative relation, through which 'values in use of one sort are exchanged for those of another sort': it appears to be 'something accidental and purely relative'.[24] '[E]xchange

---

22   *MECW*, Vol. 24, pp. 544–7.

23   *MECW*, Vol. 35, pp. 81–2.

24   *MECW*, Vol. 35, p. 46.

value, generally, is only the mode of expression, the phenomenal form, of something contained in it, yet distinguishable from it'.[25] As values, all commodities are qualitatively equal and only quantitatively different: and it is precisely this qualitative homogeneity that makes it possible to exchange one for another in determinate quantitative proportions. It is the commodity that *has* value, just as it is abstract human labour (the historical form of labour) that *creates* value: the objectivity of value is not a physical characteristic of the product, but a social element of the commodity. To *be* value, the commodity has to enter into contact with other commodities. Value is the quality common to all commodities; it exists by way of commodities. The substance of value is constituted by the labour that is socially necessary for the production of commodities. Here we have, on the one hand, the commodity as a relative form, the incarnation of use-value; and on the other, in the form of a general equivalent, the incarnation of value. Only when its own value appears in relation to another commodity does the commodity truly express itself as such.

So we need to make a rigorous distinction between the substance – the essence represented by value, which is proper to the commodity and not the product – and its phenomenal form – constituted by exchange-value, expressing the quantity of social labour objectified within the commodity. The essence of things and their phenomenal form do not immediately coincide. Marx, unlike the classical economists, shows that he recognises the opacity of the real: essence and phenomenon are non-identical.[26] Marx's reference to the real not being immediately evident is crucial for his subsequent discussion of fetishism. The immediate phenomenal forms of money and products conceal an essence: value. I cannot see or hear value: it is not empirically perceptible, and yet it subsumes use-values. Value abstracts concrete use-values, individuals, and needs of an intrinsically social character: 'Value, therefore, does not stalk about with a label describing what it is. It is value, rather, that converts every product into a social hieroglyphic'.[27] It presents both a qualitative and a quantitative dimension: the former, as emerges from what we saw already (but ignored by classical political economy) is expressed in the idea of the 'social hieroglyphic', and thus is connected to the social quality of the commodity. Yet there also exists a quantitative plane, regarding its extent: since abstract human labour is the substance of value, its extent is indicated by the labour time that is socially necessary to produce a determinate commodity – or, better, to reproduce it.

---

25   *MECW*, Vol. 35, p. 47.

26   See Geras 1971, Vinci 2011, pp. 112–13.

27   *MECW*, Vol. 35, p. 85.

It is worth specifying that the difference between value and exchange-value did not persist unchanged throughout Marx's whole *oeuvre*, but was a relatively late acquisition. Without reconstructing its various stages, I will limit myself to pointing out that even in the *Grundrisse* Marx employed value and exchange-value more-or-less indifferently, without attributing them clearly distinct functions: he even often used 'exchange-value' to mean something similar to 'value'. Between the first and second edition of Volume I of *Capital* there was a shift, in this regard, with telling alterations: in the first edition (1867), though he had introduced such a distinction – which had previously been lacking – he did not always deploy it in a rigorous and coherent manner, and these terms were sometimes confused and overlapped. In the second edition (1872), however, Marx emphasised that the commodity was the contradictory unity of use-value and value, not of use-value and exchange-value, as is often claimed in reconstructions of Marx's reflection. In his *Notes on Adolph Wagner*, Marx clearly states that 'the "*commodity*," is on the one hand, use-value and on the other, "value", not exchange value, since the mere *form* of appearance is not its own *content* ... "exchange-value" is ... only the form of appearance of value, and not "value" itself, since for me the "value" of a commodity is neither its use-value nor its exchange value'.[28] An awareness of this differentiation between value and exchange-value makes it apparent that the latter is only one manifestation of the former, and is not identical to it. The discussion we have elaborated thus far now allows us to delve into the problematic of fetishism, since within the formulation of the chapter in question this represents a sort of consequence of the commodity's own dynamics.

The Question of Fetishism: Another Name for 'Ideology'?

If the commodity is the unity of use-value, 'material content', and of value, 'social form', then its 'mystery' derives not from its 'content' – its use-value – but from its 'form', namely 'value'. As such, this 'mystery' should not be located within the dimension of utility, in the 'material content of wealth'. As values, all commodities are qualitatively equal and only quantitatively different: and it is precisely this qualitative homogeneity that makes it possible to exchange one for another in determinate quantitative proportions. It is the commodity that *has* value, just as it is abstract human labour (the historical form of labour) that *creates* value. These points should bring into clear definition the nexus among

---

28   *MECW*, Vol. 24, p. 545.

value, sociality, abstract human labour and the 'spectral objectivity' of the capitalist mode of production. The objectivity of value is not a physical characteristic of the product, but a social element of the commodity. Value, abstract human labour, a social rather than a physical reality, can be expressed only in a form that dissimulates it and makes it appear as a natural property of things.

> ... it is a definite social relation between men, that assumes, in their eyes, the fantastic form of a relation between things [*das bestimmte gesellschaftliche Verhältnis*]. In order, therefore, to find an analogy, we must have recourse to the mist-enveloped regions of the religious world. In that world the productions of the human brain appear as independent beings endowed with life, and entering into relation both with one another and the human race. So it is in the world of commodities with the products of men's hands. This I call the Fetishism which attaches itself to the products of labour, so soon as they are produced as commodities, and which is therefore inseparable from the production of commodities ... This Fetishism of commodities has its origin, as the foregoing analysis has already shown, in the peculiar social character of the labour that produces them.[29]

Marx emphasises that for the producers 'the relations connecting the labour of one individual with that of the rest appear, not as direct social relations between individuals at work, but as what they really are, material relations between persons and social relations between things'.[30] Behind this 'fetishistic' element lies the question of the transformation of products into commodities. If we want to link the position just outlined to Marx's overall analysis concerning the structure of the commodity, then clearly we must try to grasp the specificity of the problem of fetishism.

One important aspect of Marx's reflection is the relationship between representation and reality.[31] For a first approach to this question, we should con-

---

29   *MECW*, Vol. 35, p. 83.

30   *MECW*, Vol. 35, p. 84.

31   I should specify that in this chapter I substantially use the terms 'reality' and 'the real' synonymously, inasmuch as there was no distinction between them in Marx: the two dimensions mutually penetrate one another, and their intersection does not regard only theory in the strict sense, given that they are 'thought in practice' on the basis of a continuous 'exchange' between conceptual analysis and revolutionary transformation. In any case, I do consider the Lacanian distinction between reality – with its imaginary character – and the real – what actually takes place, on the basis of action – to be in

sider an analogy with the world of religion: the religious way of thinking spontaneously represents the non-intentional, non-human reality of nature as a world of persons, and moreover attributes an independent, objective existence to ideal realities that do not really exist as such. Marx conceived of religion as a fantastical aspect of social life, an illusory representation of the internal structures of social relations and of nature: religious thought and practice in reality constitute the product of determinate social relations.[32] In order to look deeper into this question, it might be useful to make brief reference to the historical origin of the notion of fetishism. I will limit myself to underlining the fact that the term appeared for the first time in a 1760 work by Charles de Brosses, *Du Culte des Dieux fétiches*, which analyses the religions of primitive peoples. In this context, 'fetishism' designated a primitive form of religion consisting in the veneration of inanimate things, plants and animals: this concept derives from *feitiço* [fetish], the term that the Portuguese used as early as the sixteenth century to denote the objects worshipped by the peoples of Western Africa. De Brosses attempted a synthesis of comparative analyses among peoples and cultures: in his view, the primitive expressions of humanity, including religious ones, ought to be analysed according to a schema of gradual progress from barbarism to civilisation. De Brosses located fetishism at the origin of religious belief, and it was defined by the absence of representation: it was the first, crude form of religion, precisely because these objects were idolised as such.[33]

It is worth emphasising that Marx had already as early as 1842 read some texts concerning the theme of fetishism, including a German translation of De Brosses's essay, and reproduced extracts from it. In his article 'Debates on the Law on Thefts of Wood', we can see clear evidence of his reading of this work. We ought not forget (among other things) that although Marx dealt with the notion of fetishism at length in the first chapter of *Capital* Volume I, this was no recent acquisition of his, having appeared in his youthful writings.[34] For example, in the 1844 *Manuscripts* 'fetishist' was used as a synonym for 'Catholic'; in the third manuscript, indeed, Marx defined Adam Smith the 'Luther of political economy' for having 'acknowledged *labour* as [his] principle', whereas 'the adherents of the monetary and mercantile system ... seem to be *fetish-*

---

part useful for the purposes of rearticulating his reasoning. Lacan 1975 is of particular significance, with regard to the reality/real relation.

32   See Godelier 1975, which examines Marx's analysis of fetishism in relation to the religious question, in many ways taking his lead from Lévi-Strauss's structuralist framework. For a more all-embracing perspective, see Lévi-Strauss 1963–76.

33   Brosses 1988; see Iacono 1985.

34   See Garo 2000a, 2000b, Garo 2012, pp. 165–184, Vincent 1973, Apter and Pietz (eds.) 1993, Assoun 2002, and Artous 2006.

ists, Catholics.[35] In Marx's early texts, fetishism designates an archaic, primitive stage, or else a backward, 'reactionary' conception, as in the case of the passage just cited. Whereas in these early texts Marx based himself on Feuerbach's analysis of religious representations, later he devoted himself to a re-elaboration, which also meant problematising this question.

As such, fetishism became the intermediate term that united the capitalist mode of production and exchange with the individual representations capable of ensuring its functioning and its reproduction: and this cannot, therefore, be considered a primitive form. With the passing of time, Marx radically rethought this concept, which could not be 'relegated' to a primitive epoch or reduced to a merely residual element that declined with the full development of capitalism. Fetishism consists, instead, in the understanding that the relations between humans are, in reality, relations between things: to the producers 'the relations connecting the labour of one individual with that of the rest appear ... as what they really are, material relations between persons and social relations between things'.[36] So fetishism is a representation that occupies a crucial function in the social and economic structure: the very nature of social relations is left opaque, or, to be more precise, becomes intelligible in a false manner.[37] Here Marx is talking about the capitalist mode of production, not precapitalist forms: the landscape painted in the first chapter of Volume I does not depict phases preceding capitalism, but capitalism itself. In capitalism we thus find ourselves faced with imaginary representations of the social production process: and among all these representations this production process no longer appears as such, but only under a different form with a different content. In capitalist society, it seems that value constitutes one property of commodities as things, and not a social relation between people who produce and exchange them. In this way, commodities and their value seem to take on a 'fantastical' character. The fetishism of the world of commodities thus consists in the capacity of the form[38] in which value presents itself to dissimulate its real essence and to appear in the guise of its opposite. It is not, then, that man tricks himself as to what reality is, but rather that reality deceives him, necessarily appearing in a form that dissimulates it and makes it appear upside-down in the spontaneous consciousness of the individuals who live in the world of commodities. The fetish character of commodities is not an effect of the alienation of consciousness, but rather an effect in and on consciousness produced by the dissimulation of

---

35   *MECW*, Vol. 3, p. 290.
36   *MECW*, Vol. 35, p. 84.
37   See Godelier 1975.
38   See Bensussan 2007, pp. 147–84.

social relations within and through the way in which they appear.[39] The basis of fetishism is found outside the sphere of consciousness, in the objective reality of historically determinate social relations.

Marx used the notion of fetishism to criticise philosophical conceptions of representation and, at the same time, to construct his analysis of the capitalist mode of production: in particular, the Feuerbachian critique of religion had proven an inadequate basis for a materialism of representation. As such, fetishism did not describe a general logic, but a determinate operation in a specific sector of social reality:[40] the fact that the specifically social character of independent private labours consists of their equal status as abstract human labour applies to the capitalist mode of production only. In Marx's vision, representation was no 'double' of the world, understood in terms of adequacy or inadequacy, but rather an active instance of the real. Fetishism marked his definitive abandonment of Feuerbach's thesis of an alienating projection: fetishism was not an archaic phenomenon, but a contemporary event, and one that imposed itself on individuals in the form of objects, rather than being a question of will. For Marx it is not consciousness that determines life, but life that determines consciousness.

This process could not be understood by reference to the dimension of consciousness, since subterranean and largely unconscious mechanisms are here at work:

> whenever, by an exchange, we equate as values our different products, by that very act, we also equate, as human labour, the different kinds of labour expended upon them. We are not aware of this, nevertheless we do it. Value, therefore, does not stalk about with a label describing what it is. It is value, rather, that converts every product into a social hieroglyphic[41]

Marx's analysis sought to demonstrate how an inversion is produced:[42] the commodity form acts on people like a looking-glass, which, as it reflects the social characteristics of their labour, converts these latter and makes them

39   See Haber 2007, and Haber 2008, pp. 33–5, which instead interprets the fetish phenomenon substantially in continuity with the young Marx's declination of the question of alienation.

40   With a somewhat different interpretation from my own, Tosel 1996, p. 88 maintains that Marx considered making fetishism into a general, trans-historical theory.

41   *MECW*, Vol. 35, pp. 84–5. Castoriadis 1975 offers very apt insights into the complex or even partially obscure aspects of subjects in capitalist society.

42   See Hatem 2006, pp. 11–46, Tomba 2011, pp. 187–8.

appear as natural elements of things. However, we ought not advance a simplified image of this question as if the inversion were an alienated moment and it would suffice to put things back in order, thus making relations transparent. Even if Marx sometimes succumbed to the temptation to think communism in terms of perfect transparency, a full 'unveiling', the central problem concerns not the inversion as such, but rather the type of conversion produced in a determinate context.

The difference between the interpretation here proposed and Lukács's approach – understanding the whole of Marxism, as a 'total philosophy', in terms of the question of commodification and the subject-object transformation – should be clear enough. Fetishism corresponds to the forms in which the internal laws of the capitalist system appear. To take this position does not mean to say that humans' fate is totally determined by the products of their labour, as if by an absolute commodification: fetishism is a necessary form of perceiving reality only in a capitalist society. It is not true that fetishism transforms the subject into an object. Lukács's perspective is based on the idea that in the world of commodity values, subjects are themselves valued and, therefore, transformed into things: Lukács here employs the term *Verdinglichung* – reification or thingification – which does not play this role in Marx's writing, where it instead indicates that the relations between commodities enjoy a certain autonomy and are thus a representation of rather than merely a substitute for the relations among people. Fetishism, unlike an optical illusion or a superstitious belief, is not an erroneous perception of reality.[43] The inversion mechanism applies to humans' real activity: thought is not pure reflection, but an active part of the real, one of its constitutive elements, a modification and transformation of it. The fetish phenomenon has to do with how reality manifests itself: and in *Capital* Marx does not counterpose appearance and reality. To counterpose a wholly transparent 'truth' to the 'falsehood' inherent to the bourgeois representation of capitalism would be to put forward a simplified, and in some senses misleading, image of Marx's reasoning. We thus return to the idea that the distinctive trait of his discourse is the fact that he points to the opacity of the capitalist mode of production.

Political economy has to deal with the contradiction that derives from the fact that it claims to be scientific, addressing a specific, determinate object, but in reality postulates the eternity of the capitalist mode of production,

---

43   See Balibar 1995, p. 80: 'Now fetishism is not a subjective phenomenon or a false perception of reality, as an optical illusion or a superstitious belief would be. It constitutes, rather, the way in which social reality (a certain form or social structure) cannot but appear'.

on the basis of an ahistorical, newly discovered 'metaphysics'. *Capital* has the subtitle *Critique of Political Economy*, thus establishing it as critique more than as science. Here, the term *critique* should be understood not only as an 'enlightened' recognition of the limits of a given paradigm, but rather as a true and proper pulling-apart of political economy.[44] Marx had made a radical break with classical political economy: in the aforementioned *Afterword to the second German edition*, he directly stated that 'Political Economy can remain a science only so long as the class struggle is latent or manifests itself only in isolated and sporadic phenomena'.[45] If classical political economy expressed the bourgeois viewpoint, then Marx's critique of political economy necessarily marked a break from it, bringing to light the proletariat's perspective: that is, a critical position: 'So far as such criticism represents a class, it can only represent the class whose vocation in history is the overthrow [*Umwälzung*] of the capitalist mode of production and the final abolition [*Abschaffung*] of all classes – the proletariat'.[46] Without the workers' 'acting in common' it would not be possible to challenge established assumptions: it is the class struggle (and not some abstract conceptual element) that 'explodes' not only classical political economy, but political economy *tout court*. We ought, however, to add to this 'class' character of his reasoning also the previous considerations we elaborated concerning the specificity of his thought and of the categorial apparatus he used to understand reality: critique, then, could not operate in absolute separation from this conceptual construct. Marx proceeded from the internal to the external: conversely, the classical economists identified 'the essential' with 'the phenomenal' and did not fully grasp the opacity of the real.

According to Marx, Ricardo – the last exponent and also the high point of classical political economy – overlooked the formal dimension, and this prevented him from understanding the two-sidedness of the commodity, and thus the formation of money. Marx believed that Ricardo had failed to bring out the link between the commodity and money, and the formal dimension of the commodity. On the basis of these presuppositions, Ricardo did not distinguish between the labour expressed in a use-value and the labour expressed in exchange-value: and as such, he confused abstract and concrete labour. For

---

44   See Althusser 1970, p. 158: '"To criticize Political Economy" means to *confront* it with a new problematic and a new object: i.e., to question the very *object* of Political Economy ... Marx's critique of Political Economy cannot challenge the latter's object without disputing Political Economy itself ... Marx's critique of Political Economy is therefore a very radical one'. See also Renault 1995.

45   *MECW*, Vol. 35, p. 15.

46   *MECW*, Vol. 35, p. 16.

Marx, even though value does also have a quantitative dimension, we cannot stop short at observing this aspect and thus totally neglect its qualitative dimension. However, we also ought to specify that Marx's evaluation of Ricardo significantly changed over time. In his 1847 *Poverty of Philosophy*, Marx's critique of Proudhon was substantially based on elements drawn from Ricardo, and in the 1850s he still accepted various among his presuppositions: only in the early 1860s did Marx feel the need to mark his distance from Ricardo.[47] And when we understand this, it becomes clear that the years between the *Grundrisse* and *Capital*, with Marx's enormous proliferation of notebooks, were decisive in producing this split.

To return to the question of fetishism, it is worth noting that Marx elaborated his critique of the classical economists precisely starting out from the conviction that they had not grasped the structural opacity of the capitalist system, instead identifying essence with appearance. For Marx, these were not the same thing, and it was not possible immediately to match one with the other. Within his analysis of fetishism, the importance of the question of appearances emerged with some force: 'appear' did not mean either wholly true or wholly false. If everything were true, then this would mean accepting the apologetic position of the exponents of classical political economy, who surreptitiously 'eternalised' capitalism. If, instead, everything were false, this would mean adopting a dogmatic position totally rejecting the acquisitions of classical political economy, as if this latter were *sic et simpliciter* an organic whole made up of mystifications. So this second framework is also inadequate, sustained as it is by an absolute counterposition of the 'truth' of Marxist science to the 'falsehood' of classical political economy. On the contrary, Marx's analysis was distinguished by its emphasis on the opacity of the capitalist mode of production, which weaved together reality and mystification. It would be an error, indeed, either to consider only the 'real' dimension or to note only the 'mystifying' one: instead, we must allow for the instability of reflection, which cannot be reduced either to perfect lucidity or to absolute darkness. Now it is time to examine the question of the relation between this study of fetishism, and the question of ideology.

---

47   Among the many letters on this subject see, for example, Marx to Engels, 2 August 1862: 'Ricardo confuses *value* and *cost price* ... Hence he denies absolute rent and assumes only differential rent. But his identification of **values of commodities** and **cost prices of commodities** is totally wrong and has traditionally been taken over from A. Smith'. All Marx and Engels texts cited in this volume without a reference from the Marx/Engels Collected Works (MECW) are taken from the Marxists Internet Archive, <http://www.marxists.org>.

My thesis, here, is that the phenomenon of fetishism in many ways came to substitute for the question of ideology, as a sort of reformulation of this latter. This statement requires certain qualifications, however, since it concerns a question that has not been defined in clear terms. Before proceeding with my reasoning, it is necessary to make a brief *excursus* on the notion of ideology. Indeed, at first glance it might seem obvious that the element of ideology plays a key role in Marx. This view is not wholly mistaken, but, expressed in such a blunt manner, it might lead to severe misunderstandings of the orientation of Marx's thinking. This notion played a decisive role in the *German Ideology*, both as an inversion and as a *camera obscura*, albeit with a number of questions left unresolved.[48] In any case, any interpretation of ideology as 'false consciousness' or as a fictitious, 'falsifying' vision, is rather unconvincing. Conversely, – as regards the *pars costruens* of Marx's reflection – we might fall into thinking of communism as the full overcoming of ideology, since it would be meaningless to speak of a proletarian ideology. After all, even if we turn to Marx's reasoning in the following years, we can see that in the *Communist Manifesto* he represented the proletariat as being devoid of a fatherland, of values – in a word, of ideologies. Here we will limit ourselves to noting the productive dimension of ideology, and its irreducibility to an element of mystification: ideologies have always existed, and thus it seems problematic to think of a perfectly transparent situation wholly devoid of ideologies.

Independently of the evaluation of the concept of ideology as discussed in the *German Ideology*, it ought to be noted that this theme largely disappeared from Marx's writing after this work. Subsequently, especially in *Capital* – beyond sporadic expressions like 'ideologies of the bourgeois class' – this notion began to 'fade away'. And within this 'void' appeared the element of fetishism, which played an ever more significant role. It should be understood that the discussion of fetishism on the one hand took its lead from an element of his analysis of ideology, and on the other hand, produces a significant 'complication' of this question. Indeed, fetishism at first appears in correlation to the question of the inversion that takes place on the basis of a logic of mystification: and this element had already been present in his analysis of ideology. A second aspect also emerges from his analysis of fetishism, connected to that which we have already noted. Fetishism consists in the understanding that the relations between humans are, in reality, relations between things: it takes the shape of a representation capable of playing a fundamental role in the capitalist structure, in which value appears to be one property of commodities as things,

---

48   See Kofman 1998, Bohlender 2010.

and not a social relation between people who produce and exchange them. The opacity of the capitalist mode of production hides, or at least renders not immediately visible, the existence of a social disciplining mechanism which has its basis outside of the sphere of consciousness, in the objective reality of historically determinate relations. This manner of interpreting fetishism on the one hand exhibits a materialist character, since it is rooted in social relations; on the other hand, it delineates an 'imaginative' dimension irreducible to superstructure, if this latter is understood in a reductive fashion, that is, based on mere deduction from the economic sphere. So we can say that imagination is constitutive of reality, thus avoiding 'crushing' ideology into the box of 'false consciousness' and mystification.[49] Even though based on a 'complication' of the question of ideology, fetishism in many ways 'takes its place', since Marx largely abandoned this question across the course of time.

The Constitution of Individuality, between the 'Economic' and the 'Juridical': The 'Eden of the Rights of Man'

If so far we have examined one important aspect of fetishism, namely the relationship that it establishes between appearance and reality, then another decisive problem concerns individuality, and thus the relation between the subjective and objective dimensions.[50] In order to delve deeper into this question, we ought to turn our attention to the second chapter of *Capital* Volume I, 'Exchange', which introduces new elements for understanding the phenomenon of fetishism. Whereas in the first chapter the owners of commodities had not entered the stage, this did come to pass in the second chapter, starting with the consideration that 'commodities cannot go to market and make exchanges of their own account'.[51] '[A] particular commodity cannot become the universal equivalent except by a social act'.[52] But there was no voluntarism in these individuals 'entering the scene': 'In their difficulties our commodity owners think like Faust: "Im Anfang war die Tat" ["In the beginning was the deed"] They therefore acted and transacted before they thought'.[53] The irruption of subjects

---

49   See the essays in Cowling and Martin (eds.) 2002, for the purposes of a study of the reality/imagination relationship which does not reduce the latter to being a mere derivative of the former.

50   See Basso 2009b.

51   *MECW*, Vol. 35, p. 94.

52   Ibid. See Bellue 1989.

53   Ibid.

is thus devoid of any 'humanist' emphasis, since they are examined on the basis of the immanence of the deed.

Marx's declension of this question worked from a dual perspective, comprising the economic and the juridical:

> [Commodity owners] must ... mutually recognise in each other the rights of private proprietors. This juridical relation, which thus expresses itself in a contract, whether such contract be part of a developed legal system or not, is a relation between two wills, and is but the reflex of the real economic relation between the two. It is this economic relation that determines the subject-matter comprised in each such juridical act.[54]

It is worth bearing in mind, here, the symmetry between economic and juridical fetishism: just as there is an economic fetishism of things, there is a juridical fetishism of persons, and, indeed, these elements constitute one same phenomenon, since the contract is the other face of exchange.[55] The aspect common to both fetishisms is generalised equivalence, which abstractly subjects individuals to a form of circulation (the circulation of values, the circulation of obligations). A qualification is in order, here: Marx examined fetishism without making reference to the activity of state apparatuses. As such, fetishism cannot immediately provide us with a theory of politics, or, therefore, of the 'sites' of the production of ideology. Obviously, to uphold such a position does not mean to assert that ideology and fetishism are two wholly separate spheres: indeed, as we have seen, we could even say that in some ways fetishism 'takes the place' of ideology. On the ideological side, he places the accent on the negation or masking of the material conditions of production, while when it comes to the theory of fetishism, he emphasises the manner in which all production is subordinated to the reproduction of value. While in the *German Ideology* Marx and Engels insisted on the fact that ideas cannot be separated from their material foundation, in *Capital* he maintained but also went beyond this acquisition, insisting on the active character of reasoning, on the fact that thought is not pure reflection, or conversely its falsification *sic et simpliciter*, but rather a manifestation of the real in a specific and determinate context.

But let's pick up the thread of our reading of the second chapter, in which Marx introduces the commodity owners. Here, the concept of the fetish returns in an explicit fashion, starting with the logic and dynamic of the commodity. The internal contradiction between the qualitative homogeneity of commod-

---

54   Ibid.
55   See Pashukanis 1978.

ities (as values) and their natural difference (as use-values) finds its solution in the differentiation of commodities into commodities and money: in the fact that the value of the commodity acquires an autonomous existence in one particular commodity, namely money. 'Money is a crystal formed of necessity in the course of the exchanges, whereby different products of labour are practically equated to one another and thus by practice converted into commodities'.[56] The 'contrast, latent in commodities, between use-value and value' is resolved through the 'differentiation of commodities into commodities and money': 'At the same rate, then, as the conversion of products into commodities is being accomplished, so also is the conversion of one special commodity into money'. Thus we pass from dealing with the simple form of the commodity, or value, to its complete form, to the form of money: the processes transforming products into commodities and transforming commodities into money take place in parallel to one another. Commodity exchange, value and money are thus revealed to be expressions of one same relation, namely the dependence of the singular on social production: from a conceptual perspective, money thus necessarily results from the form of the bourgeois production system. In this regard, Marx states that '[t]he difficulty lies, not in comprehending that money is a commodity, but in discovering how, why, and by what means a commodity becomes money'.

> In the form of society now under consideration, the behaviour of men in the social process of production is purely atomic. Hence their relations to each other in production assume a material character independent of their control and conscious individual action. These facts manifest themselves at first by products as a general rule taking the form of commodities. We have seen how the progressive development of a society of commodity-producers stamps one privileged commodity with the character of money. Hence the riddle presented by money is but the riddle presented by commodities; only it now strikes us in its most glaring form.[57]

Precisely because Marx connects the 'enigma' of money to the 'enigma' of the commodity,[58] he relates the fetishism of money back to the fetishism of

---

56   *MECW*, Vol. 35, p. 97.

57   *MECW*, Vol. 35, p. 103. On the 'fetish character of the money form', in relation to the *Grundrisse*, see Rosdolsky 1992, p. 123: 'The phenomenon of commodity fetishism is closely tied up with the formation of money'.

58   See Erckenbrecht 1976.

the commodity. In this regard, we ought to emphasise the centrality of the 'mysterious' nature of the commodity, the 'elementary form'; in addition to this consideration, however, it is necessary to note that the concept of the fetish is extended from the commodity to comprise also money. It is thus wrong to say that fetishism appertains to the first chapter alone, within a landscape lacking any intervention of the subjective.[59] Indeed, subjectivity does emerge in the second chapter, but as part of the 'spectral objectivity' of the capitalist mode of production.

We ought to make a clarification, however, as to avoid a complete misunderstanding of this reasoning. The horizon of the first two chapters we are examining concerns the simple circulation of commodities (and not the sphere of production): thus capital, labour-power, surplus-value extraction and so on are absent. Insofar as he attempts to operate a genetic reconstruction, Marx considers simple circulation as the point of departure of the concept 'capital', of which it constitutes a phenomenal form. In order to grasp the logical genesis of capital he refers back to simple circulation, and in order to grasp its factual presuppositions he invokes the production and circulation of commodities. It is the logical genesis of theory that allows him to recognise its presuppositions: neither can the latter be reduced to the former, nor vice versa. The reasoning we have laid out concerning the commodity-form *qua* elementary cell does not imply reducing Marx's *Capital* to the chapter in question, and thus to a landscape existing prior to any definition of capital and any analysis of the capitalist production process. We must always bear in mind that the first chapter is the first in the order of his exposition, and without this it is impossible to understand the structure of *Capital*. At the same time, however, we could say that the sixth chapter (in Part II, 'The transformation of money into capital') is the first in the order of his research (and here again returns the difference between exposition and research), as is evident from the fact that in the preceding chapters the category 'capital' was missing, and labour-power did not appear as a commodity.

His plane of analysis is that of the simple circulation of commodities, a landscape distinguished by freedom and equality – in a word, the reciprocity among subjects. For the purposes of deepening our understanding of this

---

59   On this point, our interpretation is rather different from that articulated in Althusser 1970 and Balibar 1974, p. 223: 'The theory of fetishism thus remains, in *Capital*, a (philosophical) genesis of the subject, comparable to others that can be found in the history of classical philosophy, but with this "critical" variation … it is a genesis of the subject *as* "alienated" subject'. Thus fetishism in Marx is 'relegated' to a preliminary phase of his reasoning. Many years later Balibar significantly changed his own reading of fetishism: see Balibar 1995.

problematic, we might look at Marx's very insightful discussion of the 'very Eden' of the rights of man:

> This sphere that we are deserting, within whose boundaries the sale and purchase of labour-power goes on, is in fact a very Eden of the innate rights of man. There alone rule Freedom, Equality, Property and Bentham. Freedom, because both buyer and seller of a commodity, say of labour-power, are constrained only by their own free will. They contract as free agents, and the agreement they come to, is but the form in which they give legal expression to their common will. Equality, because each enters into relation with the other, as with a simple owner of commodities, and they exchange equivalent for equivalent. Property, because each disposes only of what is his own. And Bentham, because each looks only to himself. The only force that brings them together and puts them in relation with each other, is the selfishness, the gain and the private interests of each. Each looks to himself only, and no one troubles himself about the rest, and just because they do so, do they all, in accordance with the pre-established harmony of things, or under the auspices of an all-shrewd providence, work together to their mutual advantage, for the common weal and in the interest of all.[60]

In the sphere of the simple circulation of commodities, individuals relate to one another as the owners of commodities, as proprietors, exchanging equivalents. Here, the end-goal is use-value, not exchange-value; in order to bring into play the conservation and expansion of value, and thus surplus-value, we must consider the production process $M-C-M'$ – though this itself presupposes circulation as its own foundation. The sphere of circulation is sarcastically defined as 'a very Eden of the innate rights of man'. Analysis of these latter appears rather complex, and charged with consequences also on the political plane: but what must be understood is whether within Marx's thought a structural 'demolition' of this element is at work, or rather, a sort of unmasking demystifying its immanent limits and internal contradictions.

If in his first writings Marx tended to diminish the role of right, considering it substantially unreal, with the passing of time he rearticulated and 'complicated' the question; though not without difficulty, given the materiality of the juridical dimension and all the consequences resulting from this, which cannot be reduced to mere superstructure. Marx did, however, maintain his youthful idea

---

60   *MECW*, Vol. 35, p. 186.

as to the non-neutrality of right, its rooting in a determinate society, and thus the illusion inherent within any uncritical and unconditional apologetics for the rights of man. In *Capital*, Marx's position on the rights of man, the fruit of the French Revolution, was founded on his identification of a relationship of interdependence between the economic and juridical spheres, two sides of the same coin. In his listing of these rights ('Freedom, Equality, Property and Bentham') there is not just *liberté* and *égalité* but also property and Bentham. As regards this first element, the structural connection between freedom and property clearly comes into view, also in the sense of the subordination of the former to the latter: freedom is effected only within a 'proprietary' logic.[61] In Marx's reasoning, Bentham – as the founder of modern utilitarianism – incarnates the search for one's own interests at all costs, to the detriment of other individuals. But the task at hand is not some moral condemnation of such a state of affairs, criticising the citizen's attachment to what is useful to him, but rather a demonstration of the contradictions existent within bourgeois representations of the rights of man: for these had not been understood as duplicitous, but instead flattened out in a superficial and uncritical image making them appear in all their pomposity and redundancy.[62]

In the field of the circulation if commodities, 'a very Eden of the innate rights of man', there emerges the juridical moment of the private (and not social) contract in which individuals recognise one another as the owners of commodities, as proprietors who exchange equivalents (the element of surplus-value does not here come into it). This relation is distinguished by the presence of a structure of freedom, equality and reciprocity, since these are juridically equal 'free agents'.[63] This reasoning is in line with the perspective of the *Grundrisse*: the 'general interest' exalted by the apologists of the existing state of affairs is in reality nothing other than the result of each person seeking her own interest. To maintain, instead, that it is the fruit of a real universality, means to trust ingenuously in 'the pre-established harmony of things' or the 'auspices of an all-shrewd providence'. These appearances conceal its attachment to the structures of domination that are present within the capitalist mode of production.

> On leaving this sphere of simple circulation or of exchange of commodities, ... we think we can perceive a change in the physiognomy of our

---

61   See Macpherson 1962.

62   Maihofer 1992, pp. 114–15.

63   [The Italian translation of the previously-cited paragraph of *Capital* Volume I, Chapter 6, says that the commodity owners 'stipulate a contract as juridically equal free individuals', not simply 'contract as free equals' – DB].

dramatis personae. He, who before was the money-owner, now strides in front as capitalist; the possessor of labour-power follows as his labourer. The one with an air of importance, smirking, intent on business; the other, timid and holding back, like one who is bringing his own hide to market and has nothing to expect but – a hiding.[64]

What are meeting (clashing) here are our '*dramatis personae*': on the one hand, the capitalist, who receives more value than he has given, and on the other hand the worker, who exchanges equivalents only apparently according to the fullest freedom and equality. We see the clear asymmetry between the worker and the capitalist, as emerges forcefully from the wage question:

> The wage form thus extinguishes every trace of the division of the working-day into necessary labour and surplus-labour, into paid and unpaid labour. All labour appears as paid labour ... here the money-relation conceals the unrequited labour of the wage labourer.
>
> Hence, we may understand the decisive importance of the transformation of value and price of labour-power into the form of wages, or into the value and price of labour itself. This phenomenal form ... forms the basis of all the juridical notions of both labourer and capitalist, of all the mystifications of the capitalistic mode of production, of all its illusions as to liberty, of all the apologetic shifts of the vulgar economists ... The jurist's consciousness recognizes in this, at most, a material difference, expressed in the juridically equivalent formula: 'Do ut des, do ut facias, facio ut des, facio ut facias'.[65]

The 'heart' of capitalist production consists in the division between necessary labour and surplus-value, and thus between paid and unpaid labour. This reasoning does not dismiss right, but rather understands it in terms of its correspondence with the economic sphere, its link with the dynamic of the capitalist mode of production, and the relations of force inherent within this dynamic: 'There is here, therefore, an antinomy, right against right, both equally bearing the seal of the law of exchanges. Between equal rights force decides'.[66] This conception is the most decisive rejection of the 'harmonies' of freedom and equality proper to the simple circulation of commodities. By no means

---

64   *MECW*, p. 35, p. 186.
65   *MECW*, Vol. 35, pp. 539–40.
66   *MECW*, Vol. 35, p. 243.

does right stand equidistant between the two parties in struggle: at the moment in which equal demands confront one another, the one that prevails is that which holds social power and is thus able to exercise *Gewalt*.[67] This latter term could be translated as either 'force' or 'violence', but we must also take account of the nexus among *Herrschaft*, *Macht* and *Gewalt* in modern political thought:[68] the use of force is intimately linked to bourgeois society's structures of subjection, in which a determinate class exercises its dominion over the working class. Marx's position is distinct from either an abstractly pacifist vision or any sort of 'bellicose' exaltation of violence; rather, here what we have is a disenchanted recognition of the relevance of violence to history, on the basis of a sort of phenomenology: 'Force [*die Gewalt*] is the midwife of every old society pregnant with a new one'.[69] An 'economic force', it 'employ[s] the power of the State, the concentrated and organised force of society'.[70]

In conclusion, we ought to repeat the fact that the 'Eden of the rights of man' denotes the sphere of the simple circulation of commodities (and not that of production), a sphere distinguished by a reciprocity between subjects. Here we have to examine the question of the subjection of individuals to a universal – whose two faces are its economic and its juridical dimension – on the basis of the symmetry between the individual as owner of commodities and the individual as owner of rights.[71] At the moment at which we pass from the simple circulation of commodities to production, this symmetry falls to pieces, and what instead emerges is a lacerated situation, a true and proper 'civil war' between the capitalists, who are 'materialisations' of capital, and the workers, who are 'materialisations' of labour. This reflection is in continuity with the overall framework of the *Grundrisse*, in which Marx notes that as we pass from the simple circulation of commodities to production, freedom and equality are converted into unfreedom and inequality. For reasons

---

67   On the question of *Gewalt* in Marx, with particular reference to the reading provided in Balibar 2001 (for a deeper examination: Balibar 2010) underlining its many strong points as well as the risk of falling into any 'total' critique of violence, which could end up becoming subaltern to capital's *Gewalt*, see Basso 2009a.
68   See Faber, Ilting and Meier 1972–90.
69   See Labica 2008, pp. 215–16.
70   Ibid. See Negri 1992, pp. 289–90: 'In the first place ... the line that goes accumulation-violence-law ... Violence is thus a constant in this process, a violence that is determined in the foundation and in the maintenance of the worker's alienation ... It begins to take on juridical forms at the moment at which it is exercised with most intensity – it can pick up or drop its "juridical labels" as required'.
71   See Goux 1973.

that we saw already, within the terms of the simple circulation of commodities we have a mystification, one that sustains the idea that the subjects in question are symmetrical. But, at the same time, an element of reality also here emerges, in that from both the economic and juridical points of view the capitalist mode of production does allow us – albeit with a series of internal contradictions – to interpret the individual in her irreducibility to a determinate horizon and in her possibility of fulfilling her own potentials, even if problematically and in the face of obstacles. So nor should the simple circulation of commodities be considered a simply fictitious sphere. But the task now incumbent on us is to examine in what sense fetishism is not reducible to the horizon of *Capital* Volume I – such as many scholars claim – but rather can be extended to the entire perspective of this work. To this end, I shall now examine some passages from the second and third volumes of *Capital*.

From the Commodity to Capital, between Production and Circulation: The 'Trinity Formula'

We could say that the entire second volume of *Capital* is underpinned by a consideration of fetishism, even if not explicitly so. Indeed, the 'complex' circulation of commodities (as distinct from the simple circulation examined in Part I of Volume I) represents the 'realm' of fetishism by a different name, since at its very basis is this same intersection of reality and mystification. In general terms – keeping the question of valorisation central – it is worth emphasising, as Marx made clear in the first volume, that this process is realised within the sphere of production, yet starting out from the presupposition of the sphere of circulation.

> This metamorphosis, this conversion of money into capital, takes place both within the sphere of circulation and also outside it; within the circulation, because conditioned by the purchase of the labour-power in the market; outside the circulation, because what is done within it is only a stepping-stone to the production of surplus-value, a process which is entirely confined to the sphere of production[72]

---

72   *MECW*, Vol. 35g, p. 205.

Earlier, we saw how circulation represents the surface-level moment in which subjects appear to be fully free and equal, based on a condition of reciprocity, whereas production instead constitutes the 'deep' moment in which such symmetries fall to pieces as freedom and equality are transformed into unfreedom and inequality, within a landscape marked by the presence of classes. In the sphere of circulation, these appearances ought not to be conceived as synonymous with unreality. The freedom and equality in question do present an aspect of mystification, but at the same time they are real, insofar as, unlike in previous productive forms, they presuppose the existence of independent individuals who have the possibility of moving around – even if in the face of a series of obstacles and limits. Moreover, we should be clear that we are here speaking not of the simple circulation of commodities, but rather of the 'final' circulation, which requires its own reproduction, comprising both production and circulation.[73] It is here worth considering some of the junctures in the second volume of *Capital* that allow us to examine the question of fetishism in a specific manner.

For example, Marx defines wages as 'but a disguised form [*eine verkleidete Form*], a form in which for instance the price of one day's labour power presents itself as the price of the labour set in motion by this labour power in one day'.[74] Here, Marx again invokes the illusory and mystifying character of the capitalist mode of production – its opacity, appearances, and disguises – as its characteristic traits. This is not a matter of reducing appearance to unreality, and thus claiming that it is a pure fiction, but nor does Marx follow the classical economists in 'sanctifying' this appearance and making it coincide with reality:

> But political economy sees only what is apparent, namely the effect of the time of circulation on capital's process of the creation of surplus value in general. It takes this negative effect for a positive one, because its consequences are positive. It clings the more tightly to this appearance

---

73   See in Volume II: 'In the production of commodities, circulation is as necessary as production itself, so that circulation agents are just as much needed as production agents. The process of reproduction includes both functions of capital, therefore it includes the necessity of having representatives of these functions ... But this furnishes no ground for confusing the agents of circulation with those of production, any more than it furnishes ground for confusing the functions of commodity-capital and money-capital with those of productive capital. The agents of circulation must be paid by the agents of production': *MECW*, Vol. 36, p. 131.

74   *MECW*, Vol. 36, p. 36.

since it seems to furnish proof that capital possesses a mystic source of self-expansion independent of its process of production and hence of the exploitation of labour, a spring which flows to it from the sphere of circulation. We shall see later that even scientific political economy has been deceived by this appearance of things.[75]

In the second volume, the question of fetishism returns in terms very similar to those used in *Capital* Volume I. Thus it seems that capital has a 'mystic source of self-expansion', belonging to the sphere of circulation; but this is an appearance, not the reality. Marx's approach pulls apart any 'imaginary' centred on circulation and thus decoupled from the 'deeper' moment, the sphere of production. Among other things, it was important to emphasise this aspect because at the time the prevalent tendency in the study of capital occluded its constitutive relation to the dimension of production, thus neutralising its asymmetries. But if the scope of the capitalist mode of production is the valorisation of capital, this process is realised within the sphere of production, and not that of circulation. We cannot, however, forget that its necessary presupposition is the sphere of circulation, and we are here denying not the importance of this latter but rather its absolute autonomy, which would even mean posing it as if it were at the basis of capital's self-valorisation.

Critically engaging with the exponents of classical political economy (in particular with Smith and Ricardo), Marx noted that in dealing with the question of fixed and circulating capital, they had concealed the origin of the element of surplus-value:

> The capital-values advanced for production in the form of both means of production and means of subsistence reappear here equally in the value of the product. Thus the transformation of the capitalist process of production into a complete mystery is happily accomplished and the origin of the surplus-value existing in the product is entirely withdrawn from view.
>
> Furthermore this brings to completion the fetishism peculiar to bourgeois Political Economy, the fetishism which metamorphoses the social, economic character impressed on things in the process of social production into a natural character stemming from the material nature of those things ... Just as was demonstrated in the case of the labour-process (Buch I, Kap. V), [English edition: Ch. VII] that it depends wholly on the

---

role which the material components play in a particular labour-process ... so instruments of labour are fixed capital only if the process of production is really a capitalist process of production and the means of production are therefore really capital and possess economic definiteness, the social character of capital. And in the second place, they are fixed capital only if they transfer their value to the product in a particular way.[76]

In this passage it is precisely the term 'fetish' that Marx uses to indicate an economic process being considered 'natural', as if it were inscribed into the very structure of things and not in a determinate activity of social domination: and here returns his critique of the 'eternalisation' of capitalism at the hands of the political economists. In reality, the means of production are capital only in particular conditions, and fixed capital only on the basis of specific presuppositions, above all starting from the condition that the production process is in general represented by the capitalist mode of production. Thus the element of fetishism plays a significant role, mostly implicitly and sometimes explicitly, within the landscape of the second volume of *Capital*. In the just-cited passage, Marx's polemic against the classical economists – already present in Volume I – flowers anew, as he finds them guilty of confusing essence and appearance. For Marx, conversely, we never find a total coincidence of these two spheres. More generally, we could say that the entire landscape of circulation presents a 'fetishist' character, this latter being understood in terms of the dimension of appearances. Thus on the one hand, circulation cannot constitute the source of surplus-value, as the fetishist 'mysticism' of political economy would have us believe; on the other hand, nor is it reducible to pure unreality.

The question of fetishism is not limited to its treatment in the first section of *Capital* Volume I, in which it is still inserted within the sphere of simple circulation, which, as we earlier mentioned, is characterised by reciprocity. Nor can it be limited within the bounds of *Capital* Volume II's portrayal of circulation. It is interesting to note, in this regard, that even in the third volume, which concerns the overall process of production and circulation, this question returns in a rather telling manner. We could even say that it is in Volume III that we find the most convincing formulation of this problematic, also providing us with the basis for understanding the discussion in the first volume. To return to the two great – mutually incompatible – readings by Lukács and Althusser,

---

 MECW, Vol. 36, p. 227.

not only is the perspective here followed substantially different from Lukács's –
for reasons that we have already explained – but we are none too convinced
by Althusser's approach in this regard, either, since the phenomenon of fetishism cannot be circumscribed within the limits of the first chapter of *Capital*
Volume I.[77] The term 'fetishism', conversely, means to point to all those situations in which the class relations within the dominant ideology come to be
reified.[78] The thesis that we want to advance here, therefore, is that fetishism
extends to the forms of capital as a whole: the fetishism of commodities, in the
first chapter of Volume I, and of money, in the second, are but a first step in the
direction of the fetishism of capital.

In order to make this journey, chapter 48 of *Capital* Volume III is particularly
significant: indeed, the question of fetishism reappears in a changed context
with respect to the first chapter of Volume I, that is to say, within the 'social
production process'. The general theme of this chapter is the 'trinity formula',
which consists of the following elements: 1) profit-capital (the capitalist's gains
plus interest); 2) ground-rent; 3) wage-labour. In synthesis, 'capital, land and
labour', the first term referring to capital not as a thing 'but rather a definite
social production relation, belonging to a definite historical formation of society' [*historische Gesellschaftsformation*].[79] Moreover, 'Wage-labour and landed
property, like capital, are historically determined social forms ... and indeed
both forms corresponding to capital and belonging to the same economic formation of society'.[80] This reasoning sets the stage for Marx's critique of political
economy:

> vulgar economy has not the slightest suspicion that the trinity which it
> takes as its point of departure ... are *prima facie* three impossible com-
> binations. First we have the use-value *land*, which has no value, and the
> exchange-value *rent*: so that a social relation [*ein soziales Verhältnis*] con-
> ceived as a thing is made proportional to Nature, i.e., two incommensur-
> able magnitudes are supposed to stand in a given ratio to one another.
> Then *capital – interest*. If capital is conceived as a certain sum of values

---

77   See Lukács 1971; and Althusser 2006, which holds that there are structural limits in Marx's
        analysis of fetishism and more generally in the idea of beginning *Capital* on the basis of
        the most simple abstraction: Marx thus remaining prisoner of 'notions from bourgeois
        juridical ideology' and 'his way of discussing value, discussing it first in order to deduce
        everything else'.

78   See Dimoulis and Milios 2004.

79   *MECW*, Vol. 37, p. 801.

80   *MECW*, Vol. 37, p. 803.

represented independently by money, then it is *prima facie* nonsense to say that a certain value should be worth more than it is worth.[81]

At the basis of this conception lies the fact that vulgar economy is 'entrapped in bourgeois production relations'. For Marx, the explanation of the 'trinity formula' consists of the dynamic according to which

> Capital yields a profit year after year to the capitalist, land a ground-rent to the landlord, and labour-power ... a wage to the labourer ... Thus, capital appears to the capitalist, land to the landlord, and labour-power, or rather labour itself, to the labourer ... as three different sources of their specific revenues, namely, profit, ground-rent and wages. They are really so in the sense that capital is a perennial pumping-machine of surplus-labour for the capitalist.[82]

Considerations touching on the fetish phenomenon reappear in this analysis in a rather telling fashion: 'Just as products confront the producer as an independent force in capital and capitalists – who actually are but the personification of capital – so land becomes personified in the landlord and likewise gets on its hind legs ... as an independent force'.[83] Among other things, Marx's emphasis on how the power of money and capital becomes autonomous from individuals, but on the basis of a social relation, is a true and proper 'red thread' running throughout his entire reflection: we need only think of his analysis in this regard as early as the *German Ideology*.[84] In any case, in the 48th chapter of *Capital* Volume III his reasoning proceeds:

> we have already pointed out the mystifying character that transforms the social relations [*die gesellschaftlichen Verhältnisse*], for which the material elements of wealth serve as bearers in production, into properties of these things themselves (commodities) and still more pronouncedly transforms the production relation itself into a thing (money). All forms of society, in so far as they reach the stage of commodity-production and money circulation, take part in this perversion [*Verkehrung*]. But under the capitalist mode of production and in the case of capital, which forms its dominant category, its determining production relation, this

---

81   *MECW*, Vol. 37, p. 804.
82   *MECW*, Vol. 37, p. 808.
83   *MECW*, Vol. 37, p. 811.
84   See Basso 2012, pp. 79–80.

> enchanted and perverted world develops still more ... Capital thus be-
> comes a very mystic being since all of labour's social productive forces
> appear to be due to capital, rather than labour as such, and seem to issue
> from the womb of capital itself.[85]

The beginning of the passage makes clear reference to the first chapter of Volume I, and thus refers back to the analysis contained therein. This landscape cannot be interpreted *sic et simpliciter* according to the much-abused category of 'absolute commodification'. On the one hand, it does provide a misleading representation that claims to be an objective conception; the classical econom-ists provided an 'ideological' framework for understanding this problematic, with the goal of fashioning a rational legitimation of capitalism. On the other hand, this should not lead us to take a caricatured view, which would be use-ful neither on the theoretical nor the political plane, that focuses exclusively on the fictitious aspect of such reasoning. Such an approach would result in an absolute counterposition between the 'falsehood' of classical political economy and the (presumed) 'truth' of Marxist science. Even ideology itself – which fet-ishism in many ways takes over from – cannot be understood as mere unreality, within any considered interpretation. Ideology does not just reflect 'the present state of things', but can exercise also a performative function, setting in motion a series of consequences of considerable importance.

In using the expression 'enchanted and perverted world' Marx is not denot-ing something purely unreal, and nor does he identify fetishism and religion: there is an analogy but not a homology between these two elements. In any case, the ideological dimension cannot be reduced to superstructure. At the same time, however, this dimension is not interpreted in an 'idealistic' manner; on the contrary, Marx's interpretation seeks out its material foundations and its rooting in determinate social relations; those relations proper to the capitalist mode of production in its specific difference from previous productive forms.

> in this economic trinity represented as the connection between the com-
> ponent parts of value and wealth in general and its sources, we have the
> complete mystification of the capitalist mode of production, the conver-
> sion of social relations into things [*Verdinglichung*], the direct coales-
> cence of the material production relations with their historical and social
> determination. It is an enchanted, perverted, topsy-turvy world, in which
> Monsieur le Capital and Madame la Terre do their ghost-walking as social

---

85   *MECW*, Vol. 37, pp. 813–14.

characters and at the same time directly as mere things. It is the great merit of classical economy to have destroyed this false appearance and illusion, this mutual independence and ossification of the various social elements of wealth, this personification of things and conversion of production relations into entities, this religion of everyday life [*Religion des Alltagslebens*]. It did so by reducing interest to a portion of profit, and rent to the surplus above average profit, so that both of them converge in surplus-value ...[86]

Thus emerges a world populated by spectres, in which social relations appear as things. Marx again proposes, in this regard, a differentiation between the 'vulgar economists', who were wholly inadequate because they were uncritical apologists for the 'present state of things'; and the classical economists, who did partially grasp 'this false appearance'. The classical economists' conception was not reducible to pure fiction; besides, Marx repeatedly stated that he preferred the rigour of Smith's approach to Proudhon's declamatory socialism, which did not provide coordinates useful for understanding the present scenario. This notwithstanding, the exponents of classical political economy remained 'more or less in the grip of the world of illusion which their criticism had dissolved' and thus ended up serving 'the interests of the ruling classes': the trinity formula 'proclaim[s] the physical necessity and eternal justification of their sources of revenue and elevat[es] them to a dogma'.[87] The classical political economists' reflection, though able to illuminate some significant aspects and 'destroying' some appearances, thus turned out to be a sort of 'theodicy' of capitalism.

The theme of fetishism is not only the horizon of the first chapter of *Capital* Volume I, but also concerns the fully-explicated categories of the capitalist mode of production, in particular capital itself. With the difference, however, that in the first and second chapters of Volume I, money – when it functions as capital – is characterised not only by being value, but also by self-valorisation, reproducing itself. In order to transform into capital and thus valorise itself, money must be able to buy on the market a commodity that is capable of creating value once it is used. This commodity does exist: labour-power. Money, therefore, becomes productive capital only from the moment in which a new social relation is established in the commodity-production process: namely, the relation between two social classes, capitalists and workers. It seems to the cap-

---

86   *MECW*, Vol. 37, p. 817.

87   Ibid.

italists and the workers that the wage pays for the entire labour provided by the worker, and thus that each social class takes its due income from the production and circulation of commodities. According to Marx, the categories wage, profit, capital interest, and income, as represented by the exponents of classical political economy, express the visible relations of everyday business practice, and as such they are of pragmatic use but not scientific value. When the circulation of commodities does not create value but realises it, and provides the means through which the surplus value created in the production process is subdivided among the various different varieties of capitalists (industrialists, financiers, landowners), assuming the form of the profits of business, interest or rent, then apparently everything happens as if capital, labour and land were autonomous sources of value that are added together and combine in creating the value of commodities.[88]

The appearance of the capitalist landscape dissimulates and contradicts its essence – that is, the hidden structure of its social relations, the mechanism by which surplus-value is formed, the fact that the wage is not equivalent to the value created by the worker, and thus the existence of a true and proper civil war between the working class and the capitalist class. Commodity fetishism and all the social forms that develop on the basis of the commodity (money, capital, interest, the wage, and so on) constitute the centre of a universe of representations that feed beliefs in the 'magical' powers of things, which are attributed an intangible character: according to Marx's sublime expression, this is the 'religion of everyday life' of the individuals living in bourgeois society. When we look at the phenomenon of fetishism, it is worth forcefully insisting that this mechanism, far from being possible to circumscribe within the context proper to the first section of *Capital* Volume I, embraces the general framework of *Capital*, its overall processes as studied in Volume III. To recapitulate, this means passing from the fetishism of the commodity to the fetishism of capital, by way of the fetishism of money.

In the fetishised representation of the agents occupied in the capitalist process, everything takes place as if the extra value created in the process of producing and circulating commodities – surplus-value – were created by capital itself and not by labour, as if it were a mysterious, autonomous, enigmatic property of capital and not the product of a social production relation between the capitalist class and the working class, based on a sharp asymmetry. In the capitalist mode of production the social structure exists independently of the institutions that regulate family, political and religious relations, and produc-

---

88   See Dimoulis and Milios 2004.

tion is essentially devoted to the production of commodities' exchange-values, management of which escapes the producers' control. Here, individuals' real relations with their material conditions are transformed not into a different set of interpersonal relations, but rather into relations among things. Classical political economy identified the capitalist mode of production's essential forms with its phenomenal forms, preventing it from grasping capitalism's opacity. Hidden within the spontaneous consciousness of the individuals who make up part of this mode of production is the internal, concealed structure of their social relations, and thus the mechanism for the formation of surplus-value. The economic dimension is depoliticised and naturalised: the social relations of dominion, which are to be found at the very origin of value, are portrayed as relations among things, thus masking the fact that it is a mode of production characterised by class antagonism, a political character distinguished by a profound internal division. It is, however, worth examining what role the subjective dimension plays in this 'fetishised' landscape.

The Person-as-Mask: A Hobbesian Marx?

For the purposes of examining this theme more deeply, the way in which Marx defines the concept 'person' in *Capital* Volume I is of very great significance:

> The persons exist for one another merely as representatives of, and, therefore, as owners of, commodities. In the course of our investigation we shall find, in general, that the characters who appear on the economic stage are but economic character masks [*die ökonomischen Charaktermasken*], facing each other as bearers [*Träger*] of these economic relations.[89]

Here Marx radicalises his overcoming – beginning with the *German Ideology* – of his anthropocentric illusions, synthesised in the Feuerbachian *homo homini deus est*: for the Marx of *Capital*, it is senseless to postulate a *Gattungswesen*, a generic being that is immediately capable of overcoming the conditions in which its activity is situated. Instead, the individual must be understood in its inter-relation with the circumstances in which it moves, the 'apparently'

---

89   *MECW*, Vol. 35, p. 95. See Lohmann 1991, particularly pp. 259–60, basing himself on a perspective different to our own; and Graham 1992, p. 16. Hegel certainly bore significant influence on Marx (though we cannot go into it here) with his discussion of the concept 'person', linked to the abstract subject of Roman law; see the *Grundlinien*, Part I, 'Abstract Right'.

objective context of the capitalist mode of production. In various passages of *Capital* he defines persons as *Charaktermasken* and *Träger* of economic relations: undoubtedly, there does exist a risk, in such a perspective, that the role of individuals is completely wiped away, being considered completely enslaved to blind economic laws that dominate the world. And we cannot deny the presence of elements in *Capital* that seem to confirm such a deterministic interpretation:

> I paint the capitalist and the landlord in no sense *couleur de rose*. But here individuals are dealt with only in so far as they are the personifications [*Personifikation*] of economic categories, embodiments of particular class-relations and class-interests. My standpoint, from which the evolution of the economic formation of society is viewed as a process of natural history, can less than any other make the individual responsible for relations whose creature he socially remains, however much he may subjectively raise himself above them.[90]

Here emerges a parallel between society and nature, where almost all of its elements (apart from the sporadic possibility of subjective impulses) seem to be inevitable. This impression seems to be confirmed by what follows: 'Intrinsically, it is not a question of the higher or lower degree of development of the social antagonisms that result from the natural laws of capitalist production. It is a question of these laws [*Gesetze*] themselves, of these tendencies [*Tendenzen*] working with iron necessity [*Notwendigkeit*] towards inevitable results'.[91] Even if it may seem possible to assimilate the study of the economic dynamic to the method of the natural sciences, thus denying the individual any margin of autonomy, it ought to be emphasised that while Marx does speak of 'laws' and 'necessity' he also speaks of 'tendencies', a term which reins in this deterministic 'gallop'. To try and identify another course, one that challenges or at least problematises any Manichean idea of 'iron necessity', it is worth remembering that 'In the analysis of economic forms, moreover, neither microscopes nor chemical reagents are of use. The force of abstraction must replace both'.[92] The

---

90   *MECW*, Vol. 35, p. 10.

91   *MECW*, Vol. 35, p. 9.

92   Ibid. In this regard, see the important work of Vadée 1992, which seeks to shake off the deterministic 'spectres' around Marx, on the contrary interpreting him as a 'thinker of the possible': according to Vadée, although there are some economistic aspects in Marx these do not represent the distinctive feature of his thought. Lefebvre 1980 had already previously advanced the thesis of Marx being a 'thinker of the possible'.

method of the physical sciences cannot be applied *sic et simpliciter* to economic inquiry, since this latter is founded on the 'force of abstraction'[93] and thus does not appear reducible to the aggregation of quantitative data.

So we ought to examine how this perspective is applied to the theme of individuality, and in particular – making reference to the above-cited passages – what it means to conceive of persons as *Charaktermasken, Träger,* and *Personifikationen* of economic relations and class interests. Telling in this regard is a passage in which Marx refers to the medieval context: 'No matter, then, what we may think of the masks in which persons present themselves in this theatre, the social relations between individuals in the performance of their labour, appear [*erscheinen*] at all events as their own mutual personal relations, and are not disguised under the shape of social relations between the products of labour'.[94] Here, Marx explicates an aspect that the definition of a person as a mask already entails analytically: namely, the 'theatrical' dimension. Among other things, it is worth noting the insertion of this acquisition within his problematisation of commodity fetishism, characterised by 'appearances'. Awareness of the identity between the notions of person and mask was not, of course, a discovery of Marx's own making, given that the term *person* itself derives from the Greek *prosopon*: mask. Without rerunning the entire history of the term, I will limit myself to invoking the discussion of this question in Hobbes's *Leviathan*, to which Marx is in many regards indebted:

> A PERSON, is he 'whose words or actions are considered, either as his own, or as representing the words or actions of an other man, or of any other thing to whom they are attributed, whether Truly or by Fiction' ... The word Person is latine: instead whereof the Greeks have Prosopon, which signifies the Face, as Persona in latine signifies the Disguise, or Outward Appearance of a man, counterfeited on the Stage; and somtimes more particularly that part of it, which disguiseth the face, as a Mask or Visard: And from the Stage, hath been translated to any Representer of speech and action, as well in Tribunalls, as Theaters. So that a Person, is the same that an Actor is, both on the Stage and in common Conversation; and to Personate, is to Act, or Represent himselfe, or an other; and he that acteth another, is said to beare his Person, or act in his name ...[95]

---

93   On the centrality of the element of abstraction – with an approach different to my own –
       see Finelli 1987. More recently: Finelli 2014.
94   *MECW*, Vol. 35, p. 88. Translation edited.
95   Hobbes 2011, p. 616.

Hobbes's brief historical reconstruction shows how in Latin this term referred to the 'disguise ... of a man counterfeited on the stage' and, sometimes, to a mask; the transferral of this notion to the juridical sphere did not at all alter its essentially theatrical character. Indeed, in everyday life just as on the stage, 'a Person, is the same that an Actor is', and 'to Personate, is to Act, or Represent'. In his *Leviathan*, Hobbes distinguishes between the natural person, who represents words or actions 'considered ... as his own', and the artificial person who plays such a function in relation 'of an other man, or of any other thing to whom they are attributed'. The link between the notions of the person and of representation is a distinctive trait of Hobbes's political theory: and within his terms, representation does not mean simply (and weakly) to delegate someone, but rather to give form to political obligation, thus escaping – partly out of rational consideration and partly for passional motives – from the natural state of *bellum omnium contra omnes*, a *fictio* necessary for the foundation of *status civilis*. In this theoretical context, the author-actor dialectic takes on a decisive role: the actor is identified as the sovereign (be it an individual or an assembly) which receives recognition of its words and actions on the part of the represented, the authors, following their previous agreement to a pact renouncing 'this naturall Right of every man to every thing'.[96] This authorisation brings about the passage from the multitude to the single person:

> A Multitude of men, are made One Person, when they are by one man, or one Person, Represented; so that it be done with the consent of every one of that Multitude in particular. For it is the Unity of the Representer, not the Unity of the Represented, that maketh the Person One. And it is the Representer that beareth the Person, and but one Person: And Unity, cannot otherwise be understood in Multitude[97]

---

96   Hobbes 2011, p. 128. The whole passage reads 'And therefore, as long as this naturall Right of every man to every thing endureth, there can be no security to any man, (how strong or wise soever he be,) of living out the time, which Nature ordinarily alloweth men to live'.

97   Hobbes 2011, p. 153. On Hobbes, within the terms of an overall analysis of modern contractualism and its significant constitutional implications, see the work of the University of Padua's research group on political concepts. Cf. Duso 1988, p. 19: 'In Hobbes's theory ... nothing preconstitutes the common body, if not individuals and their movements ... The people, understood as a unit, cannot precede the pact; rather, it is the political body which individuals contrive to bring into being. Outside of such a unit, there is only a disaggregated multitude, not a person, which means a civil person. But, then, there is no-one who can make this person's action and will present, if not he who expresses a single will and

Thus the outcome of his reasoning consists of the formation of a political
obligation endowed with an absolute character: the sovereign *qua* representative of unity (and it remains united even in the case of an assembly, if it acts as a
single body), making a scattered multitude of separate atoms into one people.

Marx was indebted to Hobbes's conception, since not only did he pick up on
the idea of the person-as-mask, but went further still, emphasising the fact that
the person is the 'personification' of determinate relations. In Hobbes, this conception appears in connection to his juridical-natural schema founded on the
dualism between the natural state and the civil state: the 'theatrical', 'representative' character of the person is seen like the actor whom the contracting parties
authorise to carry out actions and utter words 'in their stead'. Marx radicalises
Hobbes's notion of the person-as-mask; not only is the person a *Charakter-
maske* insofar as he is connected to the element of political obligation: each
individual is intrinsically a mask, the personification of someone or something.
Now it is worth turning back to the passage in the second chapter of Volume I
in which Marx goes deeper into this concept: persons exist as 'representatives
of commodities' who 'mutually recognise in each other the rights of private
proprietors', thus giving life to a juridical relation. But as well as being private
proprietors, persons also take the role of 'economic masks', 'personifications'
of economic dynamics. They are represented in the formal sense, in that they
stipulate a contract in which they receive some mutual recognition, and in the
material sense, in that they cannot step aside from the relations present in the
capitalist mode of production.

In Marx's thematisation of the notion of the person, there is not any kind
of disregard for or derision of the person's role: his critique of the capitalist
system arises precisely from his consideration of the enslavement of individuals
to social power. As such, the person is reduced to a bearer of labour-power,
which 'has a value, like all the other commodities'; not by chance, in *Capital*
Marx cites a phrase from Hobbes's *Leviathan*: 'The *value*, or *worth of a man*, is
as in all other things, his price; that is to say, so much as would be given *for
the use of his power*'.[98] We need to understand the close relation between 'man'
and 'power', along with the instrumental character of this latter: 'The POWER
of a Man, (to take it Universally,) is his present means, to obtain some future
apparent Good. And is either Originall, or Instrumentall'.[99] This consideration
of the non-absoluteness of power – in connection to the means of which it

---

action in a representative fashion, counting for the political unit as a whole'; Biral 1987,
and Piccinini 1999.
98   *MECW*, Vol. 20, p. 128.
99   Hobbes 2011, p. 96.

disposes – illuminates the meaning of the aforementioned definition of a man's value, which coincides with his price. His purpose is the search for some (more or less apparent) 'future Good', useful to himself, and certainly not the common good: its value

> is not absolute; but a thing dependant on the need and judgement of another ... And as in other things, so in men, not the seller, but the buyer determines the Price. For let a man (as most men do,) rate themselves as the highest Value they can; yet their true Value is no more than it is esteemed by others.[100]

It is precisely this understanding that allows for the fully logically coherent introduction of the notion of a man's 'price': if he is equivalent to something, indeed, his value cannot but consist of his price, what someone is ready to give for the use of his power. This provides the basis for the consideration that value cannot be something one attributes oneself: the price must be decided by the buyer. We can clearly see the influence of this reflection of Hobbes's on *Capital*'s discussion of the individual as a bearer of labour-power, which 'has a value, like all the other commodities'. It is worth noting that Marx translated 'value or worth' as *Wert* (in the sense of *Tauschwert*), 'man' as *Arbeitskraft*, and 'thing' as *Ware*, thus transposing Hobbes's context onto the conceptual structure of *Capital*. To believe in the possibility of a real equivalence between buyer and seller is a pious wish, since it is the former who determines the price, as Hobbes said: 'He, who before was the money-owner, now strides in front as capitalist; the possessor of labour-power follows as his labourer. The one with an air of importance, smirking, intent on business; the other, timid and holding back, like one who is bringing his own hide to market and has nothing to expect but – a hiding'.[101] The relation between the two figures in question – behind the appearances of the 'harmony' of freedom, equality, and reciprocity – is in reality founded on a relation of domination in which the capitalist, who buys labour-power, disposes of the means 'to obtain some future apparent Good'; he thus holds power. If we go beyond the 'surface level' represented by the simple circulation of commodities, we can take account of the fact that capital, dead labour, extorts surplus-labour from the worker, living labour, and realises it as surplus-value: the buyer makes life-and-death decisions over the seller. Marx applies Hobbes's logic to the capitalist system's

---

100   Ibid.
101   *MECW*, Vol. 35, p. 186.

mechanisms of dominion: the individual has to endure them, unable to step aside from the dynamics of production. For the Marx of *Capital*, the vulgar economists' 'apologetic shifts' chattering about man as such are thus sense-less, nothing other than a way of protracting the existing state of affairs by concealing the social power therein. As such, the individual has value *qua* bearer of labour-power, and certainly not on account of some abstract dig-nity.[102]

The 'transvaluation' brought about by the capitalist mode of production con-sists of its destruction of any community of interests and the creation of a cat-egorial context that is radically new with respect to the past, in that it is centred on the dominion of exchange-value and thus of money as a general equivalent. Persons constitute fields of forces, *qua Träger* of precise economic and class interests: and we should avoid interpreting this concept in any sort of determ-inistic terms, instead stressing the interrelation between the economic and the juridical sphere. In *Capital*, Marx looks upon individual separation with greater pessimism than he had in the *Grundrisse*, toning down some of the aspects of that revolutionary Prometheanism previously present in his perspective. Thus the individual *qua* bearer of a universal is inserted within a mechanism external and extraneous to him, a system of obligations which is both economic and jur-idical. Marx does not disregard right – which is connected to the constitution of individuality – and reduce it to a mere consequence of the economic dynamic, but examines it within the terms of its non-neutrality, its connection with the strategies of dominion inherent within the capitalist mode of production, from which it is impossible to step aside.

This perspective does not mean denying the role of the individual, as might appear at first glance, since it presents an intimately double character: the reduction of the worker to a bearer of labour-power is coexistent with her possibility of fully developing her capacities and needs. For example, Marx says of piece-wages ('the form of wages most in harmony with the capitalist mode of production') that 'the wider scope that piece-wage gives to individuality tends to develop on the one hand that individuality, and with it the sense of liberty, independence, and self-control of the labourers, and on the other, their competition one with another'.[103] The ideologues of the ruling class do not show this double – and thus problematic – character of the capitalist structure, considering it wholly natural and necessary: 'The practical agents of capitalistic production and their pettifogging ideologists are as unable to think

---

102   See J.G. Thomas 1987, p. 144.
103   *MECW*, Vol. 35, p. 554.

of the means of production as separate from the antagonistic social mask they wear today, as a slave-owner to think of the worker himself as distinct from his character as a slave'.[104]

While the freedom of the commodity-owner is not the same as the capitalist system's apologists portray it, even so it cannot immediately be reduced to a mere fiction bearing no correspondence to any reality: 'Labour-power exists only as a capacity, or power of the living individual. Its production consequently presupposes his existence'.[105] Capacity, or power, are characteristics that can be exemplified in the Greek *dynamis*:[106] here re-emerges the idea of a creative tension, susceptible to unexpected developments. The capitalist relation is founded on the difference between the labour-power of the worker-subject and the labour that is actually performed: in the sale of something that exists only as a possibility, it cannot be separated from the living individuality of the labourer, her corporeality. Within this horizon we see how crucial living labour is, namely as the use-value of labour-power which, on the one hand, is subsumed under the valorisation of capital, and on the other hand, can constitute a radical opposition to capitalist dominion. Marx's position appears wholly irreducible to any representation of living labour 'kneeling down' before the objective dimension, which would have left him unable to recognise the possibility of the workers 'acting in common'. On the contrary, the worker's body is never fully 'captured', and thus remains a potential element of resistance to capital's command. In any case, if Hobbes is right that a man's value is his price – how much someone is prepared to pay to use his power – then the bearers of labour-power are faced with the need to organise to achieve greater political power and thus to fight for legislation from the state. This latter is, of course, a far from neutral element, since it is connected to both economic and juridical mechanisms of domination.

This conception of the person as a mask for economic and class interests – with its Hobbesian 'trace' – is connected to the question of fetishism. We should reiterate that fetishism cannot be circumscribed within the landscape of the first section of *Capital* Volume I, concerning only the situation related to the simple circulation of commodities and prior to the production process; a context, that is, devoid of capital, surplus-labour extraction and labour-power. Fetishism constitutes a sort of 'red thread' throughout all of *Capital*, even if

---

104 *MECW*, Vol. 35, p. 604.
105 *MECW*, Vol. 35, p. 181.
106 See Vadée 1992.

often implicitly so: at its basis is the dimension of appearance, which ought
not to be identified with either reality or mere fiction. Contrary to what the
exponents of classical political economy argue, we are not faced with the
coincidence of essence and appearance, since the real presents an opaque
character. However, fetishism's interweaving of reality and mystification does
prove to be connected to the structure of subjectivity.

Rethinking the formation of social objectivity, Marx at the same time revolutionised the concept of the subject: the mechanism of fetishism is a worldly
construct, but it does not proceed from the activity of any already-given subject.[107] On the contrary, it forms subjects in the field of objectivity itself: subjectivity is part of the 'spectral objectivity' of capital, and thus represents an
effect of the social process. Here we have genesis of subjectivity – but as part
of the social world of objectivity. Marx's initiative is to go beyond the sub-
ject/world dualism; there are no individuals independently of a determinate
society, but only historical practices incarnated by individuals. It is not the individual who constructs the world, but, on the contrary, the world that creates
the subjectivity of the individual in capitalist society, *qua* owner of commodities and her own person. Here returns the theme of the dual stakes of Marx's
reasoning, both economic and juridical. Up till now I have examined fetishism
solely in relation to the capitalist mode of production. Among other reasons,
there were many and varied twentieth-century re-readings of fetishism that
sought to show that its character is wholly in conformity with contemporary
capitalism and its explosion of forms and images: for example, Debord provides
a representation of this in his *Society of the Spectacle*. But what we now need to
understand is whether fetishism constitutes a permanent element throughout
history – always existing across all the productive forms that have come about
across the centuries – or if it is, instead, a distinctive trait of the capitalist system.

Has Fetishism Always Existed? 'Excursus' on Precapitalist Forms

In the section in the first chapter of *Capital* Volume I that focuses on com-
modity-fetishism, Marx also takes into consideration precapitalist structures,
precisely for the purposes of understanding whether or not they conformed to
this logic. His discussion of the commodity – and his derivation, from this, of
the element of fetishism – would suggest that this is a contemporary question,

---

107   See Balibar 1995, pp. 65–7.

singularly related to the capitalist mode of production, in its specific difference with respect to the precapitalist productive forms extending across history. Moreover, the commodity – the 'beginning' of *Capital* – exists as a dominant form only in the capitalist system; indeed, capitalism appears as an 'immense accumulation of commodities'. Prior structures thus seem to be devoid of the fetish phenomenon: 'The whole mystery of commodities, all the magic and necromancy that surrounds the products of labour as long as they take the form of commodities, vanishes therefore, so soon as we come to other forms of production'.[108] He thus gives the impression that when it comes to precapitalist structures, we cannot speak of fetishism. His specific examples relate to the medieval context and a primitive situation such as that of Robinson Crusoe.[109]

> Since Robinson Crusoe's experiences are a favourite theme with political economists, let us take a look at him on his island. Moderate though he be, yet some few wants he has to satisfy, and must therefore do a little useful work of various sorts ... His stock-book contains a list of the objects of utility that belong to him, of the operations necessary for their production; and lastly, of the labour time that definite quantities of those objects have, on an average, cost him. All the relations between Robinson and the objects that form this wealth of his own creation, are here so simple and clear as to be intelligible without exertion ...[110]

The example of Robinson Crusoe is particularly charged with meaning, also because it reappears repeatedly throughout Marx's work. Extremely significant in this regard is a passage of his 1857 *Einleitung* in which he polemically uses the category of 'Robinsonades' in order to indicate the conceptions of classical political economists like Smith and Ricardo, as well as contractualists like Rousseau, who based their reasoning of the postulate of a single man in the mould of Robinson on his desert island.[111] Marx was critical of this 'Robinso-

---

108   *MECW*, Vol. 35, p. 87.
109   For an analysis of historical and imaginary situations devoid of fetishism, see Godelier 1973. On the specific role of Robinson Crusoe in economic and political reflection, see Iacono 1982.
110   *MECW*, Vol. 35, p. 87.
111   See the *Einleitung*: 'Individuals producing in Society – hence socially determined individual production – is, of course, the point of departure. The individual and isolated hunter and fisherman, with whom Smith and Ricardo begin, belongs among the unimaginative conceits of the eighteenth-century Robinsonades ... As little as Rousseau's *contrat*

nian' approach, since there has never been a fully (and perfectly) isolated man, and individuals have always moved within a determinate social context. This 'aesthetic appearance' of a natural presupposition is anything other than innocent, and is, instead, functional to the legitimation of the capitalist system's structures of domination. Marx deconstructed the 'Robinsonian' starting point of this reasoning even in works prior to *Capital*. Here, we should turn back to the previously-cited passage from *Capital* in which Marx refers to the moderation of Robinson's island. Robinson has a direct, immediate relationship with things: in this sense, the element of fetishism seems to be completely missing, since this instead refers to the opaque region founded on a separation between essence and appearance, and thus a lack of transparency and 'purity'. One complex question, in this regard, concerns communism itself (we will examine this more specifically in the fourth chapter): namely, to understand whether the transparency proper to Robinson's island is prevalent also in communist society, and if so, what the differences are between any eventual communist transparency and the 'Robinsonian' one.

Subsequently Marx described another precapitalist situation, albeit a more complex one than Robinson's island: Europe's Middle Ages.

> Here, instead of the independent man, we find everyone dependent, serfs and lords, vassals and suzerains, laymen and clergy. Personal dependence here characterises the social relations of production just as much as it does the other spheres of life organised on the basis of that production. But for the very reason that personal dependence forms the ground-work of society, there is no necessity for labour and its products to assume a fantastic form different from their reality ... the particular and natural form of labour, and not, as in a society based on production of commodities, its general abstract form ... the social relations between individuals in the performance of their labour, appear at all events as their own mutual personal relations, and are not disguised under the shape of social relations between the products of labour.[112]

---

social, which brings naturally independent, autonomous subjects into relation and connection by contract, rests on such naturalism. This is the semblance, the merely aesthetic semblance, of the Robinsonades, great and small. It is, rather, the anticipation of 'civil society', in preparation since the sixteenth century and making giant strides towards maturity in the eighteenth ...'

112 *MECW*, Vol. 35, p. 88.

This analysis in *Capital* in many ways stood in continuity with the *Grundrisse*'s discussion of 'Precapitalist Forms'.[113] Indeed, there emerges a sharp contrast between the capitalist system, which is founded on impersonal relations mediated by things, and the precapitalist orders, which were instead based on relations of personal dependence. In the medieval landscape, work did not take on a form any different from its reality: there was no 'disguise' or 'illusion', as it was totally unmediated. His reasoning with regard to Robinson returns, albeit in a more articulated way, with transparency identified as a distinctive trait of precapitalist forms, in counterposition to the opaque picture of capitalism in which essence and appearance do not coincide.

Here we ought to consider a further example from Marx, concerning a situation which is less 'dated' with respect not only to Robinson but also to the Middle Ages, concerning the patriarchial production among a family of peasants:

> For an example of labour in common [*gemeinsamer*] or directly associated [*unmittelbar vergesellschafter*] labour, we have no occasion to go back to that spontaneously developed form which we find on the threshold of the history of all civilised races. We have one close at hand in the patriarchal industries of a peasant family, that produces corn, cattle [and so on] ... The different kinds of labour ... which result in the various products, are in themselves, and such as they are, direct social functions, because functions of the family ... The labour power of each individual, by its very nature, operates in this case merely as a definite portion of the whole labour power of the family ...[114]

Even if this context appears chronologically closer to us than the previous ones, they do all share the dimension of transparency: the natural form of labour is immediately its social form, and the various different labours are immediately social functions. Here, as in the preceding structures (albeit with a series of specific differences) we have a scenario characterised by the simplicity of the relationship between men and things. Even in a situation of this type, more developed than were the previous ones, the fetishism phenomenon seems to be absent. The distinctive traits common among all precapitalist forms clearly emerge from Marx's reflection:

---

113   See Hobsbawm 1965; Terray 1969; Hindess and Hirst 1977; Carandini 1979; Sofri 1969; Jánoska (ed.) 1994, pp. 215–337; Sereni 2007, pp. 127–62; Basso 2008b.

114   *MECW*, Vol. 35, pp. 88–9.

> In the ancient Asiatic and other ancient modes of production, we find
> that the conversion of products into commodities, and therefore the
> conversion of men into producers of commodities, holds a subordinate
> place, which, however, increases in importance as the primitive com-
> munities approach nearer and nearer to their dissolution ... Those ancient
> social organisms of production are, as compared with bourgeois society,
> extremely simple and transparent. But they are founded either on the
> immature development of man individually, who has not yet severed the
> umbilical cord that unites him with his fellowmen in a primitive tribal
> community, or upon direct relations of subjection. They can arise and
> exist only when the development of the productive power of labour has
> not risen beyond a low stage[115]

In this passage, we again see the idea that the commodity becomes the dominant form only with the capitalist system: earlier, it had constituted a residual, secondary element that only appeared in the interstices of precapitalist
orders. But the way in which Marx sees the structures in question, in which
the commodity is not the dominant form, does not imply any sort of nostalgic harking back to the past. Indeed, their simplicity and transparency in
reality constitutes 'the other face' of man's attachment to the community as if
'by an umbilical cord'. Within this landscape, we cannot properly speak either
of individuals – since man does not possess any real autonomy or possibility
of movement, being entrapped within an organicist structure which 'chokes'
him – or of society as a complex web of relations. Moreover, unlike in the case
of the impersonal character of capitalism, precapitalist forms are distinguished
by the presence of personal relations. They are a 'blocked' situation, in that they
are characterised by static hierarchies and a substantial inertia.

Marx's analysis in *Capital* Volume I in many ways takes its cue from his
approach in the *Grundrisse*, which was characterised by excessive schematism
in its interpretation of the historical process: there he established an indelible
difference between the capitalist system, founded on the individual and society, and the preceding structures. The fact that these latter were not characterised by fetishism does not, in reality, indicate their superiority, in that transparency is the 'other face' of the low degree of development of the productive
forces and the presence of wholly inadequate political structures. In fact, Marx
criticised the classical political economists precisely because they considered
the communities in question to be backward: 'forms of social production that

---

115   *MECW*, Vol. 35, p. 90.

preceded the bourgeois form, are treated by the bourgeoisie in much the same way as the Fathers of the Church treated pre-Christian religions'.[116] Polemicising with the classical economists, Marx did risk – certainly in the *Grundrisse* but partly also in *Capital* – providing an over-simplified image of precapitalist structures, motivated by his desire to bring into relief the earth-shattering *novum* of the capitalist mode of production, as compared to the past.

Notwithstanding this limitation, it is worth noting that there are also other tendencies in *Capital*, complicating this picture. In order to understand in a more articulated manner his reference to precapitalist forms, or indeed anything that did not seem 'capitalistic', we must consider also other texts by Marx. These include those pieces linked to contingent events as well as the so-called *Ethnological Notebooks*, from which there emerges a complex picture, open to unexpected potentialities for the subjects involved. In any case, the fetishist character of capitalism is not an index of unreality, based on the (presumed) evanescence of disciplining mechanisms. Capital – as a social relation, and not a thing – is shot through by the asymmetries among individuals, and thus internally riven by a 'real' and indelible fracture.

116   *MECW*, Vol. 35, p. 92.

CHAPTER 2

Ethnology and Forms of 'the Common'

> If capitalism is the universal truth, it is so in the sense that makes capital-
> ism the *negative* of all social formations: it is the thing, the unnameable,
> the generalized decoding of flows that reveals *a contrario* the secret of all
> these formations ... Primitive societies are not outside history, it is capit-
> alism that results from a long history of contingencies and accidents, and
> that brings on this end
>
> GILLES DELEUZE and FÉLIX GUATTARI, *Anti-Oedipus*

∴

The 'New' Anthropology of Capitalism: From the *Grundrisse* to *Capital*

In this chapter I shall take into consideration Marx's study of precapitalist
forms, or indeed noncapitalist situations, some characteristic elements of
which became apparent at the end of the previous chapter. Within this perspective, I will also shine a light on the so-called *Ethnological Notebooks*, giving
due credit to their importance, albeit without indulging in any idealisation of
the structures that we mentioned just previously. Indeed, a distinctive characteristic of Marx across his entire trajectory was his search for individual realisation, antithetical to any type of 'communitarianism'. It is not always very clear
in what sense we ought to understand the term 'anthropology', and that goes
for Marx, too. The nineteenth-century birth of anthropology as a science and
its development in the twentieth century further complicate the picture: and
the encounter between Marxism and anthropology has been an intense one
indeed. In Marx himself, we can identify two different meanings of anthropology. The first, philosophical sense defines anthropology as a discourse on
man and his key attributes. The second, however, conceives anthropology in a
manner analogous to that adopted by anthropology as a science, and is thus
employed with particular reference to precapitalist situations and the communitarian structures present therein.[1] We will begin by addressing the former

---

1   For a differentiation between two different declinations of anthropology, see Sartre 1972. For

sense of the term, making a brief excursus across Marx's whole theoretical journey but focusing in particular on the path from the *Grundrisse* to *Capital*.

Marx's reflection was sustained by an emphasis on the individual element, as the distinctive trait of the capitalist system with respect to previous forms of production. As we already underlined in the last chapter, we cannot properly speak of the individual when it comes to precapitalist structures, since man was attached to the community as if by an umbilical cord, through the mediation of land. Such transparency in the relation between men and things, even if it is characterised by rigid hierarchies, seems wholly opposed to the fetishism that characterises capitalist society. At the base of capitalist society stands the individual, with her independence and characteristic potential for movement; this dynamism[2] must, however, be conceived in all its ambivalence, since while the single human can now take charge of her own activity, she is now developing in the context of enslavement to the social power of money and capital. Even if such an approach is present throughout Marx's entire trajectory, even from his first writings, it is without doubt in the *Grundrisse* that this logic is most fully explicated. The individual dimension here becomes central, through an irrecoverable rupture with the 'communitarian' scenario that appeared in earlier social forms.[3] According to Marx in the *Grundrisse*, what we have here is capital's 'permanent revolution' against the bonds that hold back the full development of the single person.

Such a framework presents something of a 'nineteenth-century' limitation, indulging in a 'grand narrative' with wide historical scope yet simplifying certain aspects of the situation. I do not believe that what we have here is a true and proper definition of a philosophy of history, even beyond the fact that what is meant by such a term is often opaque and far from immediately clear. In any case, it is on this basis that we find the element – present ever since the 'beginning of the epoch' in the second half of the eighteenth century – of the passage from plural *historiae* to the modern declination of history as a 'collective singularity'.[4] Certainly the *Grundrisse* present an excessively schematic

---

Sartre, philosophical anthropology is something very different from anthropology as a human science, summarising this in the formula 'in anthropology man is the object, in philosophy the subject-object'. The keystone of the crossing of paths between Marxism and philosophical anthropology, according to Sartre, lies precisely in this subjective-objective dimension, in which subjects both play a significant role and are always entering into contact with the 'practicol-inert'.

2   See Krahl 1971.

3   See Basso 2008a, pp. 153–215; Di Marco 2005; Bellofiore, Starosta and P. Thomas (eds.) 2013.

4   Koselleck 1979; Duso 1999, pp. 21 ff.

conviction that capitalism destroys all the constitutive elements of previous forms, in particular as regards erasing slave structures, on both the economic and juridical levels: in reality, these never disappeared from the horizon of capitalism.[5] Beyond such limitations, the idea that a new anthropology emerges with capitalism – almost a sort of 'genetic mutation' of humanity – remains a very important one.[6] Precisely in order to bring this change into focus, Marx stresses in an almost violent manner – even if bending the stick of historical reality – the idea that absolutely nothing remains of what determined the social structure prior to capitalism.[7] It is thus worth examining how he developed and rearticulated this theme in *Capital*, also with some important modifications.

In the first place, we should note that in *Capital* this question is problematised in view of his previous texts. He largely maintains his earlier framing of the question in terms of the radical *novum* of the capitalist mode of production compared to past ones. Yet at the same time, the problem is 'complicated', not so much in terms of the relation of past to present, between capitalism and what went before, but rather as concerns the internal articulation of capitalism in its global dimension. Indeed, in the 1840s Marx's attentions had principally concerned the European situation, above all that of Germany, France and England. Moreover, it is telling that in the *Communist Manifesto* the United States is missing from view – the most 'advanced' country – and so, too, are Russia and noncapitalist countries. In the 1850s, with his various critiques of political economy and in particular the *Grundrisse*, the picture became more complicated and he was increasingly interested in precapitalist forms; moreover, this work's *excursus* on these structures was the widest study of this theme in all Marx's work. The impression that we get from this text, albeit with a series of ambivalences (and sometimes ambiguities), is that capitalism fully destroys the preceding forms; and the image of capitalist society here presented is given the aforementioned 'progressive' characterisation, founded on the individual. It seems that he considered the situation of extra-European countries to be pre- or noncapitalist. In *Capital*, this image is not negated, but rather rearticulated.

---

5 See Moulier Boutang 1998, which brings into relief the limits of Marx's reflection in the *Grundrisse*, with his 'Prometheanism' in this regard. In this sense, the category 'wage labour' seems more appropriate than 'free labour'. On how slavery lasted into capitalist modernity and was legitimised during the Enlightenment see Benot 2003 (albeit on a basis different to our own). See also Blackburn 1997, Fogel 1989, Tomich 2004 and Linden 2005.

6 I am indebted to Ferruccio Gambino for his insights on the question of the 'new' anthropology.

7 Lefort 2005, p. 210.

Marx maintained the idea that capitalism is a break with hierarchies of a feudal imprint, which 'harnessed' man to the community without allowing him the freedom to develop his capacities and faculties. The generalisation of factory legislation

> destroys both the ancient and the transitional forms, behind which the dominion of capital is still in part concealed, and replaces them by the direct and open sway of capital; but thereby it also generalises the direct opposition to this sway. Capitalist production as a whole, the intensity of labour, and the competition of machinery with the labourer ... By maturing the material conditions, and the combination on a social scale of the processes of production, it matures the contradictions and antagonisms of the capitalist form of production, and thereby provides, along with the elements for the formation of a new society, the forces for exploding the old ones.[8]

This passage reaffirms an aspect that is continuous throughout Marx's trajectory: the capitalist mode of production destroys the previous, communitarian forms and all the veils they wrap themselves in, and thus establishes itself on the basis of direct, brutal and unscrupulous dominion.[9] This sense of capitalism casting aside all before it also appears in *Capital* Volume III:

> Domestic handicrafts and manufacturing labour as secondary occupations of agriculture, which forms the basis, are the prerequisite of that production upon which natural economy rests – in European antiquity and the Middle Ages as well as in the present-day Indian community, in which the traditional organisation has not yet been destroyed. The capitalist mode of production completely abolishes this relationship; a process which may be studied on a large scale particularly in England during the last third of the 18th century.[10]

---

8   *MECW*, Vol. 35, p. 504.

9   See Ricciardi 2010, p. 59: 'The concept of capitalism ... was constructed by way of a double negation: on the one hand, ... it denies those concepts that from within this reality refer to future constitutions of society; on the other hand, it displays another character, both precarious and fundamental, antithetical with respect to the concepts referring to past constitutions of society, whether these be defined as natural societies or more simply as communities'.

10   *MECW*, Vol. 37, p. 773.

Only on the basis of the 'revolutionising' process carried out by the capitalist system is it possible to 'think in practice' a new, yet more radical revolution – communism. It works to eat away at every previously defined community of interests:

> The guilds of the middle ages therefore tried to prevent by force the transformation of the master of a trade into a capitalist, by limiting the number of labourers that could be employed by one master within a very small maximum. The possessor of money or commodities actually turns into a capitalist in such cases only where the minimum sum advanced for production greatly exceeds the maximum of the middle ages. Here, as in natural science, is shown the correctness of the law discovered by Hegel (in his 'Logic'), that merely quantitative differences beyond a certain point pass into qualitative change.[11]

Thus capitalism grew out of feudalism, but it did so by fully negating it:

> The economic structure of capitalist society has grown out of the economic structure of feudal society. The dissolution of the latter set free the elements of the former.
> The immediate producer, the labourer, could only dispose of his own person after he had ceased to be attached to the soil and ceased to be the slave, serf, or bondsman of another.[12]

Obviously such a break did not take place abruptly, but rather gradually through the transformation of the money owner into a capitalist. Marx used a Hegelian logic, in this regard: through this process, quantity turned into quality, as Engels also often repeated. Moreover, even at the beginning of *Capital*, he had emphasised that the commodity became dominant only under the capitalist mode of production: and this was not because commodities had not previously existed, but because they played a secondary, 'minority', residual role. If quantity did turn into quality, it was only with the capitalist system that a sufficient quantity of commodities was reached. Some of the most important modern philosophers seemed fully aware of this:

---

11   *MECW*, Vol. 35, p. 313.
12   *MECW*, Vol. 35, p. 706.

Descartes, in defining animals as mere machines, saw with eyes of the manufacturing period, while to eyes of the middle ages, animals were assistants to man, as they were later to Von Haller in his 'Restauration der Staatswissenschaften.' That Descartes, like Bacon, anticipated an alteration in the form of production, and the practical subjugation of Nature by Man, as a result of the altered methods of thought, is plain from his 'Discours de la Méthode'[13]

Modern thought, paradigmatically expressed in Descartes's *Discourse on Method*, dismantled the distinctive features of ancient thought and, in so doing, reflected the material changes that modernity entailed. Referring to Aristotle, Marx explained that while use-value represented the horizon of ancient, precapitalist thought, the scope of the capitalist horizon was exchange-value, to which use-value was subsumed. In his chapter on the division of labour, Marx returned to this theme:

> In most striking contrast with this accentuation of quantity and exchange-value, is the attitude of the writers of antiquity, who hold exclusively by quality and use-value ... There is not a word alluding to exchange-value or to the cheapening of commodities. This aspect, from the standpoint of use-value alone, is taken as well by Plato, who treats division of labour as the foundation on which the division of society into classes is based, as by Xenophon, who with characteristic bourgeois instinct, approaches more nearly to division of labour within the workshop. Plato's Republic, in so far as division of labour is treated in it, as the formative principle of the State, is merely the Athenian idealisation of the Egyptian system of castes ...[14]

Indeed, in his extensive notes on ancient literary and philosophical works, Marx emphasised the fact that the forms of production in antiquity were centred on use-value, for instance in the comment that in his *Ciropedia* 'Xenophon ... lays stress exclusively upon the excellence to be attained in use-value'. Thus Marx reaffirms the supremacy of use-value over exchange-value in antiquity, as well as the inversion of this logic in modernity. It is worth specifying that even though in Marx there is a radical critique of the capitalist rule of exchange-value, this does not imply any sort of idealisation of use-value as such;

---

13   *MECW*, Vol. 35, p. 393. See Borkenau 1980, Negri 1970.

14   *MECW*, Vol. 35, p. 370.

after all, the centrality of use-value in antiquity was functional to an absolutely static order in which individual development – and, indeed, social development, in the sense of the fullness of real and ideal individual relations – was precluded. It was a 'blocked' structure, or even a caste system, closed-off to any change. Plato's Republic itself, according to Marx, was a sort of idealisation of an apparently immutable situation. Without doubt, even if on the basis of a rearticulation and 'complication' of his reasoning, Marx was here developing the *Grundrisse*'s conceptual outlook of the capitalist system's break with the forms that preceded it.

In order to understand his approach, it is worth referring not only to Hegel's *Science of Logic* but also to Marx's own study of the natural sciences: indeed, in the aforementioned passage he drew something of an analogy ('Here, as in natural science'), while a subsequent note – albeit one written by Engels – drew attention to the importance of modern chemistry. Marx very much historicised his categories: moreover, he criticised the entirety of classical political economy precisely for having 'eternalised' the capitalist mode of production, proving unable to interpret it in its specific determinations and thus in terms of its difference to previous orders. The knights were hardly a constant across all epochs: 'Don Quixote long ago paid the penalty for wrongly imagining that knight errantry was compatible with all economic forms of society'. It was similarly impossible to maintain that capital already existed in ancient Rome: 'In encyclopaedias of classical antiquities we find such nonsense as this – that in the ancient world capital was fully developed, "except that the free labourer and a system of credit was wanting"'.

At the same time, Marx devoted ever more attention not so much to pre-capitalist forms, as to the complex articulation of capitalism. *Capital* makes reference not only to countries like England, France and Germany, but also to situations that were less central or 'advanced' in a capitalist sense. For example, in his chapter on the general law of accumulation he evokes the case of Ireland: 'Ireland, with 3½ millions, is still always miserable, and miserable because she is overpopulated. Therefore her depopulation must go yet further, that thus she may fulfil her true destiny, that of an English sheep-walk and cattle-pasture'.[15] Furthermore, especially in the notes, *Capital* is full of references to extra-European countries:

---

15   *MECW*, Vol. 35, p. 702. See also the note where he refers to Ireland, also looking ahead to Volume III: 'How the famine and its consequences have been deliberately made the most of, both by the individual landlords and by the English legislature, to forcibly carry out the agricultural revolution and to thin the population of Ireland down to the proportion

In some States, particularly in Mexico, slavery is hidden under the form of *peonage*. By means of advances, repayable in labour, which are handed down from generation to generation, not only the individual labourer, but his family, become, *de facto*, the property of other persons and their families. Juarez abolished *peonage*. The so-called Emperor Maximilian re-established it by a decree, which, in the House of Representatives at Washington, was aptly denounced as a decree for the re-introduction of slavery into Mexico.[16]

He makes various references to South America, for example to its mining workers, subjected to devastating work-rhythms.[17] His reflection was rooted in a specific analysis of the crises present in each given country: 'never before was *the English crisis preceded* by tremendous crises now lasting already five years in *the United States, South America, Germany, Austria*, etc.'[18]

If we broaden our view beyond Europe and the most developed capitalist states, we understand that capitalism did not fully overcome the previous structures everywhere and in a homogeneous fashion, particularly in the case of slavery. Rather, in many parts of the world system it never disappeared, but rather proved functional to the spread of capitalism. Thus to evoke slavery is not to speak of the negation of capitalism: 'the nature of capital remains the same in its undeveloped as in its developed form'. Within the capitalist dynamic there exist not only fully developed modalities, but also incomplete ones. The question of slavery takes on an important function in terms of understanding the capitalist mode of production in its complex, articulated dimension, with the political scope of encouraging discussion of this issue:

In the United States of North America, every independent movement of the workers was paralysed so long as slavery disfigured a part of the Republic. Labour cannot emancipate itself in the white skin where in the black it is branded. But out of the death of slavery a new life at once arose. The first fruit of the Civil War was the eight hours' agitation ...[19]

---

satisfactory to the landlords, I shall show more fully in Vol. III. of this work, in the section on landed property'.

16   *MECW*, Vol. 35, p. 178.

17   See also his reference to Peru in Volume II: 'A completely isolated natural economy, such as the Inca state of Peru, would not come under any of these categories': *MECW*, Vol. 36, p. 121.

18   Marx to Danielson, 10 April 1879.

19   *MECW*, Vol. 35, p. 305.

This passage is extraordinarily alive to events, in that it shows that the capitalist mode of production did not entail the elimination of slavery, such as seemed apparent from a simplistic representation of the capitalist dynamic, sometimes visible in the *Grundrisse*.

There is also a second particularly important aspect of this question, connected to the stakes of emancipation and thus to communism. If our objective is the liberation of labour, then such a praxis cannot but entail freedom from slavery. Indeed, as long as slavery persists, there can be no prospect of communism. In the 1860s, Marx rearticulated the issue of slavery, challenging any claims as to the 'progressive' character of colonialism. We are not here attempting to identify Marx's analysis with, or 'weld' it to, the positions set out by postcolonial studies,[20] and nor do we consider Marx a 'postcolonialist'. Rather, our intention is to bring out Marx's growing awareness of the need to overcome the horizon of slavery. Moreover, we should not underestimate the significance of his reference to the United States, an interest that intensified in Marx over time. After all, the first volume of *Capital* concludes precisely with reference to migration, specifically migration toward the USA: 'The stream of emigration was only diverted from the English colonies to the United States'.[21]

---

20   Without here being able to delve deeper into the distinctive traits of postcolonial studies, which are extremely articulated and diverse, I will limit myself to noting the 'pathbreaking' role of Frantz Fanon's works (in particular Fanon 1967, 1963) and those of Edward Said (1978) as well as the attempt to interpret modernity on the basis of a plurality of locations and gazes through an intersection of political theory, sociology, anthropology, and comparative literature. This brings into question all Eurocentric approaches and appreciates the perspective of so-called 'peripheral' actors. We should stress both the numerous strong points that such a framework offers ('provincialising Europe', to quote Chakrabarty) as well as its limitations, in particular the risk of turning towards a 'culturalist' outlook that is not entirely incompatible with liberal multiculturalism. In this regard, see the observations of Mezzadra 2008a (above all pp. 10 ff.). Among the numerous texts that could be ascribed to postcolonial studies, see in particular Chakrabarty 2000, Spivak 1999, Guha and Spivak 1988, Bhabha 1994, and Young 2001.

21   *MECW*, Vol. 35, p. 760. See the continuation of this passage: 'Meanwhile, the advance of capitalistic production in Europe, accompanied by increasing Government pressure, has rendered Wakefield's recipe superfluous. On the one hand, the enormous and ceaseless stream of men, year after year driven upon America, leaves behind a stationary sediment in the east of the United States, the wave of immigration from Europe throwing men on the labour-market there more rapidly than the wave of emigration westwards can wash them away. On the other hand, the American Civil War brought in its train a colossal national debt ... The great republic has, therefore, ceased to be the promised land for emigrant labourers'.

In this ever more globalised context, pushing back the frontiers, new spaces of emancipation could emerge:

> The proper task of bourgeois society is the creation of the world market, at least in outline, and of the production based on that market. Since the world is round, the colonisation of California and Australia and the opening up of China and Japan would seem to have completed this process. For us, the difficult **question** is this: on the Continent revolution is imminent and will, moreover, instantly assume a socialist character. Will it not necessarily be **crushed** in this little corner of the earth, since the **movement** of bourgeois society is still, in the **ascendant** over a far greater area?[22]

The 'new' anthropology of capitalism, founded on the rupture with both the social structure and the imaginary that pertained to previous forms, was rooted in an ever more extensive spatial dimension. Furthermore, Marx had always emphasised that capital had a tendency to make itself a world market, thus displaying a structurally global dimension.[23] Capital was continually overcoming its confines, Europe no longer representing the centre of the world: and to understand this was of shattering importance not just for theoretical analysis, but also for political practice. The stakes of revolution could no longer be confined to the European stage, but rather had to be recalibrated according to the terms of an ever growing world. It was worth understanding the relationship between capitalism, with the aforementioned characteristics, and noncapitalist communitarian forms, above all if one maintained that the former displayed various modalities that were differentiated over space and time. That is to say, there was never any full and perfect synchronisation between different scenarios. Marx thus had to examine the distinctive traits of countries that were still not fully capitalist and yet could not be defined as 'noncapitalist'. In order to follow the path that Marx took, we have to refer back to his notes on the natural and historical sciences, in particular those concerning ethnology.

---

22   Marx to Engels, 8 October 1858: *MECW*, Vol. 40, p. 437.

23   For analysis of how the world market is a historic task of capital, see Ferrari Bravo 2001, pp. 75–145, particularly pp. 88 ff. He brings out the strong points but also the limitations of Marx's reflection in this regard, on the basis of a comparison with Lenin's theory of imperialism.

The Study of Communitarian Forms, between the Natural and Historical Sciences: The *Ethnological Notebooks*

In the last decades of Marx's production, he devoted ever greater attention to ethnological and anthropological studies.[24] More generally, it is worth noting that the late Marx did not complete many texts, apart from some political writings. Instead, he dedicated himself to re-elaborating *Capital* and to sketching out a very large amount of notes on various disciplines, largely scientific ones. As concerns *Capital*, we should remember that the second and third volumes were never published by Marx, but rather after his death by Engels. We could even say that in his last ten years Marx suspended his work on *Capital* and mainly devoted himself to studying the natural sciences.[25] Here I shall lay particular emphasis on his ethnological writings, though in reality his *Exzerpte* touched on various scientific fields.

Interpreting these notes on the natural sciences proves a rather complex task. A first key to reading them lies in understanding that the extracts in question served the purposes of his critique of political economy, and thus allow for light to be shed on some aspects of this latter: take the example of the importance of agrochemicals to crop yields. Marx was very interested in the productivity of agriculture, in an anti-Malthusian sense: and agrochemicals, geology and also physiology could all play an important role in this regard.[26] Moreover, in *Capital*, Marx deployed various metaphors from physics and chemistry: thus posing the question of whether this meant real parallels between the natural and historical sciences, and what role they played with regard to the critique of political economy. In any case, the connection (and, at the same time, the 'separation') between nature and history was a theme that ran throughout

---

24 See Krader 1978, 1966, 1976.

25 Telling, in this regard, are Engels's remarks in his preface to Volume II: 'There was another intermission after 1870, due mainly to Marx's ill health. Marx employed this time in his customary way, by studying agronomics, rural relations in America and, especially, Russia, the money-market and banking, and finally natural sciences such as geology and physiology. Independent mathematical studies also figure prominently in the numerous extract notebooks of this period': *MECW*, Vol. 36, p. 7. On the importance of the natural sciences to Marx, including the effect this had on the structure of *Capital*, see the essays in Griese and Sandkühler (eds.) 1997, AAVV 2006 and AAVV 1972.

26 See Vidoni 1982, pp. 19–135. 'In determining the possible productivity levels of land, the tools of agrochemistry seemed more useful than had the considerations of economists hitherto' (p. 46). 'It was precisely in the 1860s that the application of chemistry to agriculture spread, particularly in Germany ...' (p. 63).

Marx's whole trajectory.[27] Such a correspondence, and even the respective differences between the two fields, was further examined and developed in Marx's more mature critique of political economy. Indeed, in this critique, reference to capital's 'process of natural history [*einen naturgeschichtlichen Prozeß*]' was absolutely central. Moreover, capital was defined as an 'organism' in continual transformation. It would be too constricting to see these only as 'naturalistic' metaphors: rather, something much more significant is coming through, here.

Notwithstanding the fact that this question proved controversial and was not immediately transparent, without doubt Darwin did exercise an important influence on the architect of *Capital*.[28] It was through Darwin that Marx sought to delineate the unity of natural and human history, in counterposition to any teleological or providential vision. Human evolution is part of the evolution of the universe. For Marx, 'evolution' did not imply a uniform and unstoppable trajectory, since there were also 'leaps forward', backward steps, discontinuities, ruptures, and abrupt advances. Moreover, to bring into focus such a point of contact between Marx and Darwin does not mean failing to understand the ways in which they were clearly divided. In reality, even though Darwin's perspective was only partly compatible with that of Malthus, Marx to some degree 'associated' these two authors and marked his distance from them. Another significant author in this context was Hobbes. His task was both to grasp the full significance of the Hobbes-Malthus-Darwin 'lineage' – with

---

27   On the question of the relation between nature and history, see Schmidt 1962. This work, however, in many aspects diverges from our line of thought, tending to interpret nature according to a purely philosophical perspective and not giving due emphasis to how Marx engaged with the natural sciences.

28   In the first volume of *Capital*, Darwin's work is defined as 'epoch-defining'. On Darwin, see Engels's letter to Marx of 11–12 December 1859: 'Darwin, by the way, whom I'm reading just now, is absolutely splendid. There was one aspect of teleology that had yet to be demolished, and that has now been done. Never before has so grandiose an attempt been made to demonstrate historical evolution in Nature, and certainly never to such good effect. One does, of course, have to put up with the crude English method'; and Marx to Engels on 19 December 1860: 'I have read all sorts of things. Among others Darwin's book of Natural Selection. Although it is developed in the crude English style, this is the book which contains the basis in natural history for our view'. See Lucas 1964, Ball 1979, Heyer 1982, Vidoni 1985, Lecourt 1992. On anthropology and Darwin, and Marx's initial enthusiasm for this, followed by ever greater scepticism, see Tort 2006, pp. 115–40; and Patterson 2009 (particularly pp. 65–90), which, however, invites attention to the distinction between Darwin and social Darwinism. Indeed, there were socialist as well as conservative Darwinians.

the objective of pulling apart all theological-teleological-providential perspectives – and radically to criticise it on account of its conformity to the capitalist mode of production's mechanisms of dominion. As for his relationship with Darwin, it is worth looking into the complex question of the 'critical history of technology':

> A critical history of technology would show how little any of the inventions of the 18th century are the work of a single individual ... Darwin has interested us in the history of Nature's Technology, i.e., in the formation of the organs of plants and animals, which organs serve as instruments of production for sustaining life. Does not the history of the productive organs of man, of organs that are the material basis of all social organisation, deserve equal attention?[29]

We ought to bear in mind the fact that the recurring analogy in *Capital* between natural, biological laws and the 'laws' of capitalist production in no way implies any identification of these two spheres. Rather, the analogy brings out precisely the difference between them. Many scholars at the time made a distinction between the tangible appearance of things and their inner structure, by way of a complex series of abstractions and hypotheses. This framework proved fruitful also for the purposes interpreting fetishism – as examined in the previous chapter – on the basis of an awareness of the non-coincidence of appearance and essence, of the 'superficial' and 'profound' dimensions. The opacity of such reflection had a scientific as well as strictly philosophical foundation: science could certainly not be identified with a crude empiricist method, since the element of abstraction stood at its very basis. Moreover – again to return to themes addressed in the previous chapter – it cannot be forgotten that to define

---

29   *MECW*, Vol. 35, p. 375. On the question of technology, note also: 'The principle which it pursued, of resolving each process into its constituent movements, without any regard to their possible execution by the hand of man, created the new modern science of technology ... Technology also discovered the few main fundamental forms of motion, which, despite the diversity of the instruments used ...' (p. 489). Also worth consulting on this question are Marx's *Technologisch-historischen Exzerpte* (Marx 1981). Here (pp. 1–166) we find in particular the *Exzerpte* present in 1851's Heft B56, and subsequently those from 1859's Heft B79. Heft B56 includes extracts from Poppe on mechanics, technology, physics and the history of mathematics, from Ure on the technical dictionary, and from Beckmann on the history of inventions. See Wendling 2009. In the next chapter, we shall resume our discussion regarding his thinking on the 'critical history of technology' and the relationship between technology and technique.

the commodity as an elementary cell has a clear scientific root: it suffices to think of the scientific research of the time on cells. In general, the idea of starting out from the simplest in order to arrive at the most complex is not only a philosophical move of a Hegelian type, but also corresponds to a method typical of the sciences, particularly biology. If the first interpretation that we outlined tends to emphasise the role of the study of the natural sciences in the critique of political economy, then the second approach to this question is inclined to attribute these *Exzerpte* a great deal of autonomy from his position in *Capital*. What is central, in this latter case, is that these texts were very much internal to the debate of the time on the status of science, and thus of mathematics, physics, chemistry, and geology. In reality, these two readings do not necessarily stand in contradiction to one another, but can often intersect. For example, Marx's notes on mathematics are telling in this regard.[30]

We can immediately see the important role that mathematics played for the purposes of delineating political economy and a critique of it. Moreover, in *Capital*, in particular the second and third volumes, there were numerous mathematical constructions: think, for example, of the section in Volume III on the question of the relationship between surplus value and the rate of profit. Indeed, in his manuscripts Marx makes more calculations than is apparent from the edition published by Engels. We will limit ourselves to recalling the so-called *Mathematical Manuscripts*, which among other things belong to the last phase of Marx's output, in large part being drawn up in the late 1870s and 1880s. It is also worth remembering that in this same period Engels's interest in mathematics and (differential and integral) infinitesimal calculus also intensified, in 1877's *Anti-Dühring* and the *Dialectics of Nature* (which he worked on until 1882). This is not a matter of considering Marx's manuscripts as if they were the work of an important mathematician,[31] but rather of drawing into focus certain considerations that are important to understanding his full horizon. In the first place, the specific object of the manuscripts was differential calculus: naturally, he made reference to Leibniz and Newton, criticised on account of their 'mystical differential calculus'; to the 'rationalist method' of D'Alembert; to Lagrange's subsequent 'purely algebraic method'; and finally to Cauchy and Weierstrass. Secondly, the type of method that he used and

---

30 See Marx 1968. Many letters testify to Marx's growing interest in mathematics: see, for example, his 23 November 1860 missive to Engels: 'For me writing articles is almost out of the question. The only occupation in which I can maintain the necessary quietness of mind is mathematics'.

31 Among other things, Marx learnt much of his knowledge of mathematics from Samuel Moore, who was certainly not a great mathematician: see Matarrese 1975, Guerraggio 1982.

his approach to mathematics strongly resounded of the dialectic: indeed, he interpreted the differential by way of the dialectical negation of the negation.[32] In political economy, as in mathematics, a real process emerges through the dialectic: it is constitutive of reality, and cannot be reduced to a mere method. Thirdly, the manuscripts in question are the place where Marx elaborates the mathematical structure of his economic analysis.[33]

As well as mathematics, Marx's interest in chemistry is also of some significance: he produced numerous notes concerning either organic or inorganic chemistry, examining the most diverse questions (a great number of them corresponding to mathematical formulas), such as atoms, metals and metalloids.[34] Indeed, as well as books on chemistry in the strict sense of the word, he also considered texts concerning other natural sciences such as physics, geology and physiology.[35] Marx's studies reflected the nineteenth-century development of physics, with the advance of mechanisation. The usefulness of his studies for the purposes of analysing agriculture and industry is clearly apparent. For example, in a letter to Engels of 13 February 1866, Marx remarks upon the importance of the new agrochemistry in Germany, naming Liebig and Schönbein as significant exponents of this latter. He frequently draws analogies between the methods of political economy and those of physics and chemistry.

Also important are his notes on geology, which were heavily conditioned by his engagement with certain scholars of the time, several among them Darwinists. Among other things, the parallel that he drew between geology and political economy appears with particular clarity in some such passages: and here he was drawing an analogy, not identifying the two fields.[36] Notably, his

---

32   Consider in particular the manuscript on the concept of the derivate function, Marx 1968, pp. 45–55 (especially pp. 45–6). We think it worth noting that Hegel's *Science of Logic* had addressed the question of differential calculus: it is far from improbable that this influenced Marx. Moreover, in his *Dialectics of Nature*, Engels praised Marx's reasoning for its capacity to interpret differential calculus dialectically and bring out its dynamism: 'The differential calculus for the first time makes it possible for natural science to represent mathematically *processes* and not only *states*: motion'.

33   See Ponzio 1975, p. 34: 'The fact that in his last years Marx – as the two 1881 essays particularly testify – dedicated so much attention to differential calculus stands as a testimony to the fact that Marx had the project of constructing a mathematical theory of political economy ... the study of differential and integral calculus could give the impression that Marx had the project of realising *dynamic* mathematical models in economic analysis'.

34   See Marx 1999.

35   Jäckel 1997.

36   See, for example, *MEGA*, II, 3.6, p. 1972.

1878 *Exzerpte und Notizien zur Geologie, Mineralogie und Agrikulturchemie* were recently published in the critical edition MEGA².[37] Marx does make sporadic comments of his own, but mostly this was a matter of producing a wide catalogue of nineteenth-century texts on geology and mineralogy, dedicating considerable space to Josef Beete Jukes's text *The Student's Manual of Geology*. Particularly significant for our present purposes are his analysis of the effects of geology on agriculture and on industry, and of the connection between agriculture and colonialism, as well as his reference to labour and trade unions.[38] Moreover, Jukes's manual includes ample references to Darwin's *Origin of Species*, testifying to the very great relevance, for Marx, of the question of evolution.

Picking up on what we emphasised earlier, when we were discussing the study of the natural sciences as a whole, we can say that Marx's interest in geology was both functional to his critique of political economy (we need only think of the connection between geology and agriculture and his analysis of agrarian productivity) and also, besides that, part of a then very lively debate as to the statuses of society and their productive capacity.[39] In this regard, it is obviously worth again recalling Engels's *Dialectics of Nature*, which sought to bring together the natural sciences, theory, and political intervention, on the basis of a sort of 'politics' of science. Though we cannot here examine the relation between Engels and Marx or, more particularly, the question of to what extent Marx's horizon was distinguished by a sort of dialectics of nature (in the manner of Engels), we will limit ourselves to saying that the idea of some sort of absolute counterposition between a 'scientist' Engels and an 'anti-scientist' Marx is questionable, and even a caricature. Moreover, we cannot parenthesise the fact that while the young Marx had a philosophical training, in many senses internal to the post-Hegelian milieu, the 'old' Marx was almost completely dedicated to the study of the natural sciences. The problem that remains open, then, is the fact that the late Marx established no structural connection between the critique of political economy and his study of the natural sciences: from this point of view, it is impossible definitively to opt for either interpretative key, as either is possible. Since the specific object of this study is anthropology and the related question of communal forms, we will here particularly focus on his ethnological writings.

In order to understand the presuppositions of Marx's *Exzerpte*, it is necessary to look back to the genesis of his interests in this regard. Already in 1841,

37   Marx 2011, Krüger 2006, Griese 2006.

38   Marx 2011, pp. 9 et sqq., 6 et sqq., 107 et sqq., 100 et sqq.

39   Schiera 1987.

Marx had read Charles de Brosses's *Du culte des dieux fétiches*, and in 1851 William Coke's *Natural History of Society in the Barbarous and Civilised State*, an important text for the birth and development of evolutionism. One important period was the 1850s, during which Marx studied precapitalist forms ever more attentively: in this sense, the treatment of such forms in the *Grundrisse* is also rather telling. Starting from these years, he studied the conquest of Mexico, Slavic and Russian mythology, and travel literature. Such a research horizon was further intensified in the period in which he composed *Capital*. In this context, the element of fetishism took on ever greater importance, also with regard to the question of the relationship between capitalism, precapitalist forms and communism. It is here particularly necessary to refer to the so-called *Ethnological Notebooks*, which Marx transcribed between 1881 and 1882, soon before his death. Marx here particularly drew on Henry Morgan's 1877 work *Ancient Society* and Henry Sumner Maine's 1875 *Lectures on the Early History of Institutions*, as well as other authors such as E.B. Tylor, J. Lubbock, J.B. Phear, and M.M. Kovalevsky. These writings could be defined 'ethnological', as in the English-language reference edition, or else as 'anthropological', according to what definitions we give to the fields of anthropology and ethnology, and in particular according to whether we use the 'Anglo-Saxon' terms for these disciplines based on their substantial identification, or else the meanings given by the structuralism of Lévi-Strauss, which clearly distinguishes between them.[40] If we adopt the second approach – one that owes to the French debate – then we can also speak of anthropological notes. Thus Morgan's text, commented on by Marx, does not so much constitute a work on ethnic groups as a comparative analysis of determinate social forms – an anthropological theory in the proper sense of the word.

Later, immediately after Marx's death, Engels's work on the *Origins of Family, Private Property and the State* would take a position substantially in continuity with Marx's ethnological studies, to the extent of appearing as if it were an execution of his bequest. Marx's death had, indeed, come at a moment when he was working on a series of research projects. Moreover, Engels's exposition had been necessitated by the fact that Marx had never effected any true and proper 'welding together' of ethnology and the critique of political economy. Engels was attempting to build up a general theory from this collection of references. Beyond his high esteem for Morgan, Engels had read others among 'Marx's' authors such as Maurer, but also Bancroft, who had drawn parallels between the Germanic tribes in Tacitus and the American redskins. Ethnological works

---

40   Lévi-Strauss 1963–76, Godelier and Sève 1970.

had widened the spectrum of Marx and Engels's knowledge regarding early communities. And with Maurer, Marx had found proof for the idea that Asiatic property forms had initially prevailed in Europe. Later, including through his study of Morgan, Marx became convinced that analogous typologies were to be found also among the American Indians.[41] We can say that the course of history led to the capitalist mode of production only in a certain portion of the world, not its entirety: similar events taking place in different historical environments led to completely or partially different outcomes. As such, here there was not a rejection of Marx's conception (present in the *Grundrisse*, for example) of capitalism as the destruction of the previous communitarian forms, but it certainly was rearticulated and 'complicated'. Indeed, capitalism had not developed in a homogeneous fashion in all countries: it was not possible to adopt a single schema valid for all cases and all situations. But now let us resume our analysis of Marx's ethnological (or anthropological) notes, so that we can problematise our perspective on communitarian structures with an eye to the schema provided in the section of the *Grundrisse* that deals with precapitalist forms.

The *Exzerpte* in question dedicate particular attention to two very different authors, Maine and Morgan. As concerns Morgan, it is particularly worth bearing in mind his formulation as to the possible evolution of society 'from status to contract' and the idea that ancient societies were derived from patriarchal family orders.[42] His work reconstructed the internal lineages of ancient political orders as evolutions of smaller units based on the family and kinship: from the family to the *gens*, to the tribe, and finally the *polis*. Maine's scope was to interpret the theory of sovereignty in historicist terms, thus also displaying points of contact with Von Savigny's perspective.[43] Examining the traditional heads of the Irish septs, or clans, or the heads of the collective families and village communities in India, Maine considered these associative bodies as mere agglomerations of private families. It is worth noting, though, that when he observed Irish clans and communities he was in reality thinking of the English private family. Among other things, in his draft letter to Vera Zasulich (which we will analyse later on) Marx defined Maine as 'a keen collaborator of the British Government' and pointed to the hypocrisy of his positive evaluation of the Indian communities: 'Sir Henry Maine, for example, who was a keen collaborator of the British Government in carrying out the violent destruction of the

---

41   Iacono 2009, pp. 308–9.
42   Maine 1998. See Piccinini 2003.
43   See Capograssi Colognesi 2009.

Indian communes [*der indischen Gemeinden*], hypocritically assures us that all the government's noble efforts to support the communes were thwarted by the spontaneous forces of economic laws!'[44] In his comments on Phear's text, Marx likewise showed that he was opposed to the confusion of the public and private spheres. Maine's conception of social progress, based on evolution, presupposed that it was juridical and moral factors that determined history. Marx criticised him both for having misunderstood the crucial role of economic factors and for not having grasped the state's dependence on society. Without wishing to simplify the question of materialism, seeing it as only a matter of recognising the centrality of the economic dimension,[45] we can clearly see why Marx could not have shared Maine's position.

However, Morgan is of decidedly more importance to our present study. One of the founders of anthropological studies,[46] he considerably influenced later, twentieth-century anthropology. Morgan introduced several elements that cut through Maine's framework, including a questioning of the idea that modern societies were founded on a patriarchal-type system. In his *Systems of Consanguinity*, Morgan had torn apart the view that the patriarchal dimension was central, instead relativising different social forms. Marx had reflected on the unequal development of history and its irreducibility to a linear schema, even before reading Morgan in his final years: think, for example, of his correspondence with Engels between 1868 and 1870.[47] Engels argued that communal land ownership had existed in Ireland as late as the seventeenth century.[48] Marx assimilated the Russian commune to the primitive Germanic communities, while denouncing their undemocratic and patriarchal character.[49] He was also aware of the fact that the collective distribution of land had lasted on German territory up until the nineteenth century, as Engels repeatedly emphasised. Marx made ample use of the pointers given by the legal historian Georg Ludwig von Maurer (*Geschichte der Dörferverfassung in Deutschland*, 1865–6), in particular his thesis according to which early Europe was characterised by Asiatic typologies of property. He also held in great esteem Morgan's idea according to which the originary community displayed forms analogous also to those

---

44   Marx to Zasulich, 8 February 1881, first draft.

45   See Engels to Joseph Bloch, 21 September 1890, where he defines materialism as a conception founded on the 'production and reproduction of real life'. On materialism as a whole, see Wolf 2009, pp. 160 et sqq.

46   Morgan 1877.

47   Foraboschi 2009, pp. 21–2.

48   Engels to Marx, 29 November 1869.

49   Marx to Engels, 7 November 1868.

existing among the American Indians: a parallel between the European and American systems. Another significant author, for Marx and then Engels, was H.H. Bancroft (*The Native Races of the Pacific States of North America*, 1875–6), which compared Tacitus's Germanic tribes to the American redskins. As such, the morphology of 'the common' proved extremely complex and articulated on both the historical and geographic planes.

His historical horizon entailed an extremely differentiated analysis, in the sense that it sometimes referred to precapitalist, ancient and medieval cases, and in other cases (Germany and Ireland included) to situations existing within 'modernity'. The German context presented very particular traits, since the communitarian form in question still existed even in the nineteenth century:[50] even Hegel's *Grundlinien* were still permeated with the *ständische* dimension. As concerns communitarian structures, and the Germanic root of this question, the Prussian Haxthausen's observations also proved telling.[51] Likewise of interest were references to Ireland, where communal land ownership existed even at the dawn of the modern age.[52] It was also necessary to examine the continued existence of communitarian forms, even if on the basis of different modalities and timescales, in countries as fundamental to the 'world-system' as India, China, and Russia.

Marx's interest in the noble family emerges clearly from his notes on Maine and Morgan (as the references to ancient Greek and Roman societies testify), but so, too, does his interest in the Iroquois Indians, Celts and Hindus. Marx focused above all on the part of Morgan's *Ancient Society* dedicated to the history of the family. Thus the *gens* and the family, but also the *sept*,[53] 'complicate' his temporal framework, though also on the basis of such intricate problems as the various forms of religion and superstition. If in precapitalist phases the structure of familial relations counted for more than the type of production, then the capitalist separation must have been preceded by a change in the system of sexual relations, the formation of the monogamous family, and the introduction of structures founded on private property. On the one hand, it seems that Marx interpreted the nexus between family and kinship in terms

---

50 Marx to Engels, 25 March 1868.

51 See Engels's 'Soziales aus Rußland', *Der Volksstaat*, 16 April 1875: 'The communal property of the Russian peasants was discovered in 1845 by the Prussian Government Councillor Haxthausen and trumpeted to the world as something absolutely wonderful, although Haxthausen could still have found survivals enough of it in his Westphalian homeland and, as a government official, it was even part of his duty to know them thoroughly'.

52 Marx 1972, pp. 295, 297.

53 Marx 1972, pp. 294–5.

analogous to those he used for the relations of production and political, juridical, religious and philosophical systems. Morgan maintained that the family
had an active character, and kinship a passive one; and as Marx took up this
reasoning, he added that the same logic also applied to these latter systems.
On the other hand, Marx brought to light the fact that the modern family contains, 'in miniature', all the antagonisms that will later play out in society and
the state. Here, Marx was partly picking up on Morgan's observations on the
origins of the family, which arose after and not before the *gens*.

> Its (the gentile organization's) birth *must be sought in pre-existing ele*
> *ments of society*, and its *maturity* would be expected to occur long after
> its origination.[54]

> *Family* konnte ebensowenig – selbst d. monogamische – *natural basis*
> *of gentile society* bilden, wie heutzutage in bürgerlicher Gesellschaft *the*
> *family is not the unit of the political system* ... In the organisation of gentile
> society, the *gens is primary*, forming both the *basis* u. *unit* d. *systems*[55]

Marx in some senses adopted as his own the evolutionist thesis of a relation
between human history and natural history, within a materialist perspective.
Morgan's evolutionist conception foresaw humanity progressing through three
stages, each of them deriving from the previous one: from the savage to the barbarian to the civilised. The highest stage was reached by way of the dissolution
of the *gentes*, in the last formation of the barbarian stage. For Marx, William
Coke's text *The Natural History of Society in the Barbarous and Civilised State*
proved to be of some significance for interpreting the relationship between barbarism and civilisation. Evolution regarded the whole world, but on the basis
of different forms in different areas: in this sense, it thus 'complicated' any vision based on the unstoppable progress of the human race.[56] At the centre of
Morgan's reflection stood not the single man nor a single people, but rather
the stage of culture. We should clarify that Morgan, even if he did question the
excessive power acquired across the history of property, was no critic of the
capitalist social system: from a strictly political point of view, he was on what
we might call 'the opposite side' to Marx.

---

54   Marx 1972, p. 111. See Iacono 2009, pp. 309–310; Brown 2012.
55   Marx 1972, p. 200.
56   Krader 1978, pp. 228–31.

In Marx's *Ethnological Notebooks*, he frequently turns to Morgan's references to the Iroquois: 'Decision given by the Council. Unanimity was a fundamental law of its action among the Iroquois'.[57] Marx's interest in this author did not derive from any common basic assumptions of theirs (lest we forget that as a lawyer Morgan defended the interests of the New York State railway companies, and had nothing in common with the socialists of his day): Morgan might thus in some way be considered as one of those figures who strengthened the socialist cause against their own intentions. Rather, in Marx's view, Morgan's great merit consisted in his understanding of the importance of objective technological and institutional factors 'inventions u. discoveries came one by one; the knowledge of a cord must proceed the bow and arrow, wie gunpowder the musket, steamengine the railway and steamship ... Ebenso institutions'.[58] In this sense, Morgan presented a materialist approach, even if with elements of ingenuousness. Among the institutions that Morgan took into consideration, the *gens* is the dominant one in the context of barbarian societies. Marx applied this approach also to the theory of the historical formation of castes, which had to be interpreted on the basis of the hardening of the *gens* principle.

Equality and fraternity were put into question by the aristocratic principle based on the constitution of social classes. Private property does not, however, represent the cause of the differentiation between rich and poor, nor of the constitution of the monogamous family: it is, instead, the expression of juridical elements whose power resides elsewhere. According to Morgan, the dissolution of the *gens*, or of the kinship principle, becomes the motive force of history. This principle of Morgan's, implicitly taken up by Marx and explicitly so by Engels, contradicts Marx's formulation regarding the transition to civilised society. According to Marx, the tribes of ancient communities emerged in one of two ways, being grouped on the basis of either kinship or locality. However, he elaborated a general theory of the variegated forms of collectivism, rather than one that regarded kinship alone. The constitution of civilised society and of the state was made possible by the erosion of archaic communities (*gentes*, clans, village communities, associations) and of the equality and fraternity associated with them.

From this reconstruction there emerge traits of both continuity and discontinuity with respect to Marx's treatment of this question in the 1850s. Indeed, on the one hand he built on previously conquered ground concerning the specific

57   Marx 1972, p. 162.
58   Marx 1972, pp. 126–7.

difference of the capitalist system from precapitalist forms, and on the other hand provided a less 'flat' picture of capitalism compared to what he had proposed in the 1850s. We can say that while the classic Marxist division of the modes of production (Asiatic, classical, feudal, capitalist) is sometimes present in Marx, it does not, however, allow us to give account of the full complexity and articulation of the social and political scenario: it is problematic to attribute too great an emphasis, for example, to the idea of an Asiatic mode of production.[59] Such an articulation runs the risk of seeing a mechanical succession of stages, the first stage followed by the second, and so on. However, another approach was possible – a different object of Marx's polemic – consisting of applying the distinctive traits of precapitalist forms to certain countries in the contemporary scenario, in an 'ethnicist' manner. It was starting from this perspective that Marx heavily criticised Kovalevsky, who had applied the concept of feudalism to the Algeria that existed before French colonisation. Another of his polemical reference points was Phear, who had deployed the concept of feudalism for the purposes of an analysis of the Indian situation: 'This ass Phear calls the village's constitution feudal'.[60]

In conclusion, these communitarian forms were certainly not to be idealised and taken as a model: here, there was no 'romantic' critique of capitalism, and nor did Marx envisage a communism substantially modelled on these structures. Moreover, it emerges from Marx's ethnological notebooks, particularly those relating to Morgan, that he was operating a rearticulation of his social and political framework and a problematisation of his previous schema concerning the relation between the capitalist system and precapitalist forms, as well as

59   On precapitalist forms more generally, see p. 51. Interesting in this regard is the reading provided by Meillassoux 1975, particularly pp. 110–24, which highlights both the strong points and limitations of Marx's approach. It is not here possible to give account of the intense debates among Marxists on the Asiatic mode of production, which go so far as to exaggerate the importance of this question to Marx. In particular, see Thorner 1966, Lichtheim 1988, and Banaji 2010. Also note, with particular reference to the *Grundrisse's* 'Formen', albeit with differing approaches, Sereni 2007, p. 134 – 'What Marx termed the "Asiatic commune" was less a matter of locating the most primitive forms geographically than of a general representation, a type that covered India, China and Central Asia, combining many different heritages that conditioned this historical typology' – and Read 2003, pp. 45 et sqq.: 'According to Marx, the Asiatic mode of production, like all precapitalist modes of production, is more properly a mode of reproduction in which productive activity and development have as their telos and aim the reproduction of communal and social relations that are its presupposition'. For a rearticulation of the question of the Asiatic mode of production, see Spivak 1999.

60   Marx 1999, p. 283.

between European and extra-European countries. In reality, Marx approved of only certain aspects of Morgan's reasoning, which, among other things, was not in harmony with Maine's reflection: particularly central were his relativisation of the constitutive elements of the capitalist world – and *in primis* of private property – and his questioning of any conception that was based on considering the patriarchal dimension to be the root of modern society.

Beyond Europe

In the late Marx – or better, in Marx from the late 1860s onward – there was a 'complication' of the scenarios he observed, not only for the reasons that we have just explored but also in the sense that he widened the geographical spectrum of his reflection.[61] Indeed, it is worth remembering that up until 1848 Marx's (and Engels's) gaze was essentially turned to countries like Germany, France and England. But already in the 1850s, Marx was broadening his social and political horizons, beginning a work on precapitalist structures that would be more broadly formulated in the *Grundrisse* section on 'Precapitalist forms'. Slavic communities, in particular Russia, played a decisive role on this canvas. And later, in the 1860s, Marx made an even more marked attempt to look beyond Western Europe. Two countries that were paradigmatic for Marx in this regard, albeit very different in their social and political situation, were the United States and Russia, which had both undergone particularly significant changes: 'In my view, the most momentous thing happening in the world today is the slave movement – on the one hand, in America, started by the death of Brown, and in Russia, on the other'.[62] Many years later, in the 1882 preface to the second Russian edition of the *Communist Manifesto*, Marx made an important further specification in this regard: 'The first Russian edition of the Manifesto of the Communist Party, translated by Bakunin, was published early in the 'sixties ... Then the West could see in it (the Russian edition of the Manifesto) only a literary curiosity ... Precisely Russia and the United States are missing [in the *Manifesto*]'.[63] It had become necessary to rectify the framework that he had

---

61   See Anderson 2010, which aptly insists on the innovation that Marx's 1860s writings represented compared to his previous texts, with the 'opening up' of his geographical outlook and his questioning of any form of Eurocentrism. On the ever less 'flat' character of Marx's perspective on extra-European countries, see also Patterson 2009, particularly pp. 91–144.

62   Marx to Engels, 11 January 1860.

63   1882 Preface, second Russian edition of the *Communist Manifesto*.

previously provided, since two countries like the USA and Russia were of ever increasing significance on the world scale and yet had no place at all in the *Communist Manifesto*. In the 1850s, and ever more so from the 1860s, Marx's (and Engels's) gaze looked beyond Europe, or at least beyond the 'Western' Europe he had previously taken into consideration.

From the citations given above, two particularly telling aspects emerge. The first lies in the consideration that after 1848 Russia and the United States came to play an ever more important function in the capitalist world-system. It is necessary to add to this 'objective' element – concerning the economic and political weight of certain countries – another, 'subjective' element: the fact that there had been slave revolts within the aforementioned contexts, with all the destructuring power that implied. This was, then, not only a matter of an 'endogenous' analysis of economic processes taking place in a specific situation, but also of their interaction with class struggles, which constantly shifted the plane of reflection. As such, there could be no economic development that proceeded *iuxta propria principia*, autonomous from struggle. The 'acting in common' of working-class singularities could upset and sometimes even invert the route that capital had set out for itself, 'breaking' its 'dead mechanism'. So when it came to the question of liberation from slavery, it was necessary to emphasise that capitalism and slavery are not two mutually exclusive forces: indeed, in various historical periods and various countries, capitalism has even prospered by way of slavery, functionalising it to its own ends. We will examine, albeit cursorily, the case of the United States, as well as some of the extra-European cases to which Marx dedicated various analyses, first among them India and China.

Without here being able to run through all the stages of Marx's itinerary, we can observe that the United States was always an important point of reference for him: already in his first works, he identified this country as a sort of prototype of democracy, based on freedom and equality in all their ambivalence.[64] Indeed, we could say that in many senses such an image was present throughout Marx's whole *oeuvre*.[65] It was, on the one hand, a case of 'true' democracy, and on the other, of the greatest example of capitalist development, a 'young' country free of the stratified hierarchies that characterised the various European structures. Among other things, it is telling that Marx's and Tocqueville's analyses of the United States,[66] whatever the considerable polit-

---

64   See Basso 2001b.
65   On the USA, see Nimtz 2003, Weiner 1982. See also Sylvers 2004, pp. 42–3.
66   See Chignola 2004, p. 440, referring to Tocqueville's analysis of American democracy: '...

ical distance between the two authors, did have some points in common, in particular as concerned the democratic character of that country. For Marx, it was almost as if this were a context where the elements of modernity had developed in a particularly 'pure' way, for better and for worse: moreover, the United States had never seen feudalism. To this picture it is necessary to add, however, the fact that the USA was distinguished not only by a capitalism 'to the nth degree' but also by the enduring existence of slavery. The emancipation of labour could not proceed except by way of liberation from racial segregation. Furthermore, for the purposes of understanding Marx's journey from the 1860s onwards, reference to the American Civil War seems to be of particular importance: we could even say that for Marx this represented a sort of second American Revolution, thus endowed with extraordinary propulsive power.[67]

For a total interpretation of the world-system, with its internal differentiation and fractures, it is, however, necessary to turn our gaze further still, to non-capitalist extra-European countries like India and China – which Marx did deal with specifically. In an 1853 article Marx posed himself a radical question in this regard: 'The question is, can mankind fulfil its destiny without a fundamental revolution in the social state of Asia?'[68] In recent years, scholars' interest in Marx's interpretation of these countries has intensified, bringing out a less 'straightforward' picture than that presented in the Marxist vulgate. As concerns India, Marx's most conspicuous reflections are those dated 1853, which appeared in the *New York Daily Tribune*: among other things, it was in this period that the British Parliament reached an agreement on the definitive organisation of its Indian possessions.[69] For Marx, India's only possibility of liberation resided in its passing through the 'blood and soil' of forced industrialisation, thus carrying through the destruction of communal property. It seems clear that his reasoning on colonised India could not be disjoined from that concerning the coloniser England: at the centre of his reflection, here, was a complex web of interrelations, which were obviously not based on a symmetrical structure but rather a topology of domination. In the first lines he hammered out, it seemed that there were no expansive prospects for India: 'England has broken down the entire framework of Indian society, without any

---

the proletariat ... in which Tocqueville, importantly, *identified* the generic subject of the social movement for democracy, had to be made aware of the "price" of freedom. The concession of political and social rights, to be enjoyed by all ... was considered a means of making the democratic subject moral'.

67   See Anderson 2010, pp. 79–114.
68   'The British Rule in India', *New York Daily Tribune*, 25 June 1853. See Bologna 1973.
69   See Maffi 2008, pp. 24–5.

symptoms of reconstitution yet appearing'.[70] While the Indian order was distinguished by a communitarian dimension, 'we must not forget that these idyllic village-communities, inoffensive though they may appear, had always been the solid foundation of Oriental despotism'.[71] The category 'Oriental despotism' is a very telling one, in that shows that Marx never fell into any kind of idealisation of precapitalist forms, nor, more specifically, those of the Indian communities.

In the articles in question, there was a very critical analysis of the Indian economic situation.

> Since 1784 Indian finances have got more and more deeply into difficulty.[72]

> That there is in India a permanent financial deficit, a regular over-supply of wars, and no supply at all of public works, an abominable system of taxation, and a no less abominable state of justice and law, that these five items constitute, as it were, the five points of the East Indian Charter, was settled beyond all doubt in the debates of 1853, as it had been in the debates of 1833, and in the debates of 1813, and in all former debates on India.[73]

Indeed, Marx's evaluation of India, at least in the 1850s, seems to have been a scornful one, to the point of risking becoming a justification of colonialism, such that this country could go through the 'birth pangs' of capitalism and finally 'enter' modernity:

> A country not only divided between Mahommedan and Hindoo, but between tribe and tribe, between caste and caste ... India, then, could not escape the fate of being conquered, and the whole of her past history, if it be anything, is the history of the successive conquests she has undergone. Indian society has no history at all, at least no known history. What we call its history, is but the history of the successive intruders who founded their empires on the passive basis of that unresisting and unchanging society. The question, therefore, is not whether the English had a right to conquer

70   'The British Rule in India', *New York Daily Tribune*, 25 June 1853.
71   Ibid.
72   'The East India Company – Its History and Results', NYDT, 11 July 1853.
73   'The Government of India', NYDT, 20 July 1853.

India, but whether we are to prefer India conquered by the Turk, by the Persian, by the Russian, to India conquered by the Briton.

England has to fulfill a double mission in India: one destructive, the other regenerating the annihilation of old Asiatic society, and the laying the material foundations of Western society in Asia.[74]

As such, colonialism could bring India out of its torpor, from the medievalism in which it found itself, from its barely 'developed' social and political relations.

In the texts to which we are referring here, there returns an element already present in Marx's previous works – namely, his stress on the earth-shattering character of capitalism in regard to the forms that preceded it. In the *Grundrisse* he would even make reference to the 'civilising function' of capital, leading him to attribute it a revolutionary role in the strict sense of the word. It was problematic to associate capitalism with the dimension of revolution, even if one could note the innovation brought about by capitalism, with all its ambivalence. In reality, it was not an expansive scenario founded on emancipation, but rather a rupture with the preceding forms, and the related structures of domination. Such a transcendence, however, led to the formation of new structures of social power, which though not homologous to the previous ones were capable of bearing a devastating impact on individuals. In the Marx of the 1850s, the historical process was interpreted in an excessively linear fashion. The reflection he carried out, with all its lights and shadows, was applied to the Indian situation in the following terms: it was not a dynamic internal to the Western world, but rather a case of capitalism being 'exported' to India, a non-capitalist country, a 'non-historic people', so that it might pass from prehistory to history – to use the formulation from the 1857 *Einleitung*. The limitation of his reasoning lays in its schematism. In this context we find a rather limited interpretation of Indian society, conceived within the terms of an immutable category of 'Oriental despotism'. Since no internal resistance was possible, there had to be some intervention from the outside.

However, it cannot be said that Marx *sic et simpliciter* offered an exaltation of English colonialism in India:

> The profound hypocrisy and inherent barbarism of bourgeois civilization lies unveiled before our eyes, turning from its home, where it assumes respectable forms, to the colonies, where it goes naked ... The devastat-

---

74   'The Future Results of British Rule in India', *NYDT*, 8 August 1853.

ing effects of English industry, when contemplated with regard to India, a country as vast as Europe, and containing 150 millions of acres, are palpable and confounding. But we must not forget that they are only the organic results of the whole system of production as it is now constituted ... The bourgeois period of history has to create the material basis of the new world ... Bourgeois industry and commerce create these material conditions of a new world in the same way as geological revolutions have created the surface of the earth.[75]

There could not have been any sort of apology for English rule, in Marx, any more than for the capitalist system itself. His perspective was its abolition, since exploitation was immanent to it. In this sense, English colonialism in India brought capitalism to its extreme logical consequences, and in brutal terms. But now, in order to capture later elements of Marx's reflection concerning extra-European countries, we should look to his analysis of China, in a period not so far from the years that we have just looked at, in particular the second half of the 1850s.

The Chinese situation presented itself in different terms to the Indian one, which had been transformed as the result of English colonialism. China was an enormous territory, in which there was a patriarchal economy founded on a sort of union between agriculture and domestic industry: 'Quite apart from the opium trade, which we proved to grow in an inverse ratio to the sale of Western manufactures, we found the main obstacle to any sudden expansion of the import trade to China in the economical structure of Chinese society, depending upon the combination of minute agriculture with domestic industry'.[76] Marx's reflection on China (like that on India) must be placed within the framework of the 'idyllic processes' of primitive accumulation, to which he had devoted some attention throughout the first volume of *Capital*.[77] It was in this context that the first three opium wars took place, with various countries participating: Britain and France, then the USA and Russia, Germany and Japan, and ultimately even Italy.

---

75   Ibid. See Jaffe 2007.

76   'Trade with China', *NYDT*, 3 December 1859. See Maffi 2008, pp. 25–6.

77   'The discovery of gold and silver in America, the extirpation, enslavement and entomb-
      ment in mines of the aboriginal population, the beginning of the conquest and looting
      of the East Indies, the turning of Africa into a warren for the commercial hunting of
      black-skins, signalised the rosy dawn of the era of capitalist production. These idyllic
      proceedings are the chief momenta of primitive accumulation. On their heels treads
      the commercial war of the European nations, with the globe for a theatre. It begins

... in China, the smothered fires of hatred kindled against the English during the opium war have burst into a flame of animosity which no tenders of peace and friendship will be very likely to quench[78]

The new Anglo-Chinese war presents so many complications that it is utterly impossible to guess the turn it may take ... One thing is certain, that the death-hour of Old China is rapidly drawing nigh. Civil war has already divided the South from the North of the Empire, and the Rebel King seems to be as secure from the Imperialists (if not from the intrigues of his own followers) at Nanking, as the Heavenly Emperor from the rebels at Peking ... The very fanaticism of the southern Chinese in their struggle against foreigners seems to mark a consciousness of the supreme danger in which Old China is placed; and before many years pass away we shall have to witness the death struggles of the oldest empire in the world, and the opening day of a new era for all Asia.[79]

China, with its millennia-long tradition, found itself in a state of decadence, as well as one of extreme corruption. If the civil war had created further reasons for clashes and the country being torn apart, then the opium wars were of truly explosive significance. It was thus that Marx seemed to discern, amidst this devastating situation – following a schema that he often used – the possibility of 'a new era for all Asia'. To complete this picture, it is thus worth examining the question of the possibility or otherwise of a revolution in the country concerned, referring back to some of Marx's articles from a few years before those that we have just looked into. In 1853, Marx had spoken with great enthusiasm of the concrete hypothesis of a revolutionary ferment in China:

It may seem a very strange, and a very paradoxical assertion that the next uprising of the people of Europe, and their next movement for republican freedom and economy of Government, may depend more probably on what is now passing in the Celestial Empire – the very opposite of Europe – than on any other political cause that now exists ... But yet it is no paradox.[80]

---

with the revolt of the Netherlands from Spain, assumes giant dimensions in England's Anti-Jacobin War, and is still going on in the opium wars against China, &c.'
78   'English Atrocities in China', NYDT, 10 April 1857.
79   Engels, 'Persia-China', NYDT, 5 June 1857.
80   'Revolution in China and in Europe', NYDT, 14 June 1853.

The possibility of revolution was thus connected precisely to the intervention of the European powers, and particularly England's: 'Complete isolation was the prime condition of the preservation of Old China ... Now, England having brought about the revolution of China, the question is how that revolution will in time react on England, and through England on Europe'. For Marx, England had proven crucial for the purposes of breaking up 'the Old China', and thus of constructing a completely new scenario. Various difficulties were wrapped up in this perspective: the conditions of possibility of revolution seemed to come from the outside, from the capitalist countries. It was not, here, a matter of defending the communal property on which 'the Old China' had rested, with its apparently immutable structures of dominion, but nor of maintaining that the Chinese revolution could be some sort of consequence of English colonialism. Thus emerges the second problematic aspect of his reasoning, namely the presence therein of an excessively linear schema constituted by the succession *precapitalist forms-capitalism-communism*. Such a theoretical structure rested on the plexus *capitalist development-crisis-production of subjectivity*.

> it may safely be augured that the Chinese revolution will throw the spark into the overloaded mine of the present industrial system and cause the explosion of the long-prepared general crisis, which, spreading abroad, will be closely followed by political revolutions on the Continent. It would be a curious spectacle, that of China sending disorder into the Western World while the Western Powers, by English, French and American war-steamers, are conveying 'order' to Shanghai, Nanking and the mouths of the Great Canal.[81]

Moreover, he had already forcefully upheld such a position in an 1850 text:

> When our European reactionaries, in the course of their imminent flight through Asia, finally arrive at the Great Wall of China, at the gates which lead to the home of primal reaction and primal conservatism, who knows if they will not find written thereon the legend:
>
> *République chinoise*
> *Liberté, Egalité, Fraternité*[82]

---

81   Ibid.
82   'Review', *Neue Rheinische Zeitung*, February 1850.

As is very often the case in Marx, he here evokes the 'spectre' of the French Revolution, 'mother' of all revolutions. Here, we find a new dynamism, after centuries without movement for the country in question – as also emerges from a passage in *Capital*: 'One may recall that China and the tables began to dance when the rest of the world appeared to be standing still – *pour encourager les autres*'. It is worth remembering, however, that a large proportion of his observations on China here examined, and also of those concerning India, refer to the 1850s and thus a period prior to the one on which the present study is focused. Notwithstanding the limitations of Marx's treatment of these subjects, some important elements have emerged, here, such as the connection between crisis and the production of subjectivity. Now we need to shift our study from India and China to Russia, a country that aroused particular interest in Marx in his final years.

The Russian Commune and the Conditions of Possibility of Communism

The question of Marx's analysis of Russia is clearly both complex and extremely controversial, particularly in light of the events of the twentieth century.[83] Our interpretation of the relationship between Marx and Russia will distance itself from two opposed readings that, in our view, are both problematic and bear little fruit.

The first, proper to 'traditional' Marxism, consists of an underestimation of the role of Russia, and the insistence that it was substantially irrelevant to Marx, given that it was a peripheral country that was still not developed in a capitalist sense and was thus unable to reach communist revolution before the capitalist mode of production had fully been developed. Here, two key elements of Marx's reflection are welded together: both an underestimation of the role of Russia, and the construction of a mechanical schema for the transition from capitalism to communism, holding that the existence of a developed capitalist structure, such as was then missing in Russia, was the condition of possibility of communism. The communist revolution would thus only be able to take

---

83   On Marx's texts on Russia, with particular reference to questions of foreign policy (which will here remain on the backburner, however), see the collection Dörig (ed.) 1960. On Marx's overall analysis of Russia, Shanin (ed.) 1983 is still of key importance. For a very positive evaluation of the late Marx's position on Russia, see Dussel 2009, particularly pp. 217–31.

place in countries with advanced capitalist orders such as England and other European states.

In recent years other 'post-Marxist' approaches have followed this interpretation, integrating Marx's position with postcolonial studies in a perspective that is critical of any Western 'grand narrative' pervaded with the spirit of colonialism. This outlook attributes particular importance to the Russian situation, since this country had still not suffered the 'labour pains' of the birth of the capitalist mode of production. As such, it prefigured the possibility of a transition from the rural community to communism without first having to go through the stages of capitalism. This view exalts the characteristics of the rural commune, held to be superior to capitalist modernity. It also highly esteems the innovations that can be found in the late Marx as compared to his previous works.

The interpretation that we here propose is different from both such readings. The former is based on an excessive dogmatism in its delineation of the transition from capitalism to communism: it thus risks conceiving the entire political landscape on the basis of a single schema deduced from the experiences of the most advanced capitalist countries, without managing to grasp the great complexity of the world-system, including cases like Russia, which was not fully developed from a capitalist point of view. But if the first perspective has its limitations, the second is simply unsustainable, in that it surreptitiously characterises Marx as anti-modern, a supporter of the 'archaic' and thus marked by a sort of 'political romanticism': to problematise the framework provided by the most orthodox Marxism should not mean having to provide such a mis-shapen image of Marx.[84] Beyond our reading of Marx, there is little to be gained from a perspective substantially fixed on the most debateable positions of Russian Populism. Rather, analysis of Marx's interpretation of Russia must reject pre-established schemas, incapable as they are of grasping the complexity of his work, with its ambivalences and sometimes even ambiguities. Moreover, even though we shall be focusing particularly on Marx's writings, we will also bear in mind Engels's works from this period as well as those from after Marx's death, which provide a sort of 'bridge' to understanding the young Lenin's reflection on Russia's social structure. Among other things, one of the defects of some of the prevalent readings of Marx is that they set up an absolute counterposition between the 'antidevelopmentist' Marx and the 'developmentist' Engels.

---

84   See Bensaïd 1995 for an example of an attempt at a positive appraisal of these 'archaic' elements, unlike our own perspective, but nonetheless offering stimulating remarks.

In examining this question we ought to avoid any 'theoreticist' outlook based on some generalising schema: both a historicist and an anti-historicist reading would be abstract in character. It is worth bearing in mind firstly that in Marx there was a strong connection between theory and practice, since theory could not be conceived in separation from history, and, secondly, that there was no 'compression' of these planes such that he arrived at a fully outlined political theory. Indeed, politics never appears reducible to a mechanical derivation of theory, and does not fit into any systematic codification separate from the conjuncture in which it operates, much as theory cannot be immediately 'folded' into politics, but rather inevitably has an abstract character (the *Abstraktionskraft* to which Marx refers in *Capital*). Marx's study of Russia resounds in a dual register: on the one hand, theory must be rooted in history and in politics without, however, coinciding with these elements; on the other, politics cannot be immediately deduced from theory.

In Marx's early writings he makes only sporadic references to Russia, and they express a rather simplistic vision of a backward, 'anti-Enlightenment' country. From the 1850s – the moment when Marx began to examine precapitalist structures ever more deeply – his analysis became increasingly complex, as we can see from the substantial part of the *Grundrisse* dedicated to these structures. Here, the first precapitalist form consisted in a natural community dedicated to farming and based on the family and the union of families, the tribe, in a direct relationship with the land. One of the historical-geographical examples he provided in this regard was the Slavic community, in which there was no property but only individual possessions, since the real property owner was the commune [*Gemeine*] itself. Marx carried out research on the conquest of Mexico, on the Slavs, and in particular on Russia, as well as on travel literature. He intensified this research during the period in which he composed *Capital*, with its numerous references to these questions. Then, in a still later period, came the ethnological notebooks, which we mentioned above. After Marx's death, some of Engels's texts were of particular importance, notably 1884's *Origins of Family, Private Property and the State*, which stood in continuity with Marx's studies of anthropology. Moreover, Engels's last reflections on Russia, from the 1880s and 1890s, are also of great interest.

Marx became increasingly interested in Russia in the 1850s, and this interest continued to grow from then onwards. The principal reason behind Marx's cursory 1840s reading of the Russian situation and subsequent rearticulation of his position was connected not only to some sort of intellectual reconsideration, but also the fact that his analysis was attentive to Russia's own changing social and political conditions. It is thus worth taking a look at the characteristics of Russia's social structure, and in particular the presence therein of a series of 'communitarian' elements. The *artel* was an associative form that emerged spontaneously and concerned many fields including trade, fishing and agriculture: one of its characteristic traits was its members' responsibility of solidarity toward the community. The *obshchina* was a sort of community of peasants, co-operative usufructaries of the land that they worked.[85] The *mir* was the assembly, the decision-making body of the *obshchina*: its function was to collect taxes, distribute wages, and recruit for the armed forces. These were institutions that lasted for centuries in a Russia founded on serfdom.

In the 1840s to '50s, there were some sharp changes in Russia's social structure, in particular as the practice began to spread whereby the feudal lord exonerated his subjects of their feudal obligations: through a cash payment (the *obrok*) they could instead devote themselves to activities that would earn them money.[86] The spread of the *obrok* system began to erode – albeit only gradually and partially – the institution of serfdom. Following this, in 1861–3 Tsar Alexander II implemented certain important reforms. In 1861, the serf peasants, who had until then been tied to the land, were declared free in their civil rights and thus able, like any other subject, autonomously to stipulate contracts and to marry without the permission of the landowning lord. Thus the serfs were allowed, by way of loans from the state, to take charge from the lord over small strips of the land that they cultivated. The village assemblies, or *mir*, which assigned the peasants the communal farms to be cultivated in periods when they were not working the noble land, became the guarantors of these loans. But the instalments were too burdensome: a result of which was the series of peasant revolts from 1861 to 1863. From this brief survey of events, it becomes clear that from the 1840s to the 1860s Russia saw major transformations in the direction of capitalism, albeit in a contradictory manner and with devastating consequences from a social point of view.

Marx analysed this situation and in particular the process of the emancipation of the serfs, focusing on its fundamental ambivalence. On the one hand, its earth-shattering character was apparent, consisting of the partial overcoming of the patriarchal forms of the past: the expression 'nursery of capitalism'[87] has been used to denote the Russian situation in this period. One of Marx's letters seems particularly clear in this regard: 'To me, the movement for the

---

85   See Poggio 1978, Burgio 2000, pp. 199–235.
86   See Gitermann 1945, p. 148: 'Certainly the peasants subject to the *obrok* also continued, legally speaking, to live under the system of serfdom, but in reality they were no longer serfs in the full sense of the word. They could, freely or almost freely, dispose of their own time and labour power ...'
87   Gitermann 1945, p. 272.

emancipation of the serfs in Russia seems important'.[88] On the other hand, its deleterious aspects were also apparent (for example, the unchallenged domin-ion of the moneylenders), derived from the specific manner in which the end of serfdom had been realised: 'The peasants – taken in the mass – have been put by the redemption into a most miserable and wholly untenable position ... Such a situation is as if specially created for the usurer'.[89]

In this context, though the condition of the emancipated peasants was cata-strophic, this state of affairs did not immediately entail a true and proper devel-opment of the bourgeoisie. An unsustainable social order had been put into question, but no stable reconfiguration of social relations capable of further development had yet been reached. Marx represented the post-1861 Russian situation by making clear its ambivalent character, consisting of the overcom-ing of the past hierarchical structures but also the establishment of new rela-tions of dominion, based on an incomplete modernisation that was full of contradictions. Marx made a comparison between Russia and the USA, and in the Russian example he evoked the era of France's Sun King, thus bring-ing into focus its 'backwardness' as compared to the countries that were more developed from a capitalist point of view:

> It is ... impossible to find real analogies between the United States and Russia ... In the former the concentration of capital and the gradual expro-priation of the masses is not only the vehicle, but also the natural offspring ... of an unprecedented rapid industrial development, agricultural pro-gress, etc.; the latter reminds you rather of the time of Louis XIV and Louis XV, where the financial, commercial, industrial superstructure, or rather the facades of the social edifices, looked (although they had a much more solid foundation than in Russia) like a satyre upon the stagnant state of the bulk of production (the agricultural one) and the famine of the pro-ducers.[90]

If this was Marx's analysis of the Russian order after these changes, we must now examine the controversial question of the extent to which it was possible for Russia to pass from a not-yet fully capitalist form to communism. A study of this question must operate on what we might call a hybrid plane, since it regards not only the historical-theoretical interpretation of the Russian situ-

---

88   Marx to Engels, 29 April 1858.
89   Engels, 'Soziales aus Rußland', *Der Volkstaat*, 16 April 1875.
90   *MECW*, Vol. 45, pp. 357–8.

ation, but also the feasibility or otherwise of a revolutionary movement in such a context, thus concerning the political dimension in the narrow sense. In Marx, the relationship between theory and politics cannot be interpreted on the basis of wholly 'compressing' these two planes together: this is clear enough from his analysis of the Russian commune. Marx examined this latter as the distinctive trait of the Russian situation. The question of communal natural property is not, however, reducible to references to the Russian case alone. Indeed, as emerges from various texts by Marx and Engels, in history we find the most diverse examples of communal natural property:

> The communal property of the Russian peasants was discovered in 1845 by the Prussian Government Councillor Haxthausen and trumpeted to the world as something absolutely wonderful ... It was from Haxthausen that Herzen, himself a Russian landowner, first learned that his peasants owned the land in common, and he made use of the fact to describe the Russian peasants as the true vehicles of socialism ... From Herzen this knowledge came to Bakunin, and from Bakunin to Mr. Tkachov ... In reality, communal ownership of the land is an institution found among all Indo-Germanic peoples at a low level of development, from India to Ireland ... In Western Europe, including Poland and Little Russia, at a certain stage in social development, this communal ownership became a fetter, a brake on agricultural production, and was increasingly eliminated. In Great Russia (that is, Russia proper), on the other hand, it persists until today ... The Russian peasant lives and has his being only in his village community; the rest of the world exists for him only in so far as it interferes with his community. This is so much the case that, in Russian, the same word '*mir*' means, on the one hand, 'world' and, on the other, 'peasant community' ... very great differences in degree of prosperity are possible and actually exist among the members of the community. Almost everywhere there are a few rich peasants among them – here and there millionaires – ... Under such conditions and under the pressure of taxes and usurers, communal ownership of the land is no longer a blessing; it becomes a fetter. The peasants often run away from it ...[91]

Marx, similarly, brings out not only the ambivalence of the Russian commune, but also the deleterious elements of this arrangement: 'The whole business, *down to the smallest detail, is* absolutely identical with the *primaeval Germanic* communal system. Add to this, in the Russian case ... (1) the *non-democratic*, but *patriarchal* character of the commune leadership and (2) the *collective responsibility* for taxes to the state'.[92]

Moreover, again in his later writings from the 1870s, Marx brought into relief the emergence of elements that had provoked a major erosion of the egalitarian character of the Russian commune, entailing forms of private accumulation of mobile goods such as herds, money, and, at times, even serfs. Such mobile property, escaping from the control of the commune, played an ever more important role in the agrarian economy. Across Marx's work, there was a persistent and strong critique of any idealisation of the commune or mystical valorisation of the 'Slav mission'; this was a position that he had expressed ever since the *Neue Rheinische Zeitung*, in opposition to the pan-Slavist Herzen and the anarchist Bakunin. In this regard, however, two further points need to be specified. Firstly, it would be mistaken to represent the Populists as wholly united, since within their number there were the most diverse and articulated variants of Populism, and therefore the various thinkers connected to this tendency cannot simply be collapsed into one.[93] As well as the anarchist Bakunin and the pan-Slavist Herzen (both of them exiled in London after 1848), we should name some of the other Russian theorists studied by Marx and Engels, such as Tkachov – sometimes interpreted by Engels as a Bakuninite anarchist, but in reality largely standing by Blanquist positions –, Chernyshevsky (highly praised by Marx in *Capital*), Bervi-Flerovsky (author of *The Situation of the Working Class in Russia*), and Mikhailovsky (author of *What is Progress?*). Moreover, we cannot interpret all of the Russian Populists *sic et simpliciter* as holding to anti-modern positions: some of them, after all, also displayed aspects of 'enlightenment', to use a phrase that Lenin applied to the Russian context. In reality, there is neither always nor necessarily an absolute counterposition between Populism and 'enlightenment' in Russia. Marx, though never going so far as to idealise the Russian nation and its social structures, over time did come to show ever-greater interest in the Russian commune and its capacities for future development.

The fundamental question lay in the possibility or otherwise of the Russian commune leading to communism. More generally, it is worth focusing on Marx's historical schema and in particular on the idea that the full development of capitalism is the condition of possibility for communism. Indeed, Marx's theoretical position holds that without a full rolling-out of the capitalist

---

92   Marx to Engels, 7 November 1868.
93   See Tvardovskaja 1975, Walicki 1969, Venturi 1972, Natalizi 2006.

mode of production, communism is unthinkable, its very basis being the contradiction between capital and labour. The Russian situation thus seems rather a complicated one, since while it did not display a capitalism comparable to those existing in other European countries, it had undergone a series of significant changes in the 1860s. In his 29 November 1869 letter to Engels, Marx remarked that communal land property had existed in seventeenth-century Ireland, and he elsewhere often assimilated the Russian commune to primitive Germanic communes, criticising their patriarchal and undemocratic character. Furthermore, he was fully aware of the fact that collective distribution of land had existed on German territory up until the nineteenth century. The question of communal land could not be resolved by simply 'pigeonholing' it with reference to a long-ago past, interpreting it as a medieval residue – as demonstrated by the German case, where 'ancient' structures persisted amidst so-called modernity. Later ethnological studies further widened the scope of Marx and Engels's knowledge of agricultural communities. From this came the idea that capitalist society was fully developed in one part of the world, but not universally: comparable events taking place in different historical environments had produced at least partially different results. The topic of Russia and the Russian commune had to be inserted within an articulated framework of reference points and perspectives. In this regard, three questions are seemingly of particular relevance: analysis of the Russian historical-political context, with the changes of the 1860s; ethnological-anthropological interpretation of typologies of the commune; and a political intervention on Russia.

Marx made the following observations to the editors of *Otecestvenniye Zapisky*:

> The chapter on primitive accumulation does not pretend to do more than trace the path by which, in Western Europe, the capitalist order of economy emerged from the womb of the feudal order of economy ... Now what application to Russia can my critic [Zhukovsky] make of this historical sketch? Only this: If Russia is tending to become a capitalist nation after the example of the Western European countries ... she will not succeed without having first transformed a good part of her peasants into proletarians ... [My critic] feels himself obliged to metamorphose my historical sketch of the genesis of capitalism in Western Europe into an historico-philosophic theory of the general path imposed by fate upon every people, whatever the historic circumstances in which it finds itself ... By studying each of these forms of evolution separately and then comparing them one can easily find the clue to this phenomenon, but one will never arrive there by the universal passport of a general historico-

philosophical theory, the supreme virtue of which consists in being super-historical.[94]

Marx here rearticulates – and does not subject to critique – his analysis of primitive accumulation in *Capital*: the question of the succession of feudalism and capitalism had to be posed in more complex terms, since it presented different modalities and timescales in different countries.[95] The case of Russia is a telling one, but so, too, is that of Germany, where structures based on hierarchy lasted up to the nineteenth century. Zhukovsky, engaging with Marx's position, offered a simplified version of this, reducing it to the idea that Russia needed mechanically to pass through fully developed capitalism.

Marx always sought to hold together – albeit on the basis of an essential instability – an overarching articulation of the course of history and attention to its specific determinations, the circumstantial social context in which political activity was inscribed. This framework, which constituted a sort of destructuring of philosophy as it had been conceived up to that point, could not but reject 'an historico-philosophic theory of the general path imposed by fate upon every people' served by 'the universal passport of a general historico-philosophical theory'. In the last instance, Marx's perspective cannot be 'collapsed' either into a philosophy of history (even beyond the fact that it is not always clear what this concept means), nor any sort of anti-philosophy of history. Indeed, the counterposition here indicated is vitiated by the 'theoreticism' and the spirit of 'critical criticism' for which Marx had reproached the post-Hegelians ever since the 1840s. As such we find both a historical-theoretical critique framing Russia in an ever more complex context, and a question that is *sans phrases* political, concerning the possibility or otherwise of a revolutionary path: and these two planes are interconnected, but can never be immediately 'compressed' together.[96]

---

94   Letter from Marx to Editor of the *Otecestvenniye Zapisky*, November 1877.

95   See Patterson 2009, p. 130: 'Marx ... already had a comparative perspective on the development of capitalism in different countries. He had also commented on the inter-connections between different parts of the world: for example, of the factory workers in England, slaves in the American South, serfs in Eastern Europe, village communities in India, and immigrants to areas, like the United States or Germany, that were experiencing the growth of industrial capitalism'.

96   On this, see the apt comments in Maffi 2008, pp. 31–2: 'For Marx and Engels ... it was important to clarify through patient work the immediate *theoretical* possibilities, *practical* limits, and *environmental* conditions of the Russian historical dilemma (the possibility of reaching communism without passing through capitalism) ... This meant explaining to

In this regard, the correspondence between Marx and Vera Zasulich is interesting in several aspects. Zasulich was a Russian revolutionary with a rather complex trajectory: having started out from Populist positions, she then turned to Marxist formations, and was among the founders (along with Lenin, Martov, and others) of the review *Iskra*, before then joining the Mensheviks.[97] Marx's letter to her came within a particular context: he was suffering serious health problems and was preoccupied with 'guiding' the formation of the first Russian Marxist group. He drew up four tormented drafts far longer than the letter he did eventually send, and full of corrections. The text of the letter that he posted was shorn of the argumentation that had been present in the drafts. Marx drew attention to the ambivalence of the Russian situation, and the different outcomes that might result: 'the intrinsic dualism [of the Russian commune] allows for this alternative: either the element of private property will prevail over the collective element, or the latter over the former ... Each of the solutions is possible'.[98]

Such an approach is compatible with what we previously said about the ambiguity of the Russian commune's structure and its oscillation between communitarian elements and new dynamics toward privatisation. What was important was to understand which of these two forces in tension would prevail, though we should always bear in mind that the communitarian dimension should not be idealised (moreover, Marx's whole work, from his first writings to his last, was sustained by a tension between individual realisation and the radical critique of any kind of organicism) and that Russia did not have a democratic order in this period. This scenario presented a constitutive ambivalence, irreducible to any predetermined solutions. Thus Marx explained to Zasulich

---

Mikhailovsky that the "inevitability" of a historical advance ... is no metaphysical concept ...; of examining, in the letter to Zasulich, and indirectly to Plekhanov and Axelrod, the strong and weak points of the agricultural communes as of 1881, framing the problem, on the one hand, of the history of all the social formations of primitive communism ... and, on the other hand, the general situation of contemporary Russia ...' Conversely, according to Tomba 2011, here we have a complete rearticulation – one that is both theoretical and political – of Marx's reasoning, starting with Russia (and other extra-European and 'peripheral' realities): 'The unwritten history of the oppressed cannot be grasped with the tools of historicist historiography ... From this perspective, noncapitalist forms cannot be considered stages on the way to the capitalist mode of production and the liberation of the individual from communitarian binds, but as its contemporary alternatives ... The *obshchina* ... was welcomed by Marx, in the wake of Chernyshevsky, Kovalevsky and others, as a new possibility of human emancipation on a communitarian basis' (pp. 286–7).

97   See Geierhos 1977, Dussel 2009, pp. 226–31.
98   Marx to Zasulich, third draft.

that the schema in *Capital* neither foresaw nor ruled out the possibility of the
Russian commune transitioning to communism:

> ... the analysis given in *Capital* does not provide arguments either for or
> against the vitality of the rural commune; but the apposite study that I
> have made of it ... has convinced me that the commune is the basis of
> social regeneration in Russia. However, for it to play this function, it is
> first necessary to eliminate the deleterious influences that assail it from
> all sides, such as to secure it normal conditions for organic development.

What emerges, here, is a changeable situation that could develop in an expansive manner, but only on the basis of specific conditions. Working through this
last hypothesis, Marx brings into focus the possibility that the Russian commune might function as an element propelling the establishment of collective
production on a national scale:

> communal ownership of the land [in the Russian commune] forms the
> natural basis of collective production and appropriation ... It is precisely
> this point which demonstrates the great superiority of the Russian 'rural
> commune' over archaic communes of the same type. Alone in Europe it
> has kept going on a vast, nationwide scale.[99]

> What threatens the survival of the Russian commune is thus neither
> historical inevitability nor any theory: it is oppression on the part of
> the state and exploitation by capitalist intruders, strengthened by their
> acquisitions.[100]

> To save the Russian commune, a Russian revolution is needed ... If revolu-
> tion comes at the opportune moment, if it concentrates all its forces so as
> to allow the rural commune full scope, the latter will soon develop as an
> element of regeneration in Russian society and an element of superiority
> over the countries enslaved by the capitalist system.[101]

Within such a horizon, politics *sans phrases* forcefully bursts through. Indeed,
the problem does not appear resolvable at the theoretical level of a historical

---

99   Marx to Zasulich, first draft.
100   Marx to Zasulich, second draft.
101   Marx to Zasulich, first draft.

dialectic, but can be articulated only with the 'real movement which abolishes the present state of things', to take up the famous definition of communism from the *German Ideology*. 'To save the Russian commune', a Russian revolution would be necessary, within an adequate timescale. Certainly, there are some ambiguities in Marx's drafts of his letter to Zasulich, but it should not be forgotten that they were making a political gamble on Russia. Engels, too, some years previously, had forcefully insisted on the possibilities as well as the necessity of the Russian revolution:

> If anything can still save Russian communal ownership and give it a chance of growing into a new, really viable form, it is a proletarian revolution in Western Europe ... Russia undoubtedly is on the eve of a revolution ... a revolution that will be of the greatest importance for the whole of Europe, if only because it will destroy at one blow the last, so far intact, reserve of the entire European reaction.[102]

In this passage, even apart from Engels's considerations on the great importance of the revolution in Russia, there is another element of decisive significance, namely the relationship between the Russian revolution and the revolution in the West.

Indeed, if we carefully analyse Marx's letters to various Russian theorists and revolutionaries, as well as other writings of his from the 1870s and 1880s, we realise that Marx did not unconditionally stick to the idea that it was possible for the Russian commune to transition to communism. Rather, he identified two determining, fundamental presuppositions of such a transition. First of all, the conservation and transformation of the communitarian Russian commune in view of the establishment of communism was unthinkable unless revolution broke out shortly. According to Marx, a revolution in Russia alone could not result in a communist society. The second condition posed by Marx (and Engels) was thus that the Russian revolution had to be completed by a working-class revolution in the West. Without this latter, the Russian commune's transition to communism would prove impossible: it was wholly insufficient to resort exclusively to the propulsive dynamic of Russian associative structures. As such, the distance between Marx's outlook and the Russian Populists' thinking becomes clearly apparent, even taking into account the fact that the Populists' positions were very complex and varied and cannot be reduced to a sort of boundless idealisation of the Russian commune. Marx forcefully

---

102   Engels, 'Soziales aus Rußland', *Der Volkstaat*, 16 April 1875.

upheld the perspective here indicated in his preface to the 1882 second Russian edition of the *Communist Manifesto*, in which he brought into relief the fact that neither the USA nor Russia were considered therein:

> It was the time when Russia constituted the last great reserve of all European reaction ... in Russia we find ... more than half the land owned in common by the peasants. Now the question is: can the Russian *obshchina* though greatly undermined, yet a form of primeval common ownership of land, pass directly to the higher form of Communist common ownership? Or, on the contrary, must it first pass through the same process of dissolution such as constitutes the historical evolution of the West? The only answer to that possible today is this: If the Russian Revolution becomes the signal for a proletarian revolution in the West, so that both complement each other, the present Russian common ownership of land may serve as the starting point for a communist development.[103]

This 1882 preface, already cited above, presents various interesting themes. First of all, it underlines the fact that the *Communist Manifesto* did not have to be repudiated, but rather rearticulated on the basis of a close engagement with the historical-political events of more than thirty years of history, from 1848 to the early 1880s. This did not mean simply a change of theoretical paradigm, but an attentive analysis of the social and political changes that had taken place in recent decades. The USA and Russia, missing from the *Manifesto*, had since then come to play a crucial role, and as such the study in question could not pass over in silence the situation of these countries. As for political practice – and as will become apparent in the final chapter – the whole of Marx's trajectory in his final decades could be interpreted as a sort of continual rectification of the *Manifesto*. Indeed, in this preface he addressed the question of whether or not it was possible for the Russian commune to transition to communism. Thus the task was to understand whether the *obshchina* could serve as the starting point of communism, or whether the 'labour pains' of giving birth to capitalism, as in the West, were necessary, through a still long and complex journey. The realisation of the former hypothesis, which did not *ipso facto* foresee the full development of capitalism, would require not only a rapid revolution in Russia but also an external factor, namely the communist revolution in the West.

---

103   See Bongiovanni 1989, pp. 171–89, which also referring to this preface stresses: 'because communal property could always change course ... it was necessary to wait, as in the Germany of 1844, for the cock to crow in the West' (p. 189).

Without such mutually implicating revolutions, transformation in Russia would prove practically impossible, as Engels observed in a letter to Danielson (the Russian translator of *Capital*) ten years after Marx's death, taking on board Marx's considerations but simultaneously integrating them into a social and political dynamic in constant development:

> No doubt the commune and to a certain extent the *artel*, contained germs which under certain conditions might have developed and saved Russia the necessity of passing through the torments of the capitalistic regime. I fully subscribe to our author's letter about Zhukovsky. But in his, as well as in my opinion, the first condition required to bring this about was the impulse from without, the change of economic system in the Occident of Europe, the destruction of the capitalist system in the countries where it had originated. Our author [Marx] said in a certain preface to a certain old manifesto, in January 1882, replying to the question whether the Russian commune might not be the starting point of a higher social development: if the change of economic system in Russia coincides with a change of economic system in the West, so that both supplement each other, then contemporary Russian landownership may become as the starting point of a new social development ... If we in the West had been quicker in our own economic development, if we had been able to upset the capitalistic regime some ten or twenty years ago, there might have been time yet for Russia to cut short the tendency of her own evolution towards capitalism. Unfortunately we are too slow ... in the meantime, with you, the commune fades away.[104]

It was thus that Engels picked up the thread of Marx's discourse, attentively examining the recent development of events in Russia, which had set the 'tombstone' on any possibility of a direct transition from agricultural commune to communism. In 1894, Engels stressed that

> the initiative for any possible transformation of the Russian commune along these lines cannot come from the commune itself, but only from the industrial proletarians of the West ... The fact is: at no time or place has the agrarian communism that arose out of gentile society developed anything of its own accord but its own disintegration.
>
> ...

---

104   Engels to Danielson, 24 February 1893.

> And so the transformation of the country into a capitalist industrial nation, the proletarianisation of a large proportion of the peasantry and the decay of the old communistic commune proceeds at an ever quickening pace.[105]

Here, we are 'at the gates' of the young Lenin's reflection, which in his 1899 *The Development of Capitalism in Russia* brought into focus the growing use of technical production methods, the concentration of capital, and the proletarianisation of ever wider layers of the population (albeit with a series of qualifications noting this process's partial and incomplete character).[106] Lenin's approach proved an extremely apt one, though it displayed some excessive generalisations in terms of how the capitalist dynamic operated on Russian territory.

Working our way through this theme (including with these references to Engels and Lenin, who did not limit themselves to developing Marx's intuitions, but rather rearticulated them with reference to the changed conditions) has brought to light the existence of a change in Marx's evaluation of Russia, with respect to his first writings. It is no chance thing that in his final years Marx 'invested' so much in Russia. But to defend this position does not mean drifting toward a conception based on some sort of exaltation of Russia that makes the entire argument revolve around his letter to Vera Zasulich, a text that had very specific political motivations.

The Coexistence of Noncapitalist and Capitalist Structures

The path followed in this chapter, while constantly bearing in mind the framework established by *Capital*, has, however, also looked at a large number of Marx's excerpts – with particular reference to those of an ethnological character – as well as a series of articles, short texts and letters. This enormous mass of writings has elements of instability, of which we should take account as we examine the question of the relationship between what capitalism is, is not, and only partially is. In the first place, it should not be forgotten that in many cases these are brief texts that contain some pointers and some reflection but never take on a general value or systematic character. Among other things, this is a particularly complex problem in the case of the excerpts, since these are largely transcriptions and/or summaries of books that Marx was cataloguing,

---

105   1894 Afterword to 'On Social Relations in Russia.'
106   Lenin 1956.

with little comment of his own. Though his choice of what texts to examine is not without significance, he never truly and properly 'welds' the transcription of specific texts to the articulation of an overarching theory. It is true, however, that in *Capital* and the late Marx's economic manuscripts, there is a smattering of elements that interact with the content of these excerpts. We can also make an analogous consideration with regard to the other 'horn' of the problem, namely his analysis of 'peripheral' noncapitalist countries such as India and China as well as not-fully capitalist ones like Russia. It is in fact possible to come across some traces of this problem in various of his letters and writings, but we could hardly say that it was fully articulated. So it should be apparent from the present analysis that Marx's study of the natural and historical sciences and his examination of the situation of extra-European countries were interconnected: it is enough to think, for example, of the significant role of the Russian commune in Marx's ethnological reflection.

The lack of any solid connection between the multiplicity of Marx's writings and excerpts that address anthropological questions, and the structure of *Capital*, can be interpreted as a weak point of his reflection. Both for contingent reasons (Marx's difficult health problems in his last years) and theoretical ones, he was unable fully to work through this question. In terms of the theoretical reasons, Marx clearly faced an *impasse*, here. It should not be forgotten that in the last ten years of his life, he worked on an enormous number of excerpts, and made some not particularly substantial changes to the final two volumes of *Capital*. Indeed, Marx somewhat ground to a halt in his rearticulation of *Capital*, which meant that Engels was forced to take on not only the tasks of refining and adjusting this work, but also those of researching and completing it. As such, we can say that on the whole, Engels did not denature the sense of Marx's discourse in the second volume, but if anything sought to systematise the 'mish-mash' of manuscripts handed over to him.

It is a rather different matter as regards Volume III, since here Engels's involvement proved rather more substantial and was not reducible to the mere need to put the manuscripts in order. The third volume bears the imprint of Engels's significant contribution; and this developed in a certain manner, in many senses endowed with a 'developmentalist' character that would later proliferate in 'official' Marxism, and which many Western thinkers would inveigh against. To what extent such 'developmentalism' was in fact a characteristic trait of Marx's own perspective is a rather contested question; here, we will limit ourselves to remarking that this was something to which Marx remained open, but not the only possible alternative. Moreover, even Marx's reflection on the natural and historical sciences displays a position that is not reducible to either scientism or anti-scientism. In the previous sections, we focused on how certain elements from Darwin substantially operated, in Marx, in a fashion that was not only anti-theological but even anti-teleological. In this dance of light and shadows, Marx's reflection cannot be defined either as 'developmentalism' (aside from Engels's later contribution, which in any case pertained to a series of questions that were urgently posed at the level of political organisation) nor as twentieth-century 'anti-developmentalism', with all the difficulties it faced in reaching a satisfactory political and juridical articulation. To return to the theme with which we began, the overall structure of *Capital* doubtless poses a problem, and the fact that it was not Marx who published either its second or third volumes is proof enough of this.

However, it is possible to articulate this question in different terms, maintaining that this incompleteness is not only a problem but also a resource to draw upon, since it allows us to delineate an open perspective, susceptible to further political and theoretical declinations. In order to adopt this path, however, it is necessary to take a cue from our earlier-developed considerations of the complexity of the relationship between theory and politics in Marx's framework. The possible 'separation' of these two planes also has an important role for the purposes of understanding the horizon of this present chapter, and the results at which it has arrived concerning the relationship between what is, what is not, and what is not fully capitalist. Here, Marx's ethnological-anthropological studies (principally regarding precapitalist or at least noncapitalist communitarian forms) combine with his analyses of structures existing outside of Western Europe, such as in India, China and Russia. Indeed, his plane of argumentation proves to be a double-sided one, presenting both an objective and a subjective dimension. It is a matter, in the first place, of 'objectively' studying the relation between capitalist and noncapitalist realities, and secondly of identifying the conditions of possibility for a revolutionary political activity in noncapitalist countries, on the basis of coordination with fully capitalist situations. Moreover, the relation between the 'objective' and 'subjective' remained absolutely central throughout Marx's trajectory, and must be conceived – as in the case of the relation between theory and politics – in terms of a connection between the two elements that does not involve their being fully compacted together.

From the 'objective' standpoint, in the late Marx, there is a 'complication' of the social and political framework that he had provided in the 1848 *Manifesto*, with a growing interest in extra-European realities which he had previously examined only in cursory fashion. The world had grown both materially and metaphorically, and could no longer be confined to the boundaries of Europe alone. It was necessary to recognise that the capitalist mode of production had not spread everywhere, and that it had not spread on a fully homogeneous basis. At the same time, extra-European orders could not be considered absolutely autonomous, and thus possible to study *iuxta propria principia*, nor relegated *sic et simpliciter* to the category – somewhat prevalent in Marxist debates – of oriental despotism. British colonialism in India and Westerners' violent interventions in China in the various 'opium wars' brought to light the presence of ever stronger influences and interrelations, though these were obviously inscribed within mechanisms of domination.[107] Marx studied colonialism, at least in the 1850s, on the basis of a constitutive ambivalence (and sometimes with ambiguity): on the one hand, it had a brutal character, while on the other hand it introduced elements of capitalism and brought these countries out of despotism. From the 1860s onwards, Marx took a much more critical view, questioning the idea present in earlier texts as to the progressive character of colonialism. He increasingly understood not only the constitutively global role of capitalism (an element present throughout Marx's work), but also the specific differences of the communities operating within the world system. As such, he marked out a sort of coexistence of developed capitalist orders with noncapitalist or else not-fully developed capitalist orders. Obviously, the concrete modalities of their interrelation could not be defined once and for all time in all their complexity and internal articulation; rather, they continually had to be studied in their specificity.

In addressing this question, we must avoid two possible traps. The first would be a dogmatic reading of Marx's reflection, using a mechanical schema for the transition from precapitalist forms to capitalism. Without doubt, some elements of this are present in some parts of Marx's trajectory, but for reasons we have already mentioned, he cannot be reduced to this framework alone. Moreover, beyond interpreting Marx, such an approach would not be up to the task of grasping the distinctive traits of today's situation. Another, opposite risk lies in 'collapsing' Marx into the perspectives of so-called postcolonial studies, thus making Marx a sort of precursor of postcolonial authors.[108] Such attempts

---

107   Note Rosa Luxemburg's analysis, from which emerges the fact that the capitalist mode of production arises and develops historically within non-capitalist surroundings: Luxemburg 2003.

108   Anderson 2010, p. 6, comments: 'I argue for a move toward a twenty-first century notion of Marx as a global theorist whose social critique included notions of capital and class that were open and broad enough to encompass the particularities of nationalism, race, and ethnicity, as well as the varieties of human social and political development, from Europe to Asia and from the Americas to Africa. Thus I will be presenting Marx as a much more multilinear theorist of history and society than is generally supposed ...' Anderson's text has the notable merit of providing a broad picture, in terms with which

are again problematic both for a reason internal to Marx and for a theoretical and political reason concerning the present-day horizon. As concerns this first aspect, it is necessary to note that Marx's reflection, particularly up until the 1850s but even afterwards (think of how absolutely crucial references to England are to the framework of *Capital*), was not alien to the 'progressivist' reading that we earlier subjected to critique. As such, any attempt to make Marx immediately current by representing him as 'postcolonial' is questionable. As for the second aspect, concerning the present-day situation, we should avoid uncritically taking postcolonial studies on board without grasping the problematic character of the 'culturalism' underlying their reasoning.[109] Even considering the difficulty of identifying any common denominator with postcolonial studies, and the great interest of numerous elements in these texts, we face the risk of producing a 'dematerialised' conception in which the question of domination risks 'evaporating', losing its specific determination in relation to the node of labour. Thus it is not a matter, here, of reproducing an old vulgate from Marx, nor of presenting Marx *à la mode* such as that he is immediately employable today.

The theme of the current-day relevance of Marx's reflection is of considerable importance, but must be considered not at the immediate level, which paradoxically enough would entail a sort of dogmatism, in the sense that it would suggest that all the necessary coordinates for understanding the 'present state of things' can be found in Marx's writings. Rather – as the most fertile moments and turning points of Marxism have made clear – it is necessary to 're-run' his discourse on the basis of the newly-determined conjuncture. For example, within the present-day horizon, there is a tight interlinking of dynamics of classism and racism, a 'racism without race':[110] politically, the question of migrant subjectivity has thus proven crucial.[111] Marx certainly did provide some theoretical elements important for carrying out such a task, but they are not fully adequate to an interpretation of the present-day situation. Staying faithful to Marx's approach (and we do not use the term 'faithful' in a pejorative

---

we can largely agree, of the late Marx's itinerary, devoting attention to non-European countries that are important to the international situation, as well as peripheral European countries like Poland and Ireland. The limit of his reasoning is that this interpretation of a 'multilinear' Marx risks leading us to the idea of an immediate compatibility between Marx and the perspectives of postcolonial studies, thus anachronistically representing him as immediately current.

109   See Note 20, p. 62.
110   See Balibar and Wallerstein 1988.
111   See Gambino 2003, Sacchetto 2004, Raimondi and Ricciardi (eds.) 2004, Mezzadra 2001.

sense, but in terms of a capacity to revive the distinctive traits of his method) consists – more than in cementing a determinate content and analysis – in the capacity to combine a radical critique of the present configuration of capital with a political practice with destructive force. Moreover, the fact that these two spheres are interrelated clearly emerges from the fact that there can be no fully objective dynamic. In fact the entire 'objective' development of the capitalist system is marked by the workers' 'acting in common' in a potentially 'explosive' manner. As such, we arrive at the second 'horn' of the problem, largely linked to the subjective dimension and thus in continual interaction with political practices, in all their irreducibility to preconceived schemas.

The question of the relationship between capitalist and noncapitalist orders does indeed exhibit a subjective aspect, which is obviously connected to the objective one, but cannot immediately be deduced from it. In situations outside of Western Europe, and in particular Russia, the problem was one of identifying the conditions of possibility of a revolution, and thus the feasibility of revolution breaking out even given the absence of capitalist development true and proper: from the commune to communism. Marx's answer to this question seems rather ambivalent, if not interlocutory, neither clearly excluding nor foreseeing a revolutionary outcome. In any case, in Marx (and even more so in Engels) the reciprocal influence of revolution in the West and revolution in Russia is crucial. Thus also on the subjective plane the question of the mutual implication of capitalist and noncapitalist orders, or at least not fully capitalist ones, is placed at the centre of Marx's reasoning. Taken as a whole, we can say that one of the differences between Engels's approach and Marx's consists in the fact that for Engels the priority was the revolution in the West, to which the Russian one would be subordinate: indeed, the outbreak of revolution in the West was the condition of possibility of overhaul in Russia. In Marx, the question proves more complicated, since he defines no clear order of priority. Moreover, in terms of the subjective aspect, the aforementioned coexistence of different orders inevitably pointed to coordinates that would have to be evaluated and practiced on a case by case basis, given that action is a law unto itself, in the immanence of its development.

We will conclude our reflection by making reference to the commons and 'the common' (without identifying the two)[112] in their relation to the subjective dynamic of the question, and thus to the 'acting in common' of the singularities

---

112   There has been widespread debate on the commons in the English-speaking world: see
      Federici 2004. A problematic aspect of such approaches, though they do offer various
      fruitful elements, consists in their idealisation of premodern communal forms: see, on
      this, the observations of Mezzadra 2008b, pp. 25–52, 42. On the centrality of the question

that make up the working class. The collective dimension proper to noncapit-alist or not-fully capitalist situations (like the Russian *obshchina*) analysed in this chapter must not be either dismissed or idealised. Indeed, subjecting it to a total critique would mean adhering to a simplified, linear schema of the path of history, on the basis of an outlook conforming to the 'grammar' of Western modernity. At the same time, however, it is necessary to bring out its complex, multifaceted and sometimes even contradictory character, sweeping aside any absolutely compacted and uniform representation of it. In this sense, it is also not a matter of counterposing what is modern to what is not. It is necessary to avoid any type of political romanticism marked by a sort of nostalgia for pre-modern or even 'Robinsonian' structures.

This theme must, therefore, be interpreted very carefully at the theoret-ical and political levels, rejecting any generic or even equivocal declination of this problem based on a confusion of the Germanic, Indian and Russian com-mune [*Gemeinde*] (and nor should we identify these very diverse cases with one another), the community effected by the state form within a physically and metaphorically delimited territory, and communism.[113] The risk in several present-day readings revolving around the commons is that they operate an identification of the elements here in question, on the basis of a 'communit-arian' emphasis. In our view, throughout Marx's trajectory (even in his last writings) no such 'communitarian' approach is apparent, and as such commun-ism is not characterised in anti-individualist and organicist terms. Moreover, it should not be forgotten that by the 1870s to '80s the Russian commune, to which Marx dedicated particular attention, had undergone processes of accu-mulation: in this context, the Russian situation could thus not be considered *sic et simpliciter* as noncapitalist. The question of the communal dimension [*Gemeinwesen*] thus had to be considered as stakes in play, open to unexpected

---

of commonwealth and the common (singular not plural: thus on the basis of what is in many ways a different framework to that incardinated in the commons) for the purposes of understanding contemporary capitalism, see Hardt and Negri 2010. On a debate on 'the common', see the essays collected in Curcio and Özselçuk (eds.) 2010. On the potential and the limitations of the declinations of the 'common', see in particular the dialogue between Balibar and Negri 2010. According to a different perspective: Dardot and Laval 2014.

113   See Nancy 1996, and 2008: 'Communism, though it has put some effort into thinking the "real relation" and what defined the "individual", has still not managed to think being in common as distinct from "community"'. Nancy aptly insists on the 'separation' between the common dimension and community, but works through these elements in terms different to our own, since he conceives democracy (or communism as democracy) in terms that are more 'metaphysical' than political.

developments – but without falling into any of the frameworks criticised above, instead insisting on its ambivalences. For the purposes of understanding this problem, Marx's expression 'acting in common' is particularly fruitful, because in our view it allows us to grasp his reference to what is 'in common' and avoid any substantialist approach and any form of 'naturalism'. For example, in one passage in *Capital* (cited in the Introduction of the present work) Marx evokes 'acting in common' 'negatively', recalling the position of Le Chapelier giving the decree of 14 June 1791 in France, stating that 'the workers must not be allowed to come to any understanding about their own interests, nor to act in common [*Gemeinsam handeln*] and thereby lessen their "absolute dependence, which is almost that of slavery"'.[114] *Gemeinsam handeln* is not rooted in the structure of things, nor does it constitute a metaphysical presupposition, but rather is connected to the political activity of the working class and its attempt to 'break' the seriality of capitalism. Thus we here find a historical practice, determined in a specific way, capable of bringing individuals into being in common through a continual and mobile 'exchange' between the 'individual' and the 'collective'. The reference to the common dimension, moreover, represents a 'red thread' throughout Marx's whole trajectory, right from his first writings, as the extraordinary theoretical and political pregnancy of the concept of *Gemeinwesen* testifies.

Such a problem needs to be historicised, however, precisely on account of the fact that *Gemeinwesen* cannot be posed as a sort of abstract metaphysical assumption nor a codification of a state of things.[115] For this reason, the next chapter will be dedicated precisely to the question of the erosion of communal property carried out by the capitalist mode of production, the element of separation underlying this, and the new political spaces that it opens up. In this regard, it is worth stressing that Marx intended, in the last instance, not so much to write a history of all past productive forms as to examine capitalism in its specific differentiation from previous communities. Obviously, putting the capitalist mode of production at the heart of the argument does

---

114   *MECW*, Vol. 35, p. 731.

115   See Sereni 2010a, which focuses on the young Marx but also on the *Grundrisse* (in particular pp. 105–62), from which the centrality of *Gemeinwesen* rather than a codified *Gemeinschaft* is apparent: 'Marx tends in his mature writings to reserve "community" for precapitalist forms and "association" [*Verein*] for communism ... One of the reasons for this preference is that unlike communities, association is neither natural nor originary. To put it another way, "association" says *Gemeinwesen* but not *Gemeinschaft*' (p. 143). See also Sereni 2010b, which takes its cue from this text and particularly revolves around the late Marx.

not mean to deny the existence within it of degrees, situations, and modalities that are differentiated – if not centrifugal – or to maintain that its development is 'objective' and endogenous, since class practices continually upset and sometimes even subvert the direction that capital is trying to impose on the course of events. An analysis that looks to grasp the full complexity of the capitalist scenario cannot, however, ignore the emergence of a 'new' anthropology different to that of the past, one with a spectral and expansive character.

Individual Separation

> We undergo individual and isolated formation processes marked by all kinds of distortions and lacerations ... But at the moment at which we discover that this society is a system of total exploitation ... our formation process becomes a collective one, not in the sense of destroying our individuality, but, on the contrary, as the very constitution of individuality ... We undergo formation processes ... that reconstruct in an emancipatory way what individuality is, to the extent that we unite in the practical struggle against this system.
>
> HANS-JÜRGEN KRAHL, *Konstitution und Klassenkämpfe*

∴

'*Trennung*' and Capitalism: The Erosion of Common Property

Marx's concern was not, in the last instance, to provide a total picture of human history, but rather to examine the capitalist mode of production in its specific difference from what went before, as it breaks through all the prior communitarian, familial ties. Indeed, already in the very first of Marx's texts, like the *Critique of Hegel's Philosophy of Right* and *On The Jewish Question*, his entire reflection was sustained by an interpretation of the modern world characterised by the element of separation [*Trennung*]. Crucial, here, within a still rather generic perspective on the terrain of economic analysis, was the question of the separation of civil society and the state – which Hegel had addressed yet also mystified. With the passing of time, there was a gradual shifting of Marx's landscape, though he held onto the idea that the modern world was structurally characterised by the dimension of *Trennung*. The *Grundrisse*'s outlook stood in continuity with this approach, as emerged from our discussion of precapitalist forms in the previous chapter. More generally, capitalism is here understood in its character of 'permanently revolutionising' all communitarian ties and in posing the individual as its point of departure. After the *Grundrisse*, from the 1860s onward Marx's studies in this regard were further complicated, in terms of the internal articulation of capitalism, more than of the relationship between precapitalist communities and capitalism. In his anthropological extracts and writings largely concerning specific conjunctures, he provided a less homogeneous picture of the structure of capitalism. Capitalism did not develop everywhere in the same way, and whole areas were still excluded from capitalist development in the strict sense: Russia, India and China appearing to be particularly significant cases in point. Yet, notwithstanding the ever greater complexity of his analysis, the capitalist mode of production remained the centre of his perspective.

The whole of Marx's analysis of the capitalist system sought to bring out its character of structural separation. Even the *Grundrisse* were pervaded by the idea of a counterposition between precapitalist orders characterised by unity [*Einheit*] and capitalism, characterised by separation [*Trennung*]. If the former were distinguished by the organic unity of man and community through the mediation of the land, and thus a negation of individuality and of the possibility – even if not without contradictions – of building autonomous paths, then capitalism effected a break in this unity, thus giving life to a separation: a separation of the individual from the produce and means of labour, from objective conditions, as well as among individuals. He also brought to light the distance between each person and their own capacity to labour. Later, the entire framework of *Capital* would be sustained by the dimension of separation: most of the time *Trennung*, but also *Teilung* (particularly in relation to labour and the division of labour), and *Scheidung*, the capitalist mode of production thus being configured as a *Scheidungsprozeß*. We could interpret the whole of *Capital* in terms of this question, whose historical genealogy (or better, historical genealogies)[1] and operating mechanisms Marx tried to establish. His reference to precapitalist forms, then, still remains in the background: in order to see such a separation, it is necessary to consider that what went beforehand was a unity. In this sense, surplus-value distinguishes the capitalist mode of production from other social orders, and therefore waged labour must not be

---

1   On the structure of genealogy, note the considerations by Michel Foucault, for example Foucault 2003, pp. 9–10: 'You can see that this activity, which we can describe as genealogical, is certainly not a matter of contrasting the abstract unity of theory with the concrete multiplicity of the facts. It is certainly not a matter of some form or other of scientism that disqualifies speculation by contrasting it with the rigor of well-established bodies of knowledge ... It is a way of playing local, discontinuous, disqualified, or nonlegitimized knowledges off against the unitary theoretical instance that claims to be able to filter them, organize them into a hierarchy, organize them in the name of a true body of knowledge, in the name of the rights of a science that is in the hands of the few. Genealogies are therefore not positivistic returns to a form of science that is more attentive or more accurate ... They are about the insurrection of knowledges'. On the Foucault-Marx relationship, see Macherey 2014, pp. 149–212. See also Mezzadra 2014; Chignola 2014.

confused with slavery: 'The essential difference between the various economic forms of society, between, for instance, a society based on slave-labour, and one based on wage-labour, lies only in the mode in which this surplus labour is in each case extracted from the actual producer, the labourer'.[2]

As such there emerges – even if on the basis of a complex and articulated scenario – a situation that is new with respect to the past structures in which 'the labourer and his means of production remained closely united, like the snail with its shell'. In this context, the land played a decisive mediating role: in the communities of 'the simplest form, the land is tilled in common, and the produce divided among the members'.[3] The capitalist world is characterised precisely by the rupturing of common property and the irruption of a scenario founded on the separation of individuals, with all the ambivalence that such a state of affairs entails. As such, Marx did not pose precapitalist common property in terms of an idyll of equality, contrary to what might seem to emerge from the contemporary discussion of the commons.[4] On the one hand, Marx did historicise his reflection, and on the other he tended to see precapitalist structures generically as formations in which man was bound to the community through the mediation of the land. In reality, this approach is not a wholly satisfactory one, since there is no indistinct 'common', but rather a number of diverse structures differentiated according to their historical time and geographical location. Sometimes Marx tended, instead, to bring out a sort of generalised organicism characteristic of all precapitalist forms.

A further, more specific consideration regards the situation in England before the enclosures. As is clearly apparent also from Marx's analysis, it is wholly inadequate – both on the theoretical and the political plane – to idealise the English context that existed prior to the enclosures, as if this did not feature specific and very powerful hierarchies and as if it were not characterised by mechanisms of domination. The same argument, albeit following various different geometries, also applies to other forms existing prior to capitalism: one need only think of the slavery prevalent in the ancient world or the serfdom of the medieval period. And at the overall theoretical level, there is no basis for any idea of a truly 'egalitarian' community prior to capitalism; as such, it is fruitless and myopic to idealise such forms in function of an anti-modern perspective. At the same time, it is necessary to problematise any rigid schematising with regard to the transition from the non-capitalist to the capitalist order. Indeed,

---

2   *MECW*, Vol. 35, pp. 226–7.

3   *MECW*, Vol. 35, p. 362.

4   See pp. 104–5 footnote 112.

while it does have some internal difficulties, in *Capital* we do not find *sic et simpliciter* the idea of a mechanical succession of modes of production: the transition from one mode of production to another displays more articulated coordinates, since within one same social structure there emerge a series of differentiated levels and heterogeneous forms – sometimes coexisting, sometimes clashing – giving rise to confusion and even fractures. In the capitalist system, therefore, there are still elements from previous modes of production, existing on a more or less temporary basis.

For the purpose of delving deeper into the distinctive traits of this rupturing of common property, it is worth here introducing the concept of accumulation, which is very much present in the current debate.[5] In the first volume of *Capital*, we find a clear definition in this regard: 'Employing surplus value as capital, reconverting it into capital, is called accumulation of capital'.[6] Accumulation does not delineate a homogenous, 'pacific' space, but rather is configured in terms of a lacerating, disharmonious tension, with mutually counterposed elements and circumstantiated geometries of power at its very basis: 'The antagonistic character of capitalist accumulation, and therefore of the capitalistic relations of property generally, is here so evident, that even the official English reports on this subject teem with heterodox onslaughts on "property and its rights"'.[7] Much unlike the classical economists' apologetic, 'fetishised' way of seeing it, accumulation does not exhibit the traits of an idyll, but on the contrary is seen to be marked by structural violence and a radical expropriation: capital 'comes into the world dripping from head to foot, from every pore, with

---

5 Rosa Luxemburg's analysis of accumulation is a decisive reference point. She brings out two distinct but inter-related elements of accumulation: 'One concerns the commodity market and the place where surplus value is produced – the factory, the mine, the agricultural estate. Regarded in this light, accumulation is a purely economic process, with its most important phase a transaction between the capitalist and wage labourer ... The other aspect of the accumulation of capital concerns the relations between capitalism and the non-capitalist modes of production which start making their appearance on the international stage. Its predominant methods are colonial policy, an international loan system – a policy of spheres of interest – and war' (Luxemburg 2003, pp. 452–3). See, moreover, on the basis of various different perspectives: Harvey 2003 (which elaborates the category 'accumulation by expropriation', in his view adequate to understanding contemporary imperialism); Harvey 2010a, particularly pp. 60 sqq.; Sanyal 2007; Fumagalli and Mezzadra (eds.) 2009; Mezzadra 2008b; Sacchetto and Tomba (eds.) 2008, particularly Werner Bonefeld's contribution (English original: Bonefeld 2001); Tomba 2011, pp. 257–90.

6 *MECW*, Vol. 35, p. 578.

7 *MECW*, Vol. 35, p. 651.

blood and dirt'.[8] Indeed, it 'comprises a series of forcible methods, of which we
have passed in review only those that have been epoch-making as methods of
the primitive accumulation of capital'.[9] As such, accumulation is characterised
by the dimension of *Gewalt*: and here we should also underline the complexity
and ambivalence of the German term *Gewalt*, simultaneously both 'violence'
and 'power', since it indicates not only physical violence and brutal repression
but also the sophisticated juridical-political mechanisms that the state uses for
discipline.[10]

   If this goes for capital accumulation, then primitive accumulation could be
taken to mean

> the historic basis, instead of the historic result of specifically capitalist
> production. How it itself originates, we need not here inquire as yet. It
> is enough that it forms the starting point. But all methods for raising the
> social productive power of labour that are developed on this basis, are
> at the same time methods for the increased production of surplus value
> or surplus-product, which in its turn is the formative element of accu-
> mulation ... With the accumulation of capital, therefore, the specifically
> capitalistic mode of production develops, and with the capitalist mode of
> production the accumulation of capital.[11]

Marx forcefully reaffirms this consideration in the third volume of *Capital*: 'the
capitalist process of production is simultaneously a process of accumulation'.[12]
If we here stop and examine the 'primitive' character of accumulation, then it
is worth noting that such a position implies making reference to its 'historical
basis'. Moreover, the *incipit* of Chapter 24 on 'so-called primitive accumulation'
brings precisely this aspect into focus:

> the accumulation of capital presupposes surplus value; surplus value pre-
> supposes capitalistic production; capitalistic production presupposes the
> pre-existence of considerable masses of capital and of labour power in
> the hands of producers of commodities. The whole movement, therefore,
> seems to turn in a vicious circle, out of which we can only get by supposing

---

8   *MECW*, Vol. 35, p. 748.
9   *MECW*, Vol. 35, p. 749.
10   See p. 30.
11   *MECW*, Vol. 35, p. 619.
12   *MECW*, Vol. 37, p. 216.

a primitive accumulation ('previous accumulation' of Adam Smith) preceding capitalistic accumulation; an accumulation not the result of the
capitalistic mode of production, but its starting point.[13]

Beyond the 'theological' imaginations of the classical economists, there remains the fact that Marx uses primitive accumulation with a view to explaining
the accumulation of capitalism, as a mechanism of capital's functioning. Not
by chance, in this same chapter Marx evokes prehistory in order to denote
primitive accumulation: the relationship between primitive accumulation and
accumulation is analogous to that between prehistory and history, terminology
which brings to mind the famous passage from his 1857 *Einleitung*. We cannot
speak of a true and proper beginning, a true and proper origin: there was never
any primitive accumulation in the strict sense, any precise moment at which
capitalism began.

   Primitive accumulation is a 'fiction', though with that term we do not mean
mere un-reality: if we 'short-circuit' this interpretation with Lacanian psycho-
analysis, we could speak of a fiction charged with reality. So Marx does not
identify a beginning in the strict sense: rather, he brings together various historical examples (such as the English enclosures) that particularly effectively
bring to light how it was possible to 'spill out' of the feudal horizon. Marx brings
out the theoretical need to identify a sort of prehistory of the 'natural history'
of capital:

> In the history of primitive accumulation, all revolutions are epoch-
> making that act as levers for the capital class in course of formation; but,
> above all, those moments when great masses of men are suddenly and
> forcibly torn from their means of subsistence ... The expropriation of the
> agricultural producer, of the peasant, from the soil, is the basis of the
> whole process. The history of this expropriation, in different countries,
> assumes different aspects, and runs through its various phases in differ-
> ent orders of succession, and at different periods. In England alone, which
> we take as our example, has it the classic form.[14]

Given that his treatment of primitive accumulation speaks to a genealogical
outlook, but never arrives at a single genealogy (rather, we could recognise
various genealogies of the capitalist mode of production), the important thing

---

13   *MECW*, Vol. 35, p. 704.
14   *MECW*, Vol. 35, p. 707.

here is to understand what the distinctive characteristics of accumulation are –
even if following a sort of zig-zag approach, neither a total continuity nor
a simple iteration.[15] It is necessary to address two decisive elements of his
reasoning: in the first place, the extremely complex character of the process,
which is articulated in different phases and modalities, irreducible to any
univocal and unproblematic schema of the succession of modes of production;
secondly, the stress on one 'dominant' factor, the 'epoch-making' changes that
make possible the antagonism between the capitalist class and the working
class. As Marx made explicit in his 1857 *Einleitung*, the method he adopts is not
any sort of retrospective vision in the narrow sense: the starting point of his
reflection is the structure that has now developed, the capitalist system in its
specific difference with respect to previous modes of production.

Accumulation, thus conceived, involves a lacerating expropriation, and thus
a structural element of separation. Moreover, in the chapter on 'so-called primitive accumulation' he defines its characteristics in terms of separation:

> The capitalist system presupposes the complete separation of the labour-
> ers from all property in the means by which they can realize their labour.
> As soon as capitalist production is once on its own legs, it not only main-
> tains this separation, but reproduces it on a continually extending scale.
> The process, therefore, that clears the way for the capitalist system, can
> be none other than the process which takes away from the labourer the
> possession of his means of production; a process that transforms, on the
> one hand, the social means of subsistence and of production into cap-
> ital, on the other, the immediate producers into wage labourers. The so-
> called primitive accumulation, therefore, is nothing else than the histor-
> ical process of divorcing the producer from the means of production ...
> The immediate producer, the labourer, could only dispose of his own per-

---

15   On the relation between accumulation and the genealogical approach, with a perspective
close to that here outlined, see Balibar's 'The Basic Concepts of Historical Materialism':
'The analysis of primitive accumulation is therefore, strictly speaking, merely *the genealogy of the elements which constitute the structure of the capitalist mode of production* ...
rather than being a true history of [the] succession and transformation [of modes of production, it] is a historical *survey (sondage)* of the routes by which the separation of the
labourer from his means of production and the constitution of capital as a sum of disposable value were achieved ... For this reason, the analysis of primitive accumulation is a
fragmentary analysis: the genealogy is not traced on the basis of a global result'. Text from
the Marxist Internet Archive, at <https://www.marxists.org/reference/archive/althusser/
1968/reading-capital/cho3.htm>.

son after he had ceased to be attached to the soil and ceased to be the slave, serf, or bondsman of another ... these new freedmen became sellers of themselves only after they had been robbed of all their own means of production, and of all the guarantees of existence afforded by the old feudal arrangements. And the history of this, their expropriation, is written in the annals of mankind in letters of blood and fire.[16]

Indeed, in the third volume of *Capital*, making explicit reference to this chapter on accumulation, Marx repeats the same idea. He poses accumulation in terms of the separation between workers and the conditions of labour, the means of production, and thus between the subjective and objective dimensions:

> labour-power exists therefore separately from the means of production ... The means of production, the material part of productive capital, must therefore face the laborer as such ... We have seen on previous occasions that in its further development capitalist production, once it is established, not only reproduces this separation but extends its scope further and further until it becomes the prevailing condition.[17]

Again on Alienation?

The dynamic of separation presents an ambivalent character. Indeed, on the one hand it effectuates the destruction of feudal hierarchies, which held man fixed in place and unable to move or fulfil his capacities. But, together with this expansive aspect, it also has a 'dark side': for here we see workers being 'denuded', denied guarantees, separated from the means of production. This is the idea of accumulation-as-expropriation, which comes about through 'blood and fire', and thus through *Gewalt*: it is 'the expropriation of the great mass of the people from the soil, from the means of subsistence, and from the means of labour'.[18] This process, though it has developed gradually and in extremely diverse spatial and temporal environments, brings about the destruction of individual, personal property and the absolute rule of private property. It is important to avoid confusing individual property and private property:[19] not

---

16   *MECW*, Vol. 35, p. 706.
17   *MECW*, Vol. 36, pp. 37–9.
18   *MECW*, Vol. 35, p. 749.
19   See Di Marco 2005, p. 42: 'Communism does not entail the abolition of property as such,

only are privatisation and individualisation non-identical, but they are profoundly divergent. Moreover, across Marx's entire *oeuvre*, from his first works
to his last, communism is characterised by individual realisation, and not by
the subsumption of the single individual to the social structure with its typologies of dominion (indeed, never do we see any celebration of society as 'the
administration of things', in his polemics regarding the state sphere). At the
same time, communism does constitute a negation of private property.

Marx takes a strongly critical view of privatisation, and maintains that the
element of individual property is a stakes of crucial importance: 'Self-earned
private property, that is based, so to say, on the fusing together of the isolated,
independent labouring individual with the conditions of his labour, is sup-
planted by capitalistic private property, which rests on exploitation of the nom-
inally free labour of others'.[20] In the last instance, private property is opposed
to free individual development, in the sense that it appears to be functional
to a logic of dominion, to the exploitation of labour-power by capital. As such,
even if capitalist 'rhetoric' insists on the individual dimension, in reality what
we have is its negation, its being undermined. We have to address this question
critically, to ask 'what freedom?'[21] is being referred to, and to emphasise that it
entails an element of fiction.

On the other hand, we ought to recognise that in freedom there is not
just mystification but also reality. In this sense, it is necessary to distinguish
between waged labour and slavery, since in the capitalist mode of production it
is not the worker's body that is being sold, but rather its temporary availability:
thus emerges a corporeality configured as a permanent excess, a potential element of resistance to capitalist commands. Labour-power has an active character, in its connection to living labour and its use-value, which on the one hand
is employed for the valorisation of capital, but on the other hand constitutes a
radical opposition to capital.[22] But it is worth repeating that this antagonism

---

understood as meaning the power to appropriate for oneself the products of society, but
rather the abolition of the power to subject the labour of others to oneself by way of this
appropriation of the products of society'; Sereni 2007, pp. 203–19.

20   *MECW*, Vol. 35, p. 749.

21   Lenin 1969: see Basso 2008/2009.

22   *Operaismo* strongly emphasised the 'political' character of labour-power, in its connection
to the subjectivity of living labour. See Tronti 1980, p. 210: '*Arbeitskraft* is not only a
commodity-object that passes from the workers' hands into the hands of capital; it is an
active force ... *Arbeitskraft* can become, *must* become, *Angriffskraft*. It is the passage –
this time political – from labour-power, to working class'. On the *Grundrisse*, see Negri
1991, p. 98: 'The subjectivity of living labor opposes in such antagonistic fashion the

is not already a given, but presents a potential value, a *dynamis*: the relationship between labour-power and labour could be compared to the relationship to what exists in potential and what exists already. Moreover, in *Capital* Marx defines labour-power [*Arbeitskraft*] or the capacity for labour [*Arbeitsvermögen*] as 'the aggregate of those mental and physical capabilities existing in a human being [*lebendige Persönlichkeit*], which he exercises whenever he produces a use-value of any description'.[23]

At this point, it is necessary to investigate how and in what sense the separation outlined above – connected to the exploitation of labour-power – can be understood as alienation, and thus how adequate this latter concept is to understanding this question. Alienation has been one of the questions most debated within Marxism. The positions outlined with regard to this question have been extremely diverse, but, if we take on board the sharpest among them, we could say that in many cases there has been a sort of 'welding together' of the humanist approach and a recognition of the centrality of alienation.[24] This has

---

consolidation of dead labor into an exploiting power that it negates itself as a value, as an exploited essence, thus proposing itself as *the negation of value* and exploitation'.

23 *MECW*, Vol. 35, p. 177. On the notion of labour-power, see Vadée 1992, particularly pp. 283 sqq., which aptly brings to light the connection of labour-power – *qua* sum of physical and intellectual capacities – with the element of concrete historical possibility. While in the *Grundrisse* Marx adopted the term *Arbeitsvermögen*, in *Capital* he chose *Arbeitskraft*, which he had almost never previously used. According to Vadée, this substitution does not indicate any sharp change between the *Grundrisse* and *Capital*: instead, they stand in a line of continuity, as *Arbeitskraft* does not present a merely mechanical meaning in counterposition to the 'philosophical' *Arbeitsvermögen*, but rather is chosen because it is here more effective. On the contrary, according to Bidet 1985 (particularly pp. 69 sqq.) the use of this term denotes a complete break with the still-philosophical language of the *Grundrisse*, based on an anthropological element in which the category 'alienation' plays a still-central role. See, moreover, with differing perspectives: Dussel 1999 (particularly pp. 63–72), which insists on the idea of living labour as the source of value; and Virno 2015, pp. 159–89. On p. 168 he brings to light the breadth of the notion of labour-power, irreducible to the economic structure in the narrow sense: 'In speaking of labour-power, we implicitly refer to any sort of faculty: linguistic competence, memory, the capacity to think and so on. "Labour-power" does not indicate a circumscribed potential, but rather is the common name for various different kinds of potential; or better, the name suitable for them insofar as they are relevant to production and appear as "non-objectified labour"'.

24 For a strong emphasis on the question of reification, in connection with alienation, the decisive point of reference is Lukács 1971. Starting from a conviction as to the centrality of the concept of alienation, but on the basis of different trajectories: Pappenheim 1959, Mészáros 1970; Ollmann 1971. More recently, see Honneth 2005, which, taking a perspective different to that here outlined, tries to 'reform' Lukács's position on the basis of the

meant an emphasis on the fact that, for Marx, the key element is man, who, in capitalist society, is left distanced from his very essence, and thus in a condition of alienation: hence the attempt to conceive communism as the overcoming of this alienation and the reappropriation of man's essence.

This question must also be included as part of a study of Marx's entire trajectory, and thus the relationship between the young Marx and the 'mature' Marx. Very often, indeed, a strong focus on the concept of alienation, on the basis of a humanist approach, is associated with a positive emphasis on the young Marx's reflection, in particular texts like the *1844 Manuscripts* in which this theme plays an absolutely central role. In this regard, it is necessary to make a terminological specification: here, we are dealing with two concepts, *Entfremdung* and *Entäußerung*, which are interrelated but do not wholly coincide. Curiously, in some Italian translations, their meanings are – so to say – inverted, with *Entfremdung* rendered as 'alienation' when in fact the term 'estrangement' ought to be used, and vice versa in the case of *Entäußerung*. In German Marxism (or in philosophers who are in some way and in certain aspects close to Marxism, like Adorno and Marcuse) reference to alienation has played a decisively important role. In France, the counterposition between a humanist and an anti-humanist approach, and between a stress on the centrality of alienation and the questioning of such a stance, has proven particularly intense: one need only think of Sartre, on the one hand, and Althusser, on the other, as well as a series of other figures also involved in this debate.[25]

The path that we are taking here with regard to this thematic consists of a rejection of the humanism/anti-humanism binary: to take on the humanist or the anti-humanist option as a distinctive marker of our discourse today risks

---

theory of recognition; Fischbach 2009a, pp. 65–95; Sayers 2011. On p. 95 Fischbach 2009a critically examines Lukács's position concerning alienation-as-reification: 'The problematic of reification, proper to Lukács, was ... constituted to the detriment of Marx's [problematic] of social relations'.

25   In the French context, and on the basis of an approach founded on the humanism-alienation plexus, see Sartre 1991. Althusser 1969, which is strongly critical of Sartre, articulates an anti-humanist theoretical perspective, in which the centrality of alienation is put into question. It is necessary to underline, in this regard, that while Sartre's humanism does display some problematic aspects, it is not based on the kind of essentialist vision that Althusser's polemic seems to attribute to it. Althusser excessively rigidifies, on the theoretical plane, the theme of humanism and the critique of it. See, moreover – with a positive stress on the concept of alienation – Goldmann 1970; and Sève 1969, which is critical of Althusser but also of Sartre. For a structuralist interpretation of the problem, see Godelier 1973. A direct engagement between the counterposed theses of Godelier and Sève appears in Godelier and Sève 1970.

leading us into a dead end, and not a perspective that is productive on the theoretical and political level. This complete divarication, which had a certain meaning in the 1960s and 1970s, risks becoming a false opposite in today's scenario. In the first place, it is necessary to repeat that one of the distinctive traits of Marx's framework, at least from the *German Ideology* onward, consisted in destructuring philosophy – without this denying the need for a complex articulation of his reflection. From a certain point onward, the question of alienation lost the 'ontological' substratum that it had possessed in his early texts, particularly markedly so in the *1844 Manuscripts*.

It was not a matter of centring his reasoning upon human nature, upon the essence of man – after all, this would be negated by the historical process, since within a materialist outlook an abstract problematisation of man and his distinctive traits would be meaningless. As Marx formulated clearly already in the *German Ideology*, at the centre of his reasoning was not *Gattungswesen* – man as a generic being – but rather an investigation of 'real individuals' in their determinate activity, within the social and political ambits in which they moved, and not starting from rootless presuppositions. In this context, any form of essentialism is wholly out of place. Moreover, it is necessary to emphasise that Marx's humanism in his early writings, while having certain limitations, was in fact directed towards eroding any essentialist element, and was configured as a concrete humanism serving the *conatus* towards the realisation of individual capacities and faculties. Even when he adopted the concept of humanism, there was a 'break' with regard to Feuerbach, since *Gattungswesen* was inflected through specific social and political relations rather than being posed as an abstract hypostasis. It is true that from the *German Ideology* onwards the centrality of generic being decreased, and, at the same time, 'real individuals' and 'determinate individuals' took on a crucial function; but it is also the case that although the references to *Gattungswesen* thinned out in his later work, this category never disappeared entirely. Moreover, it is important to note that the total critique of humanism, and not just of any form of essentialism (for these two concepts never perfectly coincide) poses a series of challenges to the theorisation of individual realisation as the focal point of his reflection.

Connected to the problem of humanism, we find the question of alienation. Also in this case, the task at hand, in the first place, is to refute any 'theoreticist' approach, taking the destructuring of philosophy carried out from the *German Ideology* onwards to its full conclusions.

This same category, alienation, must therefore resound of this 'exit' from philosophy. Apparently of particular significance in this regard is Marx's statement in the *German Ideology* concerning *Entfremdung* – alienation, or, better, estrangement – 'to use a term which will be comprehensible to the philo-

sophers'. As such, his reasoning could not be fully incardinated on the basis
of *Entfremdung*: the path here taken seems similar to that subsequently followed by the structuralist Marxists, with their anti-humanist approach. On
the other hand, however, he did not abandon the category *Entfremdung*, and
indeed picked it up again in many texts following the *German Ideology*: we
need only think of the fact that it often reappears in the *Grundrisse*. As such,
it is problematic to eliminate alienation as a wholly irrelevant question, on the
basis of arguments analogous to those used with respect to humanism. If the
goal is individual realisation, and thus overcoming 'the present state of things',
then the element of alienation can persist as an attempt at a 'philosophical'
explanation of the exploitation inherent to the capitalist order. It is thus not a
matter either of centring discourse on alienation or of rejecting it. If anything,
alienation is ever more 'emptied out' from the ontological point of view, on the
basis of a materialist outlook: the central question appears no longer to be that
of one's distance from some presumed human essence. Capital's exploitation
of labour-power is Marx's focal point, along with the logic of separation underlying it.

In general, we might say that the concept of alienation no longer plays a key
role in *Capital*, such as it did in the *Grundrisse*. Indeed, in the first and third
volumes of *Capital*, *Entfremdung* reappears only rather sporadically. To uphold
such an argument does not, however, mean to indicate a diminution of the
problem that alienation denotes: the separation of objective factors from the
subjectivity of the labourer, on the basis of the – estranged and estranging –
social power of money. And this is the specific distinctive characteristic of the
capitalist system with respect to the forms of production that preceded it:

> Under the developed capitalist mode of production, the labourer is not
> the owner of the means of production ... But under this system separation
> of the producer from the means of production reflects an actual revolu-
> tion in the mode of production itself.[26]

> The relationship of capital actually conceals the inner connection behind
> the utter indifference, isolation, and alienation in which they place the
> labourer vis-à-vis the means incorporating his labour.[27]

---

26   *MECW*, Vol. 37, p. 591.
27   *MECW*, Vol. 37, p. 88. Again in the third volume, note: 'Capital comes more and more to
     the fore as ... an alienated, independent, social power, which stands opposed to society
     as an object, and as an object that is the capitalist's source of power' (p. 263). In the

Marx addressed the labourer's distance not only from the means of production, but also from his capacity to labour. Be that as it may, the central question here is not to refute categorically the humanism-alienation plexus, and thus to insist on the need to expunge every last anthropological residue as if this were the irredeemable 'downfall' of his analysis, an incapacity fully to overcome the constitutive limits of the thematisation in his early texts.[28] Rather, it is a matter of incardinating his reasoning on the element of separation, which could be considered ('to use a term which will be comprehensible to the philosophers') as a question of alienation, or, better, estrangement (to use a more precise translation of the term *Entfremdung*). But this latter cannot be studied in an abstract manner, stripped of flesh and blood; rather, it must resound of historicisation and geographical relativisation. In this sense, the problem of alienation-as-separation is inflected through the complex and articulated history of capital, thus passing through its various moments: co-operation, manufacture, and modern industry.[29]

The Moments of Separation: Co-Operation, Manufacture, Modern Industry

In the first volume of *Capital*, Marx studies historically the question of the *Trennung* of the individual within the capitalist means of production. This analysis is not only objective, but is related to a 'self-referential' history of capital which bears a radically political character and is thus shot through with the subjective dimension, with the working-class struggle that continually shifts his plane of reflection. Marx did not limit himself to mere description, but

---

first volume, we could look, for example, to the following passages: 'the character of independence and estrangement which the capitalist mode of production as a whole gives to the instruments of labour and to the product, as against the workman, is developed by means of machinery into a thorough antagonism' (Vol. 35, p. 435); 'all means for the development of production transform themselves into means of domination over, and exploitation of, the producers; they mutilate the labourer into a fragment of a man ... they estrange from him the intellectual potentialities of the labour process in the same proportion as science is incorporated in it as an independent power' (p. 639). Postone 1993, p. 31, remarks on the fact that in *Capital* alienation is inflected through the both historical and abstract constitution dynamic of the structures of social domination. On the significance of the element of temporality in this process, see Fischbach 2009b.

28   Cf. Dardot and Laval 2012.

29   See Harvey 2010b; Jameson 2014, in part. pp. 93–108.

engaged with the ambivalence of capitalist separation in his political practice. His examination of this separation always remained attached to his tendency in favour of the pulling-apart of the *status quo*, and thus a 'wager' on the future – albeit one always rooted in the given material conditions and the destructive consequences of the workers' 'acting in common'. In any case, within his historical-political reconstruction of *Trennung*, the first moment was represented by co-operation:

> When numerous labourers work together side by side, whether in one and the same process, or in different but connected processes, they are said to co-operate, or to work in co-operation ... Not only have we here an increase in the productive power of the individual, by means of co-operation, but the creation of a new power, namely, the collective power of masses.[30]

For co-operation to come about, it is necessary that a substantial number of workers are employed by one same individual capital.[31] Such a modality is not at all reducible to a mechanical sum of forces:

> When the labourer co-operates systematically with others, he strips off the fetters of his individuality, and develops the capabilities of his species ... the connexion existing between their various labours appears to them, ideally, in the shape of a preconceived plan of the capitalist, and practically in the shape of the authority of the same capitalist, in the shape of the powerful will of another, who subjects their activity to his aims.[32]

It is clear enough that 'working together' is not a mere arithmetical sum of single individuals, but a mass force. A 'multiplying' element is here apparent, one that cannot be reduced to the aggregation of existing factors: such a dynamic encourages socialisation, or the worker overcoming his own lim-

---

30   *MECW*, Vol. 35, p. 330.

31   'Capitalist production only then really begins, as we have already seen, when each individual capital employs simultaneously a comparatively large number of labourers; when consequently the labour-process is carried on on an extensive scale and yields, relatively, large quantities of products. A greater number of labourers working together, at the same time, in one place (or, if you will, in the same field of labour), in order to produce the same sort of commodity under the mastership of one capitalist, constitutes, both historically and logically, the starting-point of capitalist production' (*MECW*, Vol. 35, pp. 326–7).

32   *MECW*, Vol. 35, p. 334.

its. These limits, which do not allow the individual fully to develop his own potential, are substituted through co-operation by the development of the 'capabilities of his species' [*Gattungsvermögen*]. We must note, other than the fact that the term *Gattung* reappears here (having been very much present in the young Marx, often associated with *Wesen*), the importance of the noun *Vermögen*, with its double meaning – on the one hand capacity/faculty, on the other hand patrimony/goods. If we understand this term according to its first meaning, it can be placed alongside the Greek *dynamis*, bringing out its component of 'potential': the only condition for a different path of development and unhinging the 'present state of things'. This latter both entails devastating consequences for the workers, and yet also allows them to prefigure new scenarios in which the realisation of the 'capabilities of the species' will be possible. His analysis of co-operation forcefully brings out the dimension of socialisation, in its productive character, with all the ambivalence that this entails.

Very significant in this regard is Marx's use of Aristotle's idea of man as *zoon politikon*. He had done so already in the 1857 *Einleitung*,[33] albeit through 're-evaluating' its meaning: 'man is, if not as Aristotle contends, a political, at all events a social animal'.[34] Indeed, according to Marx, 'Strictly, Aristotle's definition is that man is by nature a town-citizen. This is quite as characteristic of ancient classical society as Franklin's definition of man, as a tool-making animal, is characteristic of Yankeedom'. But what needs to be stressed more than anything, as concerns a reflection on humanism and alienation, is that no anti-materialist critique of essentialism implies the destruction of all anthropology, but only of an abstractly philosophical anthropology. *Capital* presents elements of anthropology (among other things, the aforementioned reference to *Gattungsvermögen* seems very telling in this regard) but these must be conceived of within the framework of mechanisms of production, within the both

---

33   *MECW*, Vol. 28, p. 18: 'It is not until the 18th century, in "bourgeois society", that the various forms of the social nexus confront the individual as merely a means towards his private ends, as external necessity. But the epoch which produces this standpoint, that of the isolated individual, is precisely the epoch of the hitherto most highly developed social (according to this standpoint, general) relations. Man is a zoon politikon in the most literal sense: he is not only a social animal, but an animal that can isolate itself only within society'. See Touboul 2004, pp. 17–18. Jánoska (ed.) 1994, pp. 192–4. On the Marx-Aristotle relationship, see Vadée 1992, McCarthy 1990, Pike 1999, Schwartz 1979, Cotten 1982, and Meikle 1985. Though based on different approaches, these readings tend to note the Aristotelean ancestry of Marx's reflection. The hypothesis we here outline is, instead, an attempt to demonstrate that his reference to the *zoon politikon* entailed a substantial change of perspective as compared to Aristotle's – see Basso 2008b, pp. 208–10.

34   *MECW*, Vol. 35, p. 331.

deathly and expansive social character of capital, and certainly not on the basis
of an abstract study disconnected from material circumstances, human nature
and its distinctive characteristics.[35] What we have here is not so much a 'trace'
of Aristotle, as a bringing-into-relief of the process of individuation entailed
within the capitalist process of co-operation among many individuals and the
social potential arising from their labouring activity. 'The social' is thus shown
to be connected not so much to *polis* as to the dimension of production into
which individuals are 'thrown' – a mass force that is not only an aggregation of
individuals, but also marks a qualitative change, in that co-operation is more
than the sum of its single parts. This is not, however, to be understood in counterposition to Marx's comments on individual *Trennung* as a distinctive characteristic of the capitalist mode of production.

Marx's position is intrinsically two-sided: the separation of the single individual certainly does imply her arrival at a condition of independence, but at
the same time her enslavement to an estranged process. The worker, in fact,
does not work for herself, but for the capitalist, who does not pay the combined
labour-power of the workers, but only the value of their autonomous labour
powers:

> This co-operation begins only with the labour-process, but they have then
> ceased to belong to themselves. On entering that process, they become
> incorporated with capital. As co-operators, as members of a working
> organism, they are but special modes of existence of capital.[36]

The 'mass force' mentioned above displays a social character and activates
a web of relations, but it must not be understood in an irenic manner as if
there did not exist any hierarchy or mechanism of domination. Marx does not,
however, limit himself to noting the separation among single individuals –
rather, he emphasises the fact that there is a laceration even within each
individual. The incorporation of labour within capital means its expropriation,
and labour – as one of capital's 'special modes of existence' – has no autonomy
of its own. In many aspects, Marx's argumentation in *Capital* picks up on the
Grundrisse's thematisation of this question: capital is an organism, of which
the single individual is only one member. To bring out the 'incorporation' of
labour within capital does not at all, however, mean to attenuate the difference
between the structure of capitalism and those of previous forms:

---

35   See Roseberry 1997, Patterson 2009.
36   *MECW*, Vol. 35, p. 338.

> Co-operation, such as we find it at the dawn of human development ...
> is based, on the one hand, on ownership in common of the means of
> production, and on the other hand, on the fact, that in those cases, each
> individual has no more torn himself off from the navel-string of his tribe
> or community, than each bee has freed itself from connexion with the
> hive. Such co-operation is distinguished from capitalistic co-operation ...
> The capitalistic form, on the contrary, pre-supposes from first to last, the
> free wage-labourer, who sells his labour-power to capital.[37]

Unlike two moments that we will go on to examine, co-operation doubtless has
the peculiarity that it cannot be precisely located in a determinate historical
moment, present as it is in both precapitalist orders and the capitalist system.
To maintain this position does not mean to deny the specific difference of the
latter with regard to the former, which are distinguished by communal property
and the individual being denied any possibility of autonomy and independence
from the *Gemeinwesen*. Marx sought to reject any nostalgic take on the past:
'Those ancient social organisms of production are, as compared with bourgeois
society, extremely simple and transparent. But they are founded either on the
immature development of man individually, who has not yet severed the umbilical cord that unites him with his fellowmen in a primitive tribal community,
or upon direct relations of subjection'.[38] Here again we have the image of the
umbilical cord, which had already been used to good effect in the 1857 *Einleitung*, where it connoted the link between the individual and the *Gemeinwesen*.

It is here necessary to examine the condition of the individual within the
capitalist mode of production, moving forward from co-operation to manufacture, which developed 'from the middle of the 16th to the last third of the 18th
century':[39]

> Manufacture proper not only subjects the previously independent work-
> man to the discipline and command of capital, but, in addition, creates a
> hierarchic gradation of the workmen themselves ... Not only is the detail
> work distributed to the different individuals, but the individual himself
> is made the automatic motor of a fractional operation ... the manufac-
> turing labourer develops productive activity as a mere appendage of the
> capitalist's workshop.[40]

---

37   *MECW*, Vol. 35, p. 339.
38   *MECW*, Vol. 35, p. 90.
39   *MECW*, Vol. 35, p. 341.
40   *MECW*, Vol. 35, p. 365.

In manufacture as in co-operation, we find the worker being subjected to the command of capital, but the difference is that manufacture brings about a transformation in the 'mode of working', as compared to co-operation. The effect of this process is the division of the individual, reduced to an 'appendage' of capital, 'where the workshop may ... be considered as an engine, the parts of which are men'.[41] As such the individual is structurally prevented from turning the situation in his own favour, since the mode of production is a mechanism that 'crushes' him: 'Division of labour within the workshop implies the undisputed authority of the capitalist over men, that are but parts of a mechanism that belongs to him'.[42] There is a separation not only between the workers and the overall mechanism, but also a mutual separation among the individuals existing within the capitalist system: indeed, competition within capitalism is marked by coercion, deriving from a divergence of interests which cannot be resolved through a logic of mediation. This duress is intimately linked to the formation of a mass of unskilled workers:

> Manufacture begets, in every handicraft that it seizes upon, a class of so-called unskilled labourers, a class which handicraft industry strictly excluded. If it develops a one-sided speciality into a perfection, at the expense of the whole of a man's working capacity [*Arbeitsvermögen*], it also begins to make a speciality of the absence of all development. Alongside of the hierarchic gradation there steps the simple separation [*Scheidung*] of the labourers into skilled and unskilled.[43]

With manufacture, labour takes on an even more hierarchical connotation: the new discriminating factor is the presence or absence of skills within the individual *Arbeiter*. Marx notes the universal character of this specialisation, and its negation of labouring capacity by way of a process of separation – *Scheidung* – according to the criterion of greater or lesser skill. Here emerges a reference to the capitalist division between the 'manual' and the 'intellectual':

> Intelligence in production expands in one direction, because it vanishes in many others. What is lost by the detail labourers, is concentrated in the capital that employs them. It is a result of the division of labour in manufactures, that the labourer is brought face to face with the intellec-

---

41   *MECW*, Vol. 35, p. 367.

42   *MECW*, Vol. 35, p. 361.

43   *MECW*, Vol. 35, p. 355.

tual potencies of the material process of production, as the property of another, and as a ruling power.[44]

The 'intellectual potencies' of production, with its intimately social character, now belong to capital: they form a social power alien to the workers as single individuals. Marx reconstructs this process historically, from its genesis in simple co-operation to its development in manufacture and full expansion in modern industry. The question of *Spaltung* takes on ever more marked connotations in modern industry. The substitution of 'the workman, who handles a single tool, by a mechanism operating with a number of similar tools and set in motion by a single motive power' represents an undeniable change from the previous situation centred on the worker's labour:

> Machinery also revolutionises out and out the contract between the labourer and the capitalist, which formally fixes their mutual relations. Taking the exchange of commodities as our basis, our first assumption was that capitalist and labourer met as free persons, as independent owners of commodities; the one possessing money and means of production, the other labour-power. But now the capitalist buys children and young persons under age. Previously, the workman sold his own labour-power, which he disposed of nominally as a free agent. Now he sells wife and child. He has become a slave-dealer.[45]

With the development of the automatic system of machines, conversely, every element of reciprocity is destroyed. Here, the mystification inherent to the categories of freedom and equality – as analysed by Marx – is not only confirmed, but intensified, through the extreme acceleration of processes. Machinery increases both the degree of exploitation and the amount of human material that is exploited, since it 'spreads the value of the man's labour-power over his whole family. It thus depreciates his labour-power'.[46] Modern industry, based on the automatic system of machines, is partly connected to manufacture and yet displays a significant difference from it:

> In handicrafts and manufacture, the workman makes use of a tool, in the factory, the machine makes use of him ... In the factory we have

---

44   *MECW*, Vol. 35, p. 366.
45   *MECW*, Vol. 35, p. 399.
46   *MECW*, Vol. 35, p. 398.

a lifeless mechanism independent of the workman, who becomes its mere living appendage ... Every kind of capitalist production, in so far as it is not only a labour-process, but also a process of creating surplus value, has this in common, that it is not the workman that employs the instruments of labour, but the instruments of labour that employ the workman. But it is only in the factory system that this inversion for the first time acquires technical and palpable reality. By means of its conversion into an automaton, the instrument of labour confronts the labourer, during the labour-process, in the shape of capital, of dead labour [*tote Arbeit*], that dominates, and pumps dry, living labour-power [*die lebendige Arbeitskraft*].[47]

The factory effects a transformation of the worker's relation to the tool. With the development of the automatic system of machines, the 'vampiric' character of capital forcefully emerges, as it feeds on the living labour of the single worker: 'But capital has one single life impulse, the tendency to create value and surplus value, to make its constant factor, the means of production, absorb the greatest possible amount of surplus labour. Capital is dead labour, that, vampire-like, only lives by sucking living labour, and lives the more, the more labour it sucks'.[48] Capital's end goal is its own valorisation, and hence its quest for a continual augmentation of surplus-value: taking possession of the living labour of others is the condition of its very existence, or better, of its continual 'revival'. In the last instance, capital's 'social brain' resides precisely in this effort to subordinate the working process to the process of valorisation:

> It is now no longer the labourer that employs the means of production, but the means of production that employ the labourer. Instead of being consumed by him as material elements of his productive activity, they consume him as the ferment necessary to their own life-process, and the life-process of capital consists only in its movement as value constantly expanding, constantly multiplying itself.[49]

In order to delve deeper into the question of capital's self-valorisation, and its consequences for the single labourer, it is necessary to look at the relationship between absolute surplus-labour and relative surplus-labour, and thus the rela-

---

47   *MECW*, Vol. 35, p. 425.
48   *MECW*, Vol. 35, p. 241.
49   *MECW*, Vol. 35, pp. 314–15.

tionship between formal and real subsumption. While the production of absolute surplus-labour, deriving from the lengthening of the working day, proved
'to be independent of any change in the mode of production' – seeing that
'capital subordinates labour on the basis of the technical conditions in which
it historically finds it'[50] – the production of relative surplus-value, and thus
real subsumption, leads to the incorporation of the working process within the
process of the valorisation of capital: 'The technical and social conditions of
the [working] process, and consequently the very mode of production must
be revolutionised, before the productiveness of labour can be increased'.[51] As
Marx forcefully argues in the draft sixth chapter: 'With the real subsumption of
labour under capital there takes place a complete [and a constant, continuous,
and repeated] revolution in the mode of production itself, in the productivity of labour and in the relation between capitalist and worker'.[52] Moreover,
even the position that the chapters on co-operation, manufacturing and modern industry are given within *Capital* is very telling: they appear in the fourth
section, entitled 'Production of relative surplus-labour', indicating how significant this latter is for interpreting these processes. Marx's analysis brings out the
political character of real subsumption, in that the working class is no longer
considered external to social relations, but rather as internal to them, though
having a contradictory character. This antagonism does not represent a mere
effect of the capitalist system, but rather its fundamental condition: the capitalist mode of production is based on a true and proper civil war between
the capitalist class and the working class. When interpreting this scenario, it
is necessary to avoid falling into any moralistic approach, and always to bear in
mind that capital is not a thing, but rather a social relation. This stress on the
relational dimension does not of course imply any sort of irenic vision, since

---

50   See the whole passage (ibid.): 'At first, capital subordinates labour on the basis of the tech-
      nical conditions in which it historically finds it. It does not, therefore, change immediately
      the mode of production. The production of surplus value – in the form hitherto considered
      by us – by means of simple extension of the working day, proved, therefore, to be inde-
      pendent of any change in the mode of production itself … If we consider the process of
      production from the point of view of the simple labour process, the labourer stands in
      relation to the means of production, not in their quality as capital, but as the mere means
      and material of his own intelligent productive activity … it is different as soon as we deal
      with the process of production from the point of view of the process of creation of surplus
      value. The means of production are at once changed into means for the absorption of the
      labour of others'.
51   *MECW*, Vol. 35, p. 320.
52   *MECW*, Vol. 34, pp. 108–9. See also Badaloni 1980, pp. 51–2; Tosel 1995; Di Marco 2005,
      pp. 59 sqq.

these relations are asymmetrical and constantly shot through by topologies of domination.

As is clearly apparent also from the *Grundrisse*, capital is an earth-shattering force that destroys every pre-given community of interests. A distinctive trait of the capitalist structure is its constant revolutionising of its own limits, which is possible only through the production of relative surplus-value – and thus within the terms of real subsumption. This latter is fully realised with modern industry and the automatic system of machines, which represents the most important form of fixed capital – in its turn, the decisive element of capital in general:

> Modern industry never looks upon and treats the existing form of a process as final. The technical basis of that industry is therefore revolutionary ... By means of machinery, chemical processes and other methods, it is continually causing changes not only in the technical basis of production, but also in the functions of the labourer, and in the social combinations of the labour-process.[53]

Unlike precapitalist communities, which display a 'conservative' character, capitalism treats every *Grenze* [limit] as a *Schranke* [obstacle] and brings about a continuous revolutionising of pre-existing suppositions. This fluidity denies the workers any tranquility or security: and precisely in order to illustrate this situation, one of Marx's notes in *Capital* cites a passage from the *Manifesto*: 'All that is solid melts into air, all that is holy is profaned, and man is at last compelled to face with sober senses his real conditions of life, and his relations with his kind'.[54] The transparency of the capitalist mode of production allows us to see the real condition of the dominated class – Marx refers to 'the most reckless squandering of labour-power' and the 'devastation caused by a social anarchy'.[55]

The individual finds herself in a situation of extreme laceration: 'The special skill [*Das Detailgeschick*] of each individual insignificant factory operative vanishes as an infinitesimal quantity before the science, the gigantic physical forces, and the mass of labour'.[56] Again, here, we have the theme – present as early as the *German Ideology* – of the separation [*Scheidung*] between manual

---

53   *MECW*, Vol. 35, p. 489.
54   Ibid.
55   *MECW*, Vol. 35, p. 490.
56   *MECW*, Vol. 35, p. 426.

and intellectual labour, functional to capital's rule over labour: machines accentuate the *Trennung* between capital and labour to the point of paroxysm, enslaving labour to a global order that is not reducible to the economic sphere alone. The single individual does not enjoy any real autonomy, but rather appears as an 'infinitesimal quantity' – such as to unleash a true and proper competition between worker and machine, from which the former risks emerging defeated: 'The self-expansion of capital by means of machinery is thenceforward directly proportional to the number of the workpeople, whose means of livelihood have been destroyed by that machinery'.[57] But while the aspect here emphasised is very important to understanding the labour-capital dynamic, it must not be interpreted in a unilateral manner missing the structural two-sidedness of Marx's argumentation, which on the one hand demonstrates the devastating side of this situation and on the other brings to light the possibility of overcoming it. The exploitation by capital of the worker's labour-power, and the reduction of this latter to a partial element – a mere tool, or, literally, the bearer of a social function – are indelibly bound up with the possibility of considerable individual growth. These are two sides of the same coin, but at the same time they are in conflict with one another, and this tension must be politically 'acted' and not just described: to make use of this contradiction is the necessary condition of even thinking about putting the 'current state of things' into question.

Decisive, in this regard, are machines and their ambivalence: they make the worker ever more an organ of production, yet also open up new perspectives to her.[58] Marx recognised their propulsive role and thus did not risk falling into any sort of 'political romanticism'; but nor was he an uncritical spokesman of 'magnificent and progressive destinies',[59] and he identified the unsustainable elements of the technological process. The object of his critique was not machinism as such, but the manner in which it was used by capitalism: 'The contradictions and antagonisms inseparable from the capitalist employment of machinery, do not exist, they say, since they do not arise out of machinery,

---

57   *MECW*, Vol. 35, p. 433.
58   We should here note the sharp difference between Marx's position on technique and its ambivalent character, and the reflection carried out by the Frankfurt School, which sometimes resulted in a total – and in many senses undynamic – denunciation of the role of progress. See, for example, Adorno and Horkheimer 1999. On the question of machinism, from Smith to Marx, see De Palma 1971. On the question of technique (and following different approaches) see, among others, Axelos 1965; Di Marco 1984, pp. 109–77; Cotten 1993, pp. 29–65; and more recently, Touboul 2010, pp. 78–127.
59   [A reference to the poet Giacomo Leopardi – DB].

as such, but out of its capitalist employment! Since therefore machinery, considered alone, shortens the hours of labour, but, when in the service of capital, lengthens them ...'.[60] This consideration did not imply that technique could possibly be neutral: on the contrary, he emphasised that the working class could – and thus had to – deploy a 'counter-use' of it in order to achieve its own political objectives. The development of machinism on the one hand rendered the worker ever more subjugated to the production process, and on the other hand provided her with the possibility of directly opposing such a situation:

> If the general extension of factory legislation to all trades for the purpose of protecting the working class both in mind and body has become inevitable, on the other hand, as we have already pointed out, that extension hastens on the general conversion of numerous isolated small industries into a few combined industries carried on upon a large scale; it therefore accelerates the concentration of capital and the exclusive predominance of the factory system ... but thereby it also generalises the direct opposition to this [dominion of capital].[61]

Such a reorganisation of the factory system meant a transformation of working processes, one which led to the 'concentration of capital'. And the developed capitalist form – characterised by the big industrial system and thus the structure of machinism – brought naked reality into sharp focus. Marx's argumentation presented not only an 'objective' aspect but also a subjective one, connected to a conflict of general significance. His concepts did not merely describe a given state of affairs, but bore an earth-shattering political character. Moreover, struggles constantly shifted his plane of reflection: there was no self-referential development of capitalism that could not be permeated by these conflicts.

This situation was characterised by the existence of a structure of separation: 'The capitalist system presupposes the complete separation of the labourers from all property in the means by which they can realize their labour. As soon

---

60   MECW, Vol. 35, p. 444. Note the immediately subsequent passage: 'No doubt [the bourgeois economist] is far from denying that temporary inconvenience may result from the capitalist use of machinery. But where is the medal without its reverse! Any employment of machinery, except by capital, is to him an impossibility. Exploitation of the workman by the machine is therefore, with him, identical with exploitation of the machine by the workman. Whoever, therefore, exposes the real state of things in the capitalistic employment of machinery, is against its employment in any way, and is an enemy of social progress'.

61   MECW, Vol. 35, p. 504.

as capitalist production is once on its own legs, it not only maintains this separation, but reproduces it on a continually extending scale'.[62] Within the 'brain'
of the capitalist system there was an expropriation of the worker, now distanced from the 'social means of subsistence and of production', which were
transformed into capital: 'The separation of labour from its product, of subjective labour-power from the objective conditions of labour, was therefore the
real foundation in fact, and the starting-point of capitalist production'.[63] This
separation, inherent to the capitalist system, is identified with the separation
between the objective and subjective dimensions represented by labour-power
and its potentially revolutionary energy. If we consider the case of the reproduction process, the figures that incarnate this separation – worker and capitalist –
no longer appear on the market simply as buyer and seller:

> Capitalist production ... reproduces and perpetuates the condition for
> exploiting the labourer ... Capitalist production, therefore, under its as-
> pect of a continuous connected process, of a process of reproduction,
> produces not only commodities, not only surplus value, but it also pro-
> duces and reproduces the capitalist relation; on the one side the capitalist,
> on the other the wage labourer.[64]

We must always bear in mind the significance of reproduction, which points
to both the permanence and the changeability of the conditions of production. Within this scenario, the working class seems to represent a mere cog in
a machine that is extraneous to it. In any case, there is an irresolvable asymmetry between the two personifications of this *Trennung*, the worker and the
capitalist:

> The labourer produces, not for himself, but for capital ... Hence the notion
> of a productive labourer implies not merely a relation between work and
> useful effect, between labourer and product of labour, but also a specific,
> social relation of production, a relation that has sprung up historically and
> stamps the labourer as the direct means of creating surplus value.[65]

In *Capital*, people are interpreted as personifications, as masks of determinate class interests: the worker is the 'figure' of labour, the capitalist the 'figure'

---

62   *MECW*, Vol. 35, p. 705.
63   *MECW*, Vol. 35, p. 570.
64   *MECW*, Vol. 35, p. 577.
65   *MECW*, Vol. 35, p. 510.

of capital. The anti-substantialist implications of such an approach are obvious, pulling apart as they do any form of essentialism in the delineation of the relationship between class and individual. Moreover, by adopting this position Marx makes clear that his critique is not directed against individual 'bad' capitalists, but against capital itself, of which individual capitalists are but representatives. In this context, the worker's productivity is functional to the valorisation of capital; if productive labour is the point of departure, the destination is productive capital, in which workers find the exclusive terrain of their subsistence.[66]

Here returns the idea that capital is a force capable of constantly overcoming its own limits, thanks to the incorporation of labour-power for the purposes of creating surplus-value. It must be understood that Marx's position is foreign both to a preaching, moralistic socialism that does not grasp the earth-shattering role of capitalism, and to bourgeois ideologues who focus only on liberation from feudal relations and hide away the exploitation[67] connected to this liberation, and thus the 'blood' and 'fire' inherent to the expropriation of the workers: 'the capitalist mode of production and accumulation, and therefore capitalist private property, have for their fundamental condition the annihilation of self-earned private property; in other words, the expropriation of the labourer'.[68] Freedom and expropriation are not mutually exclusive, but rather wrapped up in each other; freedom, though not merely a label that immediately corresponds to its opposite, entails a radical mystification – and what is neces-

---

66 Cohen 1978, p. 31.

67 There has also been a wide debate on the notion of exploitation in the English-speaking world, in so-called analytical Marxism, with the goal of establishing whether this notion is a descriptive one deriving from economic analysis, or a moral, value judgement. In order to frame this discussion, it is particularly worth referring to Roemer (ed.) 1986, in which we find a review of the most significant positions: see especially pp. 260–82, which maintains that Marx's critique of exploitation is a critique of the injustice of the capitalist system, and thus displays a moral connotation; Wood 1986, on the contrary, holds that Marx's stance is not based on a logic of rights and justice. Analogous to Roemer, Lukes 1985 and Elster 1985 (a text that has provoked a wide debate) insist – with different emphases – on the 'prescriptive' character of Marx's position. The perspective here outlined cannot be reconciled with these approaches, since it rejects the 'analytical' dichotomy between the descriptive and moral, prescriptive dimensions: among other things, such a dualism masks the intrinsically politically character of Marx's reflection, as demonstrated by these interpretations' under-evaluation and 'functionalisation' of class, as they attempt to 'reform' Marx's position and make it compatible with a political economy derived from Keynes.

68 *MECW*, Vol. 35, p. 761.

sary is to bring out the structural limits of this notion, its double-sidedness. So it is clear from the discussion in this chapter that though there are points of continuity between the different moments – co-operation, manufacture and modern industry – it is doubtless also true that there are elements of discontinuity, and in particular that the capitalist mode of production in the strong sense of the term only comes about with modern industry, including the aforementioned mutual imbrication of freedom and expropriation. Moreover, here we are referring not only to an objective dynamic internal to the (real or presumed) laws of capital, but also a subjective dynamic constantly shot through with the class struggle, which only emerges in true and proper form with the formation of the factory.[69]

The Factory and Class Formation

From the 1850s to 1860s, Marx strengthened his critical emphasis on the role of machines within the capitalist mode of production, and thus began to back away from the idea that these elements were of an immediately expansive character: he did not disavow or question his analysis of the general intellect in the *Grundrisse*, but rather 'complicated' it. Here, is necessary to add a further consideration, namely a recognition of the need to avoid arriving at an antimodern, anti-technological understanding – for this does not correspond to Marx's approach. In fact, Marx's critique was not levelled against machines as such, but rather the capitalist use of them. Marx distinguished his own position from that of the machine-breaking Luddites, declaring his awareness of the need to direct his attacks 'not against the material instruments of production, but against the mode in which they are used'.[70] It is worth emphasising, on this point, that Luddism in fact represented a rather complex, articulated movement which is not reducible to the mere sabotage of machinery out of some sort of ingenuously anti-modern and anti-technological outlook.[71]

Marx's perspective proved wholly irreconcilable with that of the bourgeois economists, who did not conceive of any use of machinery apart from a capitalist one, or, for that matter, any other mode of production, having natural-

---

69   The reading which I here propose is intended to question – or, at least, problematise – the famous statement in the *Communist Manifesto* according to which 'The history of all hitherto existing society is the history of class struggles'. We will delve deeper into this question in the fourth chapter, in our discussion of the status of class.

70   *MECW*, Vol. 35, p. 432.

71   See Thompson 1963.

ised and thus 'eternalised' capitalism: '[the bourgeois economist] is far from denying that temporary inconvenience may result from the capitalist use of machinery. But where is the medal without its reverse! Any employment of machinery, except by capital, is to him an impossibility'.[72] Indeed, with the development of machinism came 'the physical deterioration as well of the children and young-persons as of the women', along with 'the enormous mortality, during the first few years of their life, of the children of the operatives'.[73] This also had strong moral and intellectual implications: Marx referred to the 'moral degradation' to which Engels had devoted extraordinary pages in his *Condition of the Working Class in England*, the true and proper 'intellectual desolation artificially produced by converting immature human beings into mere machines for the fabrication of surplus value'.[74]

The tendency of capital, materialised in the capitalist, was to make the worker labour as much as possible, 24 hours a day; but this obviously found its limit precisely in the presence of the worker and his possibilities of resistance – for capital did not buy the worker as such, but a determinate temporal availability. So there was still something left over, represented by the living corporeality of the labourer. With machinism, however, came an ever-more docile female and child labour force. There is an 'immanent contradiction [*ein immanenter Widerspruch*]' within this process. On the one hand, this system leads to an increase in the number of wage labourers, directly regimenting all the members of the working-class family, without distinction of age or sex, under the empire of capital. Machines, therefore, increased and extended the exploitation of labour-power, with the well-known excesses which factory legislation would later propose to mitigate. On the other hand, the tendency to improve labour productivity in order to increase relative surplus-value pushed the capitalist to transform a previously-variable part of capital, either turning it into living labour-power, machinery, or into constant capital which does not produce surplus-value.

Capital's aspiration is, on the one hand, to extend the working day, with the maximum possible number of simultaneous working days, thus increasing the labouring population; on the other hand, to reduce the necessary labour-time to a minimum, and thus also the necessary number of workers, thus arriving at a relative diminution of the working population. This 'immanent contradiction' is part of the structure of the capitalist mode of production, but plays out in

---

72   *MECW*, Vol. 35, p. 445.
73   *MECW*, Vol. 35, p. 401.
74   *MECW*, Vol. 35, p. 403.

full only with machinism and modern industry: and this latter, in turn, drives capital to lengthen the working day in order to compensate for the relative diminution of the number of exploited workers. Extremely interesting, in this regard, is Marx's 'Workers' Inquiry', some of whose questions seek precisely to bring out the difficult material condition of the workers and the possible increase in unemployment resulting from the development of machinery.[75] One development apparent throughout his argument is the intensification of exploitation, a historical reconstruction of which appears in *Capital*:

> in England, during half a century, lengthening of the working day went hand in hand with increasing intensity of factory labour ... So soon as the gradually surging revolt of the working-class compelled Parliament to shorten compulsorily the hours of labour ... from that moment capital threw itself with all its might into the production of relative surplus value, by hastening on the further improvement of machinery.[76]

Marx brings to light the counter-measures that capital took once the working-class struggle had obtained the reduction of the length of the working day. Exploitation was not weakened, but rather strengthened through the intensification of labour, thus rendering the possibilities of breaking with the 'spectral objectivity' of the capitalist mode of production seemingly ever more remote. However, with machinism and thus the concentration of an ever greater number of workers in the same production site, at least potentially their resistance would be ever more accentuated – hence the earth-shattering aspects of the aforementioned 'mass force', which could open up space for the workers 'to act in common'. When we speak of machinism, however, this is not a merely technical consideration but also concerns the creation of a social form increasing the productive force for the production of relative surplus-value. With the growth of constant capital to the disadvantage of variable capital, the workers find themselves competing not only amongst themselves, but also with the machine. With the development of the machine system, labour productivity increases: the goal is to have more labour in the same time, sped up by machinery.

---

75   See, on this, Renault 1995, p. 58: 'the range of his questions represents an attempt to grasp the concrete experience of the worker, considered in all its dimensions – an objective that is both useful and hardly compatible with the disciplinary slicing-up and specialisation that are so common in the contemporary social sciences'.

76   *MECW*, Vol. 35, p. 412.

At the commencement of this chapter we considered that which we
may call the body of the factory, i.e., machinery organised into a system.
We there saw how machinery, by annexing the labour of women and
children, augments the number of human beings who form the material
for capitalistic exploitation [*das menschliche Exploitationsgrad*], how it
confiscates the whole of the workman's disposable time, by immoderate
extension of the hours of labour, and how finally its progress, which allows
of enormous increase of production in shorter and shorter periods, serves
as a means of systematically getting more work done in a shorter time, or
of exploiting [*ausbeuten*] labour-power more intensely.[77]

In this context, Marx examines the position of Dr. Ure, whom he defines as
the 'Pindar of the automatic factory'. The reference to Pindar makes clear his
sarcastic tone in dealing with the Scotsman Ure, who was not only the theorist,
but, so to say, the 'poet' of the automatic factory: his 1835 work *Philosophy of
Manufactures* is repeatedly cited in *Capital*. Indeed, Ure describes 'the central
machine, from which the motion comes, not only as an automaton, but as an
autocrat'. As compared to manufacture, there appears 'in the automatic factory,
a tendency to equalise [*Gleichmachung*] and reduce to one and the same level
[*Nivellierung*] every kind of work that has to be done by the minders of the
machines'.[78] There is a true and proper disciplining – if not a regimentation –
of each single worker by drawing him into an objective order from which he
cannot deviate.

   The distinctive markers of machinism fully emerge in the factory, which represents the ensemble of the machine system. The automatic factory is founded
on the levelling-down of job tasks, the diminution if not destruction of the
qualitative dimension, and thus the emptying-out of the individual according to a dead mechanism that mortifies the capacities and faculties of the
single worker: here returns the metaphor of capital-as-vampire. Marx does not
address scientific and technological development uncritically, as if these could
be presumed to be immediately expansive: in reality, machines become the
bosses of science, employing it for their own consumption and usage. Indeed,
the question of the conjugation of science with production is a very significant one: machines embody science, technique and knowledge in general, such
that science if subsumed under capital.[79] The capitalist use of machines proves

77   *MECW*, Vol. 35, p. 420.
78   *MECW*, Vol. 35, p. 423.
79   See Krahl 1971.

to be the exact opposite of what bourgeois ideology would have us believe. Marx's deconstruction, here, is a radical one: within the capitalist system, he argues, there was never any phase in which science developed autonomously of the mechanisms of production, and thus the logic of command, just as there was never any phase in which work was realised outside of the 'meat grinder' of valorisation, thus one in which the worker acted as a truly free subject.

It is necessary to be clear, however – if we are to avoid entirely misunderstanding Marx's perspective – that the polemical reference point of his reflection was the capitalist use of machinery, and not machines themselves, since this was not the only possible way of using them. Indeed, at the base of his discourse is the idea that, unlike previous, conservative modes of production, the technical basis of industry had displayed a revolutionary character; later, in the twentieth century, its earth-shattering novelty would consist in the fact that for the first time in history peasants did not constitute the majority of the population.[80] The inversion that Marx invokes – where it is the conditions of production that 'employ' the worker, and not vice versa – is a characteristic trait of the capitalist mode of production, but only with machines does it acquire 'technical and palpable reality',[81] and thus achieve its maximum development:

> The technical subordination [*Unterordnung*] of the workman to the uniform motion of the instruments of labour, and the peculiar composition of the body of workpeople ... give rise to a barrack discipline [*Disziplin*], which is elaborated into a complete system in the factory, and which fully develops the before mentioned labour of overlooking, thereby dividing the workpeople into operatives and overlookers, into private soldiers and sergeants of an industrial army ... The factory code in which capital formulates, like a private legislator, and at his own good will, his autocracy over his workpeople, unaccompanied by that division of responsibility, in other matters so much approved of by the bourgeoisie, and unaccompanied by the still more approved representative system, this code is but the capitalistic caricature of that social regulation of the labour-process ... The place of the slave-driver's lash is taken by the overlooker's book of penalties.[82]

---

80   See Hobsbawm and Ranger 1983.
81   *MECW*, Vol. 35, p. 426.
82   *MECW*, Vol. 35, pp. 426–7.

So 'Is Fourier wrong when he calls factories "tempered bagnos"'?[83] These passages in Marx's analysis, including extensive quotations from the Factory Reports as well as a long section from Engels's *Condition of the Working Class in England*, provide an incisive description of the conditions in the factories: as Engels emphasises, 'These workmen are condemned to live, from their ninth year till their death, under this mental and bodily torture'.[84]

With the factory – unlike in the cases of co-operation and manufacture – labour-power becomes a partial function: we see the decline of the worker performing many tasks, while the previously-established relationship between the worker and the means of labour is wholly transformed. It should be noted that Marx constantly combined an overall analysis of the capitalist mode of production and its means of functioning with a historical reconstruction examining the transformations that had taken place. There is, indeed, no bifurcation between logic and history: the conceptual structure of *Capital* is continually shot through by history. This element is worth repeating, as against those 'logicist' interpretations of *Capital* that mask – or at least neutralise – the historical dimension, as well as the political dimension, of Marx's reflection. Modern industry was paralysed so long as it was linked to individual skill: the mechanism of production here became an objective process of which the worker was not just a part but an appendage, since the means of labour were now the axis of production. As such, the fundamental principles of machinism were the substitution of skilled labour with simple labour, increased productive force, and the transformation of simple natural forces into the potential of social labour. Within this landscape, marked by a 'violent' socialisation of capital, valorisation – and thus the subsumption of productive activity to it – were ever more intensified, as skill was transferred to the machines. Capital could substitute unspecialised workers for skilled ones, and thus more easily make the labour force subject to its own control. The moments of unused time became ever briefer: the machinery forced a more rapid expenditure of labouring capacity. Rather than making the worker more independent and alleviating her exploitation, the machine served to confiscate an ever greater part of her working time as surplus-labour, and thus to strengthen and perpetuate the power of capital, opposed to her.

According to Marx, modern industry represented the production model most adequate to the capitalist system, insofar as it marked a fundamental passage in the new determination of the concept of labour in general, which

83 *MECW*, Vol. 35, p. 430.
84 *MECW*, Vol. 35, p. 427.

now concerned the means of labour rather than labour-power. In this process, indeed, capital did not only augment the productive forces, but also profoundly altered its own technological-organisational basis. The question posed by Marx's reasoning was the need to maintain an approach highly critical of 'the capitalist use of machines', and to hold this together with due stress on the revolutionary significance of capitalism, in counterposition to the conservative character of the previous modes of production:

> The principle which [modern industry] pursued ... created the new modern science of technology [*Wissenschaft der Technologie*] ... The technical basis of that industry is therefore revolutionary [*revolutionär*] ... By means of machinery ... it is continually causing changes not only in the technical basis of production, but also in the functions of the labourer, and in the social combinations of the labour-process ... the historical development of the antagonisms [*Entwicklung der Widersprüche*], immanent in a given form of production, is the only way in which that form of production can be dissolved [*Auflösung*] and a new form established [*Neugestaltung*].[85]

One element of particular significance emerges clearly from this passage, namely the science of technology. In the previous chapter on the forms of the 'common', we underlined the fact that Marx saw the need for a 'critical history of technology', a work that has still not yet truly been carried out:

> A critical history of technology would show how little any of the inventions of the 18th century are the work of a single individual. Hitherto there is no such book ... Technology discloses man's mode of dealing with Nature, the process of production by which he sustains his life, and thereby also lays bare the mode of formation of his social relations, and of the mental conceptions that flow from them.[86]

The technological dimension, which cannot be reduced to technique alone – since it also concerns the active behaviour of man in relation to nature – was, in Marx's view, a stakes to be fought over, one whose fate could not be determined in advance. Moreover, he posed himself the question of advancing from the theoretical level ('the history of technology') to a directly political one – even if there was no one-dimensional, cause-and-effect relationship

---

85   *MECW*, Vol. 25, pp. 280–1.
86   *MECW*, Vol. 25, pp. 375. See p. 66 of this book, and Panzieri 1961.

between these two levels. Machines ought not be rejected from some romantic standpoint, but rather collectively reappropriated. Marx gives us a glimpse of how working-class management of machinery could put the extraction of surplus-value into question, thus leading to the dissolution of the capitalist mode of production: the communist horizon is instead characterised by a plan devoted to the realisation of *Gattungsvermögen* [capabilities of the species], as mentioned earlier. The 'realm of freedom' – the full valuation of the individual – does not mean the negation of technology but rather its reappropriation on a new basis, quite unlike the capitalist order. The problem left open, here, is that Marx does not determine specifically the political modality in which this 'counter-use' of technology is meant to be realised.

It is necessary, however, to keep in mind the ambivalence of his reasoning, rejecting both an apologetic vision of technology (obviously) and a total critique of it. In this sense, Marx has two polemical referents. The first is bourgeois science, which functionalises technology to capitalist development as if there were a science that is *per se* expansive, and neutral with respect to the relations of production: here we again see the question of the relationship between science and production. As Marx unveils the adaptation of this relation to the capitalist mode of production's disciplining mechanisms, we can see that he is operating a critique of capitalist ideology; but we must here add a further specification, picking up on our first chapter's comments with regard to fetishism and its relationship – in many aspects a relationship of continuation and 'complexification' – with the question of ideology. It would be totally reductionist to conceive of ideology as mere un-reality, a deliberate mystification showing the opposite of what is really taking place.[87] It could only be called a fiction if we were to understand that in Lacanian terms – as an element constantly producing new images – in chiaroscuro tones. Marx's analysis of fetishism does insist precisely upon the opacity of the capitalist system: but what is at issue, here, is to understand that ideology deeply permeates the existing structures, rather than reject it *en bloc* as a pure falsification. Any reading that attempts to suggest an absolute counterposition between Marxian science and 'false' science – the ideology (in the reductive sense of the term) inherent to Smithian political economy, simplistically understood as an apology for the 'animal spirits' of capitalism – is thus wholly inadequate.[88]

---

87 The delineation of ideology in this chapter is influenced by Althusser's framing of this question. For an overall analysis of ideology in Althusser's thinking, see Raimondi 2011. See also Raimondi 2004.

88 Winch 1978 is among the most important readings of the political implications of Smith's

This problematisation of the question of ideology leads us to a second important consideration. Here emerges not only a critique of technology, but also its appreciation: the search for a 'counter-use' of technology. Though technology could not be exalted as such – as if it were not connected to the mechanisms of production – still less could it be criticised *en bloc*, as if technology *per se* had destructive characteristics. Moreover, the late Marx's interests in the natural science – as examined in the previous chapter – undoubtedly show his quest for scientific status, through a complicated interweaving of the social and natural sciences. Merely to level the charge of scientism is not the end of the matter. Apart from anything else, at the very basis of his reference to *Naturwissenschaft* is the idea that science cannot be understood in a merely empiricist manner, since it is founded on the method of abstraction: the passage 'from the abstract to the concrete' peculiar to Marx's reflection is not in contradiction with his invocation of scientific disciplines. Marx's science with regard to classical political economy was characterised by his fully assuming both a non-coincidence between essence and appearance, and the irreducibility of this latter to mere un-reality – as is clear from his discussion of fetishism. At the same time, it should be noted that science remained a somewhat problematic question for Marx, never being defined once and for all time. Marx usually denotes his own conceptual mechanism with the term 'critique' rather than 'science' (the word 'critique' being present in the title or subtitle of almost all of his 'mature' works).[89] No homology with bourgeois science is possible, here, and it is critique – understood not in purely enlightenment terms but as the true and proper pulling-apart of the object under discussion – that plays a crucial role.

However, this was not critical theory – as would appear in the twentieth century (moreover, Marx's polemic of the 'critical criticism of Bauer and friends' remains unsurpassed) – but rather a critique of theory, a radical questioning of the relationship between thought and reality as it had always hitherto been understood,[90] on the basis of a continual 'exchange' between conceptual

---

discourse. On Smith, see Zanini 1997, and Arrighi 2007, p. 43: independently of whether or not we can share his analysis of the contemporary Chinese situation, he does convincingly deal with Adam Smith, 'pulling apart' a series of myths regarding his work: 'The dogmatic belief in the benefits of minimalist governments and self-regulating markets typical of the nineteenth-century "liberal creed" or ... of "shock therapies" advocated by the Washington Consensus in the late twentieth century, were completely alien to Smith'.

89   Rancière 1965.

90   On the relation between thought and reality, see Althusser 1970, pp. 86–7: 'The decisive point of Marx's thesis concerns the principle distinguishing between the *real* and *thought*

analysis and social and political transformation.[91] As clearly emerged in the 1857 *Einleitung*, with the delineation of a complex and articulated 'whole' characterised by a 'dominant' factor, Marx's most earth-shattering acquisition as compared to Hegel resides precisely in the different manner in which he interprets the relationship between thought and reality, pulling apart any homology between the two and grasping within a materialist perspective the 'gap' between the object of theory and the real object.[92] Such a non-immediate understanding of this relation should not be seen in terms of 'theoreticism': the twists and turns of practice have continual repercussions on theoretical reflection, and at the same time this latter remains partially autonomous from them.

It is, then, possible to speak of science – but on condition that it is not understood in a purely theoretical manner, but rather on the base of the violent irruption of revolutionary practice.[93] Indeed, in the postscript to the second edition of *Capital*, Marx emphasises that bourgeois science can only remain such as long as the class struggle is still dormant (see p. 2 of this book). When this struggle 'explodes', it opens up the space for a new science, one related to 'the

---

... This principle of distinction implies two essential theses: (1) the materialist thesis of the primacy of the real over thought about the real presupposes the existence of the real independence of that thought ... (2) the materialist thesis of the specificity of thought and of the thought process, with respect to the real and the real process'. Althusser aptly brings into relief the 'gap' between these elements. The difficulty of Althusser's discourse, as emerged in our previous discussion of anti-humanism, consists in the move from this assumption to his articulation of the subjective element. For a different perspective on the reality-action nexus, see Lefort 1978, which insists on the radical 'politicisation' imbuing Marx's reflection: 'The need for action should not be added to the need for consciousness; still less should it be understood as heralding a revolt against the real ...' (p. 185). As such, 'the good and the bad are determined only within the terms of revolutionary action ... in its complete form, *reality is politics*' (p. 192).

91   For a reading that appreciates not only the revolutionary act, but also the delineation of a new modality of social relations: Lefebvre 2002, p. 23: 'To transform the world was, for Marx, also and above all to transform the human world: daily life'.

92   We here outline his distance from Hegel in terms different to those in Colletti 1973's interpretation – however significant some of its theoretical acquisitions may be. Following in the wake of Della Volpe's approach, Colletti insists on Marx's 'Galileism'. See also Colletti's lectures on the first chapter of *Capital*: Colletti 2011; on Hegel, see pp. 79–81, for example.

93   See Tronti 1980, p. 220: 'working-class science will never offer itself up to the "scientist" in an internally finished form. The working-class point of view – *qua* science – is already a contradiction. For this not to be so, it must be not only science, the cognitive grasping and prediction of phenomena; it must be a revolution, an active process of overthrowing what exists'.

real movement which abolishes the present state of things'. Thus emerges a science that 'takes sides', a science from the partial and destructive perspective of the working class. The production process, which science proposes to examine, cannot be separated from class practices: there is no purely objective capitalist development that cannot be permeated by class struggles. Rather, these latter shift the political terrain and thus the plane of analysis itself. The tendency towards communism is constantly present in Marx's analysis of the capitalist mode of production. The theoretical and political search for a working-class science is, however, of an unstable character: this science is not analogous to bourgeois science, and the critique of political economy clearly does not mean constructing another political economy, since this latter represents a distinctive trait of the capitalist mode of production.[94]

For Marx, what is important is not only to develop a critical theory that brings out the mystifications of classical political economy: his reflection furthermore advances onto the terrain of politics, or better the *conatus* towards revolutionary transformation, entering into the fractures of the 'social' and demonstrating its unsustainability. It follows that his reflection does not only work on the conceptual terrain, but interacts with the dimension of politics *sans phrases*, on the basis of a continual 'exchange' between consciousness of reality and its transformation. The relation of theory to praxis is not only a connection, but also a possible 'leap': practice cannot be deduced from theory, nor theory from practice. Indeed, the critique of political economy does involve subjects, but no immediate subjectivations: these latter cannot be fully identified with an overall conceptual structure, and must instead be continually rearticulated on the basis of the conjuncture within which they are inscribed. As such, it is necessary to see *Capital* in interaction with Marx's late political-historical writings, from which the workers' 'acting in common' forcefully emerges – this latter being irreducible to any general schema, and appearing in a specific determination which is not *sic et simpliciter* the fruit of pre-existing dialectical moments. And it is within this complex landscape that we must articulate (and practice) a 'partial' science of the working class, the 'collective singular' that brings individuals together on the basis of a movement seeking to destroy the modern separation between the 'social' and the 'political'.

---

94   See Lebowitz 2003, based on an outlook partly different from that outlined in these pages,
      on the 'political economy of the working class'.

Subjectivity and Class: The Space of Politics

[T]he working class can never express itself completely as an active political subject: there will always be zones or regions or sectors which, because of historical reasons of development, will remain serialized, mas-
sified, alien to the achievement of consciousness. There is always a residue. There is a strong tendency today to generalize the concept of class
consciousness and of class struggle as pre-existing elements antecedent
to the struggle. The only a priori is the objective situation of class exploitation. Consciousness is only born in struggle: the class struggle only exists
insofar as there exist places where an actual struggle is going on.

JEAN-PAUL SARTRE, *Masses, spontaneity, party*

∴

The 'Political Character' of Class: From the *German Ideology* to *Capital* Volume III

In the course of this work, in particular in the previous chapter, we have
insisted on the fact that Marx's conception of class – which was absolutely
central across his itinerary, from his first texts to his last – was based on the
logic of its specific determinations. Marx sought to study class without falling
into any sort of hypostatisation, be it ontological or sociological in character.
In his research, Marx examined the distinctive traits of class, its relationship
with the dimension of subjectivity, the difference between the proletariat and
the working class, and to what extent this question was trans-historical in
character: that is, understanding whether all epochs were characterised by the
presence of class or whether it 'exclusively' appeared as an element of the
capitalist mode of production, in its specific difference with respect to the
preceding forms. Finally, he sought to understand the articulation of the 'acting
in common' of the individuals making up a class, with its potential to break up
the 'present state of things'.

For the purposes of this study of the problem of class, it seems particularly
worthwhile to refer to two works by the young Marx, namely his *Contribution to the Critique of Hegel's Philosophy of Law*, and the *German Ideology*. In

the first text, we see the 'capture of speech'[1] by the proletariat, the 'class with radical chains',[2] the incarnation and materialisation of 'tort', given its radical asymmetry with respect to the bourgeoisie. Indeed, while this latter has particular interests and thus seeks to fulfil a particular goal, the proletariat instead appears as a non-class class, the bearer of a sort of 'partial universalism' since, unlike the bourgeoisie, it has no particular interests to defend. We can speak of the dimension of universalism because the proletariat tends toward the overcoming of class society, and thus its own existence as a class, on the basis of a full negation of all particularisms.[3] At the same time, however, this universalism is rooted in a determinate portion of society, is not neutral with regard to existing social positions, and thus assumes the 'guilty' perspective of the proletariat. This paradox of the non-class proletarian class is extremely productive on the theoretical and political planes, but at the same time presents certain difficulties.

The second text mentioned, the *German Ideology*, presents a consideration of great importance for our analysis of this problem: 'The separate individuals form a class only insofar as they have to carry on a common battle against another class'.[4] The thing that unites the individuals who come to constitute a

---

1 Certeau 1998.
2 *MECW*, Vol. 3, p. 186.
3 See Žižek 2004, pp. 297–8: 'the only universal class whose singularity (exclusion from society of property) guarantees its *actual* universality, is the proletariat ... In Alain Badiou's terms, proletariat is not another *particular* class, but a *singularity* of the social structure, and *as such* the universal class, the non-class among the classes'. See also Žižek 2008. For further insight on this declination of the proletariat, see Badiou 1992, which articulates a 'politics of emancipation', which 'exists in sequences' and is dependent on the 'chance of the event' that prescribes it; Badiou 1998 and 2009. On Badiou and Marxism, see Toscano 2007. We agree with some aspects of Badiou's reflection on the proletariat as a partial universalism, but we consider this concept's lack of specific determination problematic; indeed, this naturally flows from a conception of politics incardinated on the dimension of the event. A rather different perspective is the 'democratic' outlook of Rancière 1995a, with its theorisation of the 'part of those who have no part', the 'recognition' of wrong. See also Rancière 1995b, which addresses the paradox of the proletariat as a non-class class, interpreting subjectivation as the process of 'disidentification' or 'declassification'. For a comparison between Badiou and Rancière, see Visentin 2009. Another framework incardinated on the element of democracy, though articulated in a manner different to Rancière's, is that of Laclau and Mouffe 1989, in certain respects drawing on Gramsci's notion of hegemony. However, with this approach the question of domination risks losing its constitutive reference to the 'bond' of labour. On Laclau and his engagement with Gramsci see Frosini 2009, pp. 105–20.
4 *MECW*, Vol. 5, p. 77.

class is not some fixed 'substance', but rather a conflict that is mobile and thus irreducible to any predetermined solutions. A further aspect also thus emerges, here: classes cannot be defined once and for all on the theoretical plane in the narrow sense. There is, then, a binding link between class and practice: to radicalise this discourse, we might say that classes only exist in the class struggle, and have no determination independent of the conjuncture of the struggle in which they are inscribed. Class is, therefore, an eminently political notion, though it demands a refoundation of politics radically different from the way in which politics was hitherto conceived.[5] Class is an element that must be 'practiced', which is why it is impossible to find any definition of it that is valid across all historical and geographic situations.

The development of Marx's reflection following these two texts, during 1848 and its defeat, was also extremely significant in this regard. To see the 'political character' of class, it is enough to recall the passage of the *Poverty of Philosophy* in which Marx states that the struggle of one class against another is a political struggle. It is not a merely 'economic' fact, but has a political dimension that enters into the 'folds' of the social. Thus emerges the idea of a continual exchange between the social movement and the political movement, not only reprising the French Revolution, but 'going beyond' its constitutive limits. After all, on the one hand the social movement displays a political character, while on the other hand the political movement is rooted in the class dynamic of society. This interaction between the 'social' and the 'political', which is not 'peaceful' but rather in permanent tension, reached an important point of condensation in the *Communist Manifesto*, which emphasised the potential opportunities opened up by the events of 1848. In particular, in the French context – analysed in *Class Struggles in France* – Marx discerned the first emergence of a true and proper class struggle: in this scenario, the political significance of class 'exploded'.

It is precisely when we fully take on board the 'political' character of class that it becomes clear that it was in Marx's historical-political writings that the workers' 'acting in common' emerged most sharply, since these texts were con-

---

5   In this regard, *operaismo* was of fundamental importance in stressing not only the political character of class and the primacy of political practice, but also the non-immediacy of the coincidence between theory *qua* anticipation and practice *qua* intervention. As Tronti 1980, p. 188 writes: 'the theory of revolution is wholly contained within the political definition of the working class'. On the question of class, see the more recent Tronti 2008, p. 69, referring to 'class not as an economic category or sociological determination, but a political concept founded on an economic fact. But this political concept is continually fleeing from the economic prison'. See n. 22, p. 116.

nected to the 'real state of things', examining a unique and specific situation, rather than putting forward an overall and inevitably generalising schema. Marx sought continually to recalibrate his reflection on the basis of the complex changes taking place within the social stratigraphy, in both time and space, 'deploying' the question of class within the contexts in which it was inserted. History and politics thus 'violently' entered into his reasoning on class, which could not be addressed once and for all time in abstract terms. The late Marx's writings represented a constant effort to rearticulate his political discourse: a sort of correction to the framework established in the *Communist Manifesto*. A further cue for reflection, in this sense, is provided by a text that appeared much later in time than those we have mentioned thus far, namely *Capital* Volume III, which features a chapter on 'Classes'. Before anything else, even beyond the fact that this was the final chapter of *Capital* (and, we ought to remember, one from a volume published not by Marx, but by Engels) it is important to note that this chapter was never finished, even if Marx did have time to do so (after all, the third volume was written before the first). He produced less than two pages of it.[6] This consideration provides further testimony of the difficulty, if not impossibility, Marx faced in defining class once and for all time, uncoupling it from either a purely 'objective' role, with the class of capitalists in function of capital and the working class in function of labour – that is, one based on the 'materialisation' of the capital-labour contradiction – or a purely 'subjective' role, which could, however, be captured in a conjunctural perspective rooted in a specific social and political situation.

In the chapter 'Classes', Marx outlines the theme of class:

> The owners merely of labour-power, owners of capital, and land-owners, whose respective sources of income are wages, profit and ground-rent, in other words, wage-labourers, capitalists and land-owners, constitute then three big classes of modern society based upon the capitalist mode of production.
>
> In England, modern society is indisputably most highly and classically developed in economic structure. Nevertheless, even here the stratification of classes does not appear in its pure form. Middle and intermediate strata even here obliterate lines of demarcation everywhere (although incomparably less in rural districts than in the cities) ... We have seen that the continual tendency and law of development of the capitalist mode of production is more and more to divorce the means of production from

---

6   See Krätke 2003.

labour, and more and more to concentrate the scattered means of production into large groups, thereby transforming labour into wage-labour
and the means of production into capital. And to this tendency, on the
other hand, corresponds the independent separation of landed property
from capital and labour, or the transformation of all landed property into
the form of landed property corresponding to the capitalist mode of production.[7]

Beyond the aspect that we mentioned in the previous chapter regarding the
centrality of the question of separation for the purposes of understanding class
structure, here emerges an element that complicates Marx's previous representation of the capitalist system, but also the landscape presented in *Capital*
Volume I founded on a two-sided structure (class of capitalists and working
class). After all, here he represents not two, but three classes, composed of
wage-labourers, capitalists and landlords: the personifications of wages, profit
and ground-rent respectively. He also provides a geographical reference point
in this regard, highlighting the fact that this dynamic is most clearly expressed
in England (moreover, in many ways the image of the capitalist mode of production presented in *Capital* reflects the situation in that country), though adding
that even in that context these figures cannot be discerned in a perfectly pure
fashion. Indeed, in other contexts we find even more hybrid dynamics and situations. Thus emerges a social stratification of decisively greater articulation and
complexity than the various ones that Marx himself presented. The continuation of the passage cited above poses a question of crucial significance:

> What constitutes a class? – and the reply to this follows naturally from the
> reply to another question, namely: What makes wage-labourers, capital-
> ists and landlords constitute the three great social classes?
>   At first glance – the identity of revenues and sources of revenue. There
> are three great social groups ... However, from this standpoint, physicians
> and officials, e.g., would also constitute two classes, for they belong to two
> distinct social groups, the members of each of these groups receiving their
> revenue from one and the same source. The same would also be true of
> the infinite fragmentation of interest and rank into which the division of
> social labour splits labourers as well as capitalists and landlords ...[8]

---

7 *MECW*, Vol. 35, pp. 870–1.
8 Ibid.

What is at issue, therefore, is to understand what it is that makes a class a class. The only solution he presents in this regard takes a 'negative' route, so to speak. Marx emphasises that despite the importance of reference to income, this does not alone define class. We thus have further confirmation that class is never fully 'theorisable': though we can identify some of its salient traits, for example sources of revenue, it can never be entirely unbound from the political context in which it is inscribed. Moreover, it is very telling that in *Capital* Marx constantly speaks of classes and yet there is never any overall theoretical thematisation of class – and, where it should have appeared, in Volume III, it was left unfinished. The above-cited passage is also evidence of the fact that Marx's treatment of classes was, in the last instance, part of a study of the constitutive elements of the capitalist mode of production.

This consideration ought to be examined in light of the *Communist Manifesto*'s claim that the history of all hitherto existing societies rested on classes and the class struggle. In Marx's later work, it becomes ever more apparent that classes and the class struggle in the strict sense only come about with the capitalist mode of production – when social relations are depersonalised and historicised, and for the first time there emerges a truly social form, in the both spectral and expansive sense of the term. Only capitalism has a two-sided social structure (the class of capitalists and the working class) in which antagonism is not an effect, but rather the *sine qua non* condition of its coming-into-being. Marx's reflection on classes, strictly speaking, concerns only the capitalist mode of production, in its specific determination and difference with regard to previous forms. Fully taking on board the rooting of classes in the capitalist order, it is, however, necessary to note that their status is extremely complex, presenting a series of antinomies, sometimes internal contradictions, or even breaking points.[9]

First of all, it is true that classes – in the strong sense of the word – exist only within the class struggle, but at the same time the landscape of classes is an articulated one, and however accurate the idea of a more or less latent 'civil war' between the classes may be, the question cannot be wholly identified with this element. Here, we refer the reader back to the anti-substantialist statement outlined above, according to which class cannot be hypostatised, that is, decoupled from the conjuncture in which it is inscribed. In this regard, it is necessary always to bear in mind the relation between the working class, the workers' movement and working-class organisation (unions, parties or other forms of co-operation). The working class cannot be defined outside the

---

9 Balibar 1997.

terms of the workers' movement, and this latter cannot be considered outside the terms of working-class organisation. We ought to reactivate the theme, formulated already in the *Poverty of Philosophy*, of the transition from the 'class in itself' to the 'class for itself' (this not being understood *sic et simpliciter* as a succession of stages), which implies the necessity not only of a movement, but also of organisation.

> In this struggle – a veritable civil war – all the elements necessary for a coming battle unite and develop ...
>
> Economic conditions had first transformed the mass of the people of the country into workers. The combination of capital has created for this mass a common situation, common interests. This mass is thus already a class as against capital, but not yet for itself. In the struggle, of which we have noted only a few phases, this mass becomes united, and constitutes itself as a class for itself. The interests it defends becomes class interests. But the struggle of class against class is a political struggle.[10]

To assume this connection between the working class, workers' movement and working-class organisation does not, however, mean working through this question by way of a complete 'compression' of the objective and subjective factors. We find ourselves faced with the essential instability of these elements, as well as their 'impurity': in fact, only in abstract theorisation can they take on a pure character, whereas in historical and political practice they always appear in an impure and articulated form. The workers' movement has, therefore, never been the bearer of all class practices, and it has never been entirely and only anti-capitalist: in this sense, some have referred, in expansive terms, to 'another' workers' movement.[11] Here, we will overlook the question of ground-rent, mentioned in the previously-cited passage: in the landscape presented in the third volume Marx identified not two, but three classes, thus adding landowners into the mix and problematising the theme that we are examining. Furthermore, Volume III shows itself to be particularly attentive to the concreteness of the existing dynamics: indeed, only on an abstract plane can we speak of two classes, whereas actual reality poses us with a more articulated stratigraphy. In any case, up till now I have taken class to mean the working class, probably the only class that emerges in true and proper form in *Capital*.

---

10   *MECW*, Vol. 6, p. 211.

11   On the possibility of 'another' workers' movement different from the 'dominant' one in some senses embroiled in the state's disciplining mechanisms, see Roth 1974.

There are ambivalences and ambiguities also in Marx's delineation of the capitalist class, or better, the class of capitalists. In concrete history there is never a perfectly compact capitalist class; rather, there exist capitalists of different types, whose unity is made possible thanks to the role of the state.

We ought to mention another aspect that plays an important role in the thematisation of this chapter, based on the one hand on *Capital*, and on the other hand on Marx's historical-political writings: namely, the fact that there is a difference in the register of these works, including in terms of the status that each of them gives to class. In the perspective that we have delineated up till now, we have rejected any dichotomy between *Capital*, understood in a purely theoretical-categorial sense, and Marx's historical-political texts, as if these were contingent interventions lacking any overall theoretical inspiration. Such a choice does not mean taking his thought and insisting on a full, immediate identification among the writings in question, which do, after all, have different registers. As regards the element of class, we must observe that his historical-political writings present classes, and in particular the working class, as collective subjects that play an earth-shattering role in the development of events. Moreover, these works were inscribed in specific conjunctures in which classes were either on the move in revolutionary activity (think of the *Class Struggles in France* or his writings on the Paris Commune); found themselves amidst a sort of 'revolution from above' (a rather problematic expression, used by Engels to indicate the role played by Bismarck);[12] or directly faced a counter-revolutionary involution (think, for example, of the *Eighteenth Brumaire*). Precisely because they were conjunctural, these writings 'photographed' the class in a specific moment, often a particularly telling one, and in a specific place, itself also often of significance. But even insofar as he sometimes delineated a complex social stratigraphy, there did nonetheless seem to emerge a representation of a coherent collective subject with a revolutionary function.

In *Capital*, the question is posed in partly different terms, in the sense that the capitalist and the worker constitute the 'figures', the personifications of capital and labour: more than the struggle between two social classes, what emerges here is the contradiction between capital and labour. As we emphasised in the first chapter, Marx desubstantialises this discussion: each person, with their both economic and juridical roles,[13] is a mask for economic and class interests. However, even within this logic there is an asymmetry between the class of capitalists and the class of workers: to be precise, we could say that the

---

12   In his 1895 introduction to *The Class Struggles in France*, in MECW, Vol. 27, pp. 506 et sqq.
13   See Pashukanis 1978.

only true class, in *Capital*, is the working class, whose presence is the *sine qua non* condition for the valorisation of capital. We must reiterate that this framework does not imply denying the significance of the element of class struggle, or more generally a rejection of a political reading of capital, since the pages of the work in question are constantly traversed by history and politics. In this regard, it is worth delving deeper into an aspect that until now remained in the shadows, namely the relationship between working class and proletariat. Indeed, up till this point we have in general referred to the working class, and sometimes used the term 'proletariat' in a manner that almost presupposed a substantial coincidence between these two terms.

If we examine *Capital*, in particular the first volume, we see that Marx spoke of the working class [*Arbeiterklasse*] more than of the proletariat [*Proletariat*]: this latter term appears only sporadically throughout the text. Other than in the dedication to Wilhelm Wolff, it appears in the chapter on the transformation of surplus-value into capital and in the 'Afterword' to the second edition of *Capital*. This last reference is of particular significance, since here Marx incisively brought out the perspective that underlay his own critique of political economy: 'So far as such criticism represents a class, it can only represent the class whose vocation in history is the overthrow of the capitalist mode of production and the final abolition of all classes – the proletariat'.[14] Here we apparently see the return of the distinctive traits of the proletariat such as we previously saw them in Marx's youthful texts, in particular its existence as a non-class class and its 'partial universalism', directed toward the overcoming of class structures and thus of its own class position, even if starting out from a determinate portion of society. In reading the lines just cited, we ought not forget that the 'Afterword' to the second edition of *Capital* was written in 1873, and was thus heavily imbued with the political experience of the Paris Commune and the 'subjective' role Marx had ascribed to this latter. The proletariat thus bore a radically 'political' character: later on, we will return to the question of proletarian politics, which is not without its antinomies.

Even if the word 'proletariat' did not disappear entirely in *Capital*, without doubt here Marx's key term for denoting workers as a whole was 'working class' and not 'proletariat'; just as it is clear that in his analysis of the production process, and the exploitation underlying it, he referred always to the working class and not to the proletariat. In *Capital* there is both an economic theory founded on the valorisation of capital, and a political theory of classes linked to the active struggles that sought to challenge the 'present state of things'.

---

14   *MECW*, Vol. 35, p. 16.

As we emphasised in the previous chapter, Marx was attempting to give life to a working-class science, a science on the 'side' of the workers, which was, however, continually traversed by politics and not identified with theory, as abstractly understood. On the basis of these presuppositions, it seems that Marx was differentiating between the working class as an economic class and the proletariat as a political subject, the 'universal class', the class *par excellence* with its revolutionary character. However, this distinction should not be rigidly taken for granted, since it continually changed across the passing of time and was never given any fully defined formulation. Indeed, in this context the definition of 'economic' and 'political' has an essential instability. Particularly important for a concrete analysis of the relationship between the working class and political action in *Capital* is the tenth chapter of Volume I, 'The Working Day', focusing as it does on the working class's struggles for the shortening of working hours.

The Struggle over the Working Day: Between Reforms and Revolution

The chapter 'The Working Day' appears in the third section of Volume I, concerning the production of absolute surplus-value, and thus the increase of the length of the working day. However, this capitalist objective met with the resistance of the working class, which sought to reduce its time at work: 'The establishment of a normal working-day is the result of centuries of struggle between capitalist and labourer'.[15] Within this landscape, it is worth bearing in mind the significance for Marx's analysis of two moments of economic crisis: namely, 1857–8 (the first crisis of overproduction) and 1861–5. But the history of the limiting of the working day is, above all, a history of class struggles, which started from the most advanced sectors (cotton, wool, linen, and silk production) and then extended to a succession of other industries. The working class's need to fight to resist capital derives from the fact that this latter works by all means to increase its own self-valorisation:

> The labourer is nothing else, his whole life through, than labour-power ... all his disposable time is by nature and law labour-time, to be devoted to the self-expansion of capital ... in its blind unrestrainable passion, its were-wolf hunger for surplus-labour, capital oversteps not only the moral,

---

15   *MECW*, Vol. 35, p. 276.

but even the merely physical maximum bounds of the working-day. It usurps the time for growth, development, and healthy maintenance of the body.[16]

The capitalist is nothing if not capital personified, in Marx's anti-substantialist vision: 'Free competition *brings out the inherent laws of capitalist production, in the shape of external coercive laws* having power over every individual capitalist'.[17] The labourer is reduced to mere labour-power and her available time becomes identified with working time, and thus the period necessary for the valorisation of capital, as the labour process is incorporated into the process of valorisation. The activity of capital, the 'were-wolf's hunger for surplus-labour', is completely devoted to overcoming 'not only the moral, but even the merely physical maximum bounds of the working-day': for capital, every *Grenze* [limit] is a *Schranke* [obstacle], a barrier to be eliminated as soon as possible. Left to its own devices, capital would exploit the worker as much as possible, even twenty-four hours a day, if it could:

> To appropriate labour during all the 24 hours of the day is, therefore, the inherent tendency of capitalist production ... The workers consist of men and women, adults and children of both sexes. The ages of the children and young persons run through all intermediate grades, from 8 (in some cases from 6) to 18. In some branches of industry, the girls and women work through the night together with the males.[18]

The worker's physical limits and the possibility of resistance, and certainly not the goodwill of the capitalist, render this aim impossible to achieve. The idea of capital as an objective social power is connected with the problem of time: the stealing of the worker's available time is the 'heart' of capitalist domination. This is clearly apparent in Marx's references to the murderous rhythm of labour in the English factories of the early nineteenth century:

> If, therefore, in our historical sketch, on the one hand, modern industry, on the other, the labour of those who are physically and legally minors,

---

16   *MECW*, Vol. 35, pp. 270–1. Note also the words that follow on from this: 'It steals the time required for the consumption of fresh air and sunlight ... Capital cares nothing for the length of life of labour-power. All that concerns it is simply and solely the maximum of labour-power, that can be rendered fluent in a working-day'.

17   *MECW*, Vol. 35, p. 276.

18   *MECW*, Vol. 35, pp. 263–4.

play important parts, the former was to us only a special department, and the latter only a specially striking example of labour exploitation.

...

After capital had taken centuries in extending the working-day to its normal maximum limit, and then beyond this to the limit of the natural day of 12 hours, there followed on the birth of machinism and modern industry in the last third of the 18th century, a violent encroachment like that of an avalanche in its intensity and extent. All bounds [*Schranke*] of morals and nature, age and sex, day and night, were broken down ... Capital celebrated its orgies.

As soon as the working-class, stunned at first by the noise and turmoil of the new system of production, recovered, in some measure, its senses, its resistance [*Widerstand*] began, and first in the native land of machinism, in England.[19]

Capital seeks to destroy any community of interests, overcoming any limits relating to age, sex, and working time. The landscape depicted thus far stands in continuity with Engels's unsurpassed work *The Condition of the Working Class in England*, which Marx often cited, though he did also delve into other contexts. A particularly interesting point of reference in *Capital* is the United States, which had an advanced capitalist order, albeit one based on slavery. But this problem also presents an aspect of more general importance than this reference to the United States, since it concerns the fact that the emancipation of labour would be impossible without emancipation from slavery. Thus emerges Marx's understanding of the centrality of the question of slavery and its permanence within capitalism, at least in determinate regions and moments: capitalism and slavery are not mutually exclusive. As the American case demonstrates, the end of slavery meant not only the end of unacceptable discrimination against part of the population, but also 'lit the touch-paper' for working-class struggles to reduce the working day.

The development of capital on the one hand places the working class in a tragic position, on account of its structures of ever-increased exploitation; on the other hand, it allows it to organise its resistance with an ever-greater sense of consciousness. The reduction of the individual to a seller of her own labour-power implies her destitution, since everything that belongs to her is stolen; yet at the same time it opens up the opportunity for her to follow a different course of development seeking the realisation of her own capacities

---

19   *MECW*, Vol. 35, p. 283.

and faculties. This objective could only be reached by way of a long series of struggles, opening out into a true and proper civil war:

> The history of the regulation of the working-day in certain branches of production, and the struggle still going on in others in regard to this regulation, prove conclusively that the isolated labourer [*der vereinzelte Arbeiter*], the labourer as 'free' vendor of his labour-power, when capitalist production has once attained a certain stage, succumbs without any power of resistance. The creation of a normal working-day is, therefore, the product of a protracted civil war [*Bürgerkriegs*], more or less dissembled, between the capitalist class and the working-class[20]

Such invocations of the Hobbesian *bellum omnium contra omnes* represent a characteristic trait running throughout Marx's entire work, from his first writings to his last: there is ceaseless struggle in which all certainties are destroyed. Marx does not speak generically of a struggle among individual atoms counterposed to one another, but rather brings out the 'class' connotation of this fight, which is a true and proper civil war between the two classes.[21]

Even apart from the fact that this civil war develops slowly and is often latent rather than fully unleashed, it is worth noting that while the dimension of politics is connected to that of war, Marx's position here must be taken with a pinch of salt,[22] since to consider the working class and the capitalist class as two stable, fixed armies does not correspond to the complexity of his articulation of class. As such, affirmation of the political connotation of this struggle does not just mean exaltation over 'the civil war being waged'; it also means that the working class must adopt a strategy aimed at achieving legislation more appropriate to its own needs than what exists already:

> For 'protection' against 'the serpent of their agonies', the labourers must put their heads together, and, as a class, compel the passing of a law, an all-powerful social barrier that shall prevent the very workers from selling, by voluntary contract with capital, themselves and their families into slavery

---

20 *MECW*, Vol. 35, p. 303.

21 See J.G. Thomas 1987, p. 207.

22 On the relation of politics to war, see Gramsci 1975, pp. 120–2: 'comparisons between military art and politics, if made, should always be taken *cum grano salis* – in other words, as stimuli to thought ... in military war, when the strategic aim – destruction of the enemy's army and occupation of his territory – is achieved, peace comes ... The political struggle is enormously more complex'.

and death. In place of the pompous catalogue of the 'inalienable rights of man' comes the modest Magna Charta of a legally limited working-day, which shall make clear 'when the time which the worker sells is ended, and when his own begins'.[23]

If we assume that the class only exists, in the true and proper sense, within a dynamic of conflict, and thus on the terrain of practice, then we should also note that the individuals united by a common condition and thus a common need for struggle must seek to increase their collective political weight, toward the end of securing the passing of a law: therefore, in order to improve its situation the working class is compelled to make a pact with capital. The theme of reducing the length of the working day frequently reappears in a position of strategic importance throughout Marx's works in these years: we need only think of his invocation of this topic in the passage on the 'realm of freedom' in *Capital* Volume III, as well as in his writings on the First International. Moreover, in Marx's so-called 'Worker's Inquiry', which we mentioned in the previous chapter, several questions in one sense or another related to the length of the working day and its shortening by way of trade-union and political practice.

If we accept that it is this important for the working class to obtain legislation from the state, then this means admitting that law is not just of an unreal character, or entirely enslaved to capitalist interests. What Marx unmasks is its pretence to stand entirely autonomous of the determinate mechanisms of the capitalist system. Precisely because law is not an end in itself, but rather an instrumental element endowed with a structural duplicity, the working class must apply pressure on it, seeking to 'exploit' its potentials and opportunities, thus 'using it' as a weapon. Thus emerges a consciousness of the fact that the working class must be united if it wants to acquire political weight sufficient to obtaining its demands: division is synonymous with its total isolation in the face of capitalist domination. In contrast to the 'pompous catalogue of the inalienable rights of man' heralded by the French Revolution, the legislation obtained through the struggle to shorten the working day is but a 'modest Magna Charta'. The adjective 'modest' is deployed in ironic counterposition to the 'pompous' Freedom, Equality, Property and Bentham: through this legislation the workers can achieve a reduction in their exploitation, so to speak, but certainly not complete liberation, which is impossible as long as the capitalist mode of production remains in place. Marx's purpose in *Capital* is not

---

23   *MECW*, Vol. 35, pp. 306–7.

abstractly to counterpose revolution to the struggle to conquer certain reforms. Very telling, in this regard, is a passage in his *Class Struggles in France, 1848 to 1850*:

> The first draft of the constitution, made before the June days, still contained the *droit au travail*, the right to work, the first clumsy formula wherein the revolutionary demands of the proletariat are summarized ... The right to work is, in the bourgeois sense, an absurdity, a miserable, pious wish. But behind the right to work stands the power over capital; behind the power over capital, the appropriation of the means of production, their subjection to the associated working class, and therefore the abolition of wage labor, of capital, and of their mutual relations. Behind the '*right to work*' stood the June insurrection.[24]

This right may at first seem 'an absurdity, a miserable, pious wish'. In reality, it cannot be wholly reduced to that, since it does represent an attempt to turn the tables on the current situation, to the advantage of the worker: its end goal is domination over capital, and thus the destruction of the present production relations. Obviously, in order fully to achieve such objectives, there would need to be a change in the mode of production: and from that point of view, this perspective is an insufficient one. However, when Marx defines it as a 'first clumsy formula', he does not stop at highlighting this limitation, but rather recognises the importance of the struggles waged by the workers demanding that this right be promulgated. This slogan may be awkward and not wholly satisfactory, but it is nonetheless the first attempt to pull apart the *status quo*. For Marx, the problem is not whether or not to take a stance in favour of the reforms themselves, but rather, to understand whether a specific piece of legislation corresponds to a class practice capable of shaking up the present horizon. The slogan 'the right to work' was, therefore, not accepted theoretically, but activated politically.

Whatever the tensions in Marx in this regard,[25] he did not *sic et simpliciter* show disdain for right, but understood it in terms of its mutual penetration with the economic sphere, its link with the dynamic of capitalism, and thus the rela-

---

24   *MECW*, Vol. 10, pp. 77–8.

25   For example, for an apparently total critique of right, see not only Marx's early writings – above all his *Critique of Hegel's Doctrine of the State* and his *On the Jewish Question*, in which he brings out its 'unreality' – but also one of his last political texts, the *Critique of the Gotha Programme*, in which he speaks of his intention to go beyond the 'narrow horizon of bourgeois right'.

tions of force that traversed it. This conception was posed as the most decisive rejection of the 'harmonies of freedom, equality, etc.' proper to the simple circulation of commodities. By no means does right stand in equidistance between the two parties in struggle: at the moment in which equal demands confront one another, the one that prevails is that which holds social power and is thus able to exercise *Gewalt*.[26] The use of force proves to be intimately linked to the capitalist mode of production's structures of subjection, in which a determinate class exerts domination over the working class. Marx's position was distinct from either an abstractly pacifist vision or any sort of bellicose exaltation of violence. Rather, what we have here is a demystified, so to speak 'phenomenological' recognition of the relevance of *Gewalt* to history. Marx notes the importance of this element in the birth and development of bourgeois society, which has devastating effects on the colonial world through its dependence upon 'brute force'[27] and the separation that it introduces:

> *Tantae molis erat*, to establish the 'eternal laws of Nature' of the capitalist mode of production, to complete the process of separation [*Scheidung-sprozess*] between labourers and conditions of labour, to transform, at one pole, the social means of production and subsistence into capital, at the opposite pole, the mass of the population into wage labourers, into 'free labouring poor,' that artificial product of modern society. If money, according to Augier, 'comes into the world with a congenital blood-stain on one cheek,' capital comes dripping from head to foot, from every pore, with blood and dirt.[28]

The dominion of capital, reinforced by the state structure – 'the concentrated and organised force of society' capable of imposing capital's own law – provokes a process of separation among the wage-labourers. This landscape is not 'one-dimensional', since even when the class of capitalists tries to increase the length of the working day, the working class fights to reduce it: in this context, managing to achieve legislation that while unable to eliminate exploitation does diminish its burden. In this regard, it is worth repeating that in *Capital*, except on a few rare occasions, Marx uses the term 'working class' [*Arbeiterklasse*] and not 'proletariat'. In the passage cited above, he counterposed the working class to the capitalist class, or better, the class of capitalists

---

26   See p. 30 of this book.
27   *MECW*, Vol. 35, p. 739.
28   *MECW*, Vol. 35, p. 747.

(as if it were impossible to refer to it as a unitary subject, since the subject is capital itself rather than a capitalist class). But if the use of 'working class' instead of 'proletariat' signals the difficulty inherent to any immediate representation of the proletariat as a universal class, this does not, however, mean reducing it to an economic class in the narrow sense of the word, lacking any subjective – and thus political – connotation. It was necessary to hold open the relationship between the working class and 'the working-class movement that daily grew more threatening'.[29] Again, here, we see the working class – class struggle – workers' movement nexus. Even legislative measures were the outcome of a class practice: they 'were not at all the products of Parliamentary fancy. They developed gradually out of circumstances as natural laws of the modern mode of production. Their formulation, official recognition, and proclamation by the State, were the result of a long struggle of classes'.[30] It sometimes appeared that the 'antagonism of classes had arrived at an incredible tension'.[31]

There is not always such a violent 'explosion', however. Indeed, the connection between class and class struggle is often not immediate in character: a very complex process takes place, in which the aforementioned elements do not always coalesce. Moreover, it is necessary to emphasise the structural duplicity of labour-power: on the one hand, the individual worker is relegated to her function as a labourer, but on the other hand there do open up some spaces of subjectivation, since the capitalist does not buy labour-power, but rather avails himself of it temporarily. Labour-power cannot be separated from the living corporeality of the worker, which poses a potential element of resistance against the 'meat grinder' of valorisation. We must continually insist on the fact that the ambivalence of her condition has to be 'activated' politically, precisely on the basis that the worker's body cannot itself be 'cashed in'. In any case, within this representation the state is understood not on the basis that politics – or at least the state sphere – is directly derived from the economic sphere, constituting a mere reflection of or deduction from it. The state sphere obviously is closely linked to the interests of the class of capitalists, but at the same time it is configured as a field of forces whose outcome can seemingly not always be taken for granted. At this point, it is necessary to study more closely Marx's analysis of the state sphere, with particular reference to his historical-political writings, all the while bearing in mind that the two principal positions

---

29   *MECW*, Vol. 35, p. 247.
30   *MECW*, Vol. 35, p. 287.
31   *MECW*, Vol. 35, p. 296.

that Marx opposed, but did, however, maintain some ambiguous closeness to (now with one, now with the other) were Bakunin's anarchism and Lassalle's statism.

Class and Organisation, between Anarchism and Statism: Marx *versus* Bakunin and Lassalle

From the discussion that we have developed thus far, the importance of the theme of the state sphere is clearly apparent, and indeed it has constituted one of the most discussed, most controversial questions in Marxism.[32] Many have spoken of the absence of any Marxist theory of the state, seeing this element either as an insurmountable problem and index of Marxism's inability to articulate the political dimension;[33] or, on the contrary, as a paradoxical opportunity, since it leaves space open for a proletarian politics without too tight a 'strait-jacket' denying room for manoeuvre.[34] For the sake of a brief overview of Marx's itinerary prior to his last period – the object of the present analysis – it is worth emphasising that in his first texts (for example, the *Critique of Hegel's Doctrine of the State* and *On the Jewish Question*) there was a true and proper devaluation of the role of the state, which he even interpreted as a fiction, an offshoot of politics, comparable to religious mystification as identified by Feuerbach. With the passing of time, this simplistic reading was dropped, and the idea of the state as the 'executive committee of the bourgeoisie' – as he particularly clearly termed it in the *Communist Manifesto* – took shape. This definition, though a genial description of the situation in Britain, was, however, a reductionist one, since it conceived of the state mechanically as a product of bourgeois class interests. Marx was thus compelled to recognise the state's partly autonomous role, as was made clear by the case of Bonapartism, where there was a sort of 'exchange' where the bourgeoisie 'traded' political authority – or, at least, direct political authority – for economic power. As emerges in the *Eighteenth Brumaire*, Marx no longer understood the state as the immediate reflection of bourgeois interests. More generally, from the 1860s onward

---

32 Among others, see Lefebvre 1976, which sheds light on the various stratifications of this concept and the problems that remain unresolved.

33 For an interpretation very critical of Marxism's lack of any theory of the state, see Bobbio 1976. On Marx see the texts collected in Bobbio 1997.

34 For a text attributing political value to the incompleteness and non-systematic character of Marx's interpretation of the state, see the works of Negri, particularly those compiled in Negri 2006.

Marx paid more attention to the state sphere than he had done previously, also because the state itself necessarily changed, increasingly operating at a rhythm different from the primordial instincts and instances of capital. Here, we ought to specify that in Marx's discussion of the state there emerged two different usages of this term, which were correlated amongst themselves but not wholly coincidental. The first – strongly present already in his youthful writings – concerned the modern state as a territorial entity. The second – very important for the late Marx (and, subsequently, Lenin) – concerned the state-machine, the state in its separate, executive, governmental function.

Seemingly decisive in this regard is an analysis of the relationship between the capitalist mode of production and the state, according to a perspective that seeks to bring out both the impossibility of immediately deducing the latter from the former, and the extreme importance of the state for the production and reproduction of capital. This problem is also of considerable significance for a study of the spaces of class subjectivity. Indeed, as we have seen in our discussion of the struggle for the shortening of the working day, even if the state is functional to the class of capitalists, it also plays a significant role as a battlefield that the working class must 'use' in order to secure legislation serving to improve its conditions. Obviously such a 'Magna Carta' cannot be identified with communism, and nor will it necessarily produce communism even over time; but nor can it simply be dismissed by branding it as 'reformism'. The question left open concerns the specific function of the state with regard to the workers' 'acting in common'. We will here attempt to show how Marx's position in this respect differed from both Bakunin's anti-state anarchism and Lassalle's statism, to name but two approaches (and political practices) of particular significance. Certainly, Marx's approach did seek to differentiate the political dimension from the dimension of the state, but it is also clear that this distinction cannot count always and everywhere, in relation to all historical and geographical situations.

A comparison of Marx with Bakunin apparently displays signs of an absolute opposition, an irreconcilable polemic that sometimes took on rather virulent tones.[35] In reality, the question was posed in more complex terms. Indeed,

---

35   Important, here, are the two volumes edited by Wolfgang Eckhardt: Bakunin 2007 and 2011. These volumes, which collect the writings of Bakunin and other writers on the question of the state, provide a developed portrayal of the relation between Marx and Bakunin. Eckhardt's 2011 *Einleitung*, of sweeping scope, is useful on account of the great quantity of information that it offers on the historical-political landscape, within which this polemic was inscribed. I do not, however, share the perspective he outlines in its final part, entirely conditioned as it is by the desire to 'defend' Bakunin against Marx's accusations. The work

initially their relations were not negative ones, but with the passing of time tensions did arise, and these tensions were enormously aggravated with the formation and development of the First International. Marx was not the leader of the International, but was in many senses its inspirer (though in its first years Marx's perspective was not dominant within it, whereas the trade unions' role was considerable)[36] since he elaborated documents of decisive importance to its foundation, namely the 'Inaugural Address' and the 'Provisional Statutes'. Subsequently, the London Conference of 1871 was of particular significance, this being the first international congress that was truly and properly under the direction of Marx and Engels.[37] They were attempting to unite the various 'souls' of the working class, providing it with an international platform. This political commitment took place in the context of Marx's work on *Capital*. For example, the question of machines seems to have been particularly important to Marx, who in an intervention at the International's general council in 1868 emphasised both their functionality to the capitalist mode of production, and the possibility of a 'counter-use': 'on the one side machinery has proved a most powerful instrument of despotism and extortion in the hands of the capitalist class; ... on the other side the development of machinery creates the material conditions necessary for the superseding of the wages-system by a truly social system of production'.[38]

   With the passing of time, Bakunin and the Bakuninists created what was in truth an autonomous group within the International, the 'Alliance of Socialist Democracy', which came to represent a sort of 'International within the International' enjoying roots above all in Italy and in Spain. Bakunin (together with the other members of the Alliance) was accused of mounting a true and proper conspiracy, seeking to oppose itself not so much to the exploitation of labour-power by capital, as to the International itself: as Engels put it, 'we are dealing with a genuine conspiracy against the International. For the first time in the history of the working-class struggle, we stumble upon a secret conspiracy plotted in the midst of the working class, and intended to undermine, not the existing exploiting regime, but the very Association in which that regime finds its

---

of Barker 1986 is dedicated to the Marx-Bakunin relationship – or better, that between Marxism and anarchism more generally – though it is too categorical in affirming the absolute 'incompatibility of Marxism and Anarchism' (p. 213).

36   On this, see Cole 1954. However, Cole attempts to 'weld' Marx's position together to a championing of the role of trade unions. The present reading moves in a very different direction to that outlined by Cole.

37   See Vanzulli 2008, Vanzulli 2009.

38   *MECW*, Vol. 21, p. 9.

fiercest opponent'.[39] Bakunin's Alliance came to become a real 'thorn in the side' of the International (just as subsequently, and in a different sense, there would be robust polemics with Blanqui and the Blanquists) to the extent that it led to a split. In an 1871 interview Marx remarked on the 'pluralist' character of the International, which did welcome different political positions in its ranks, albeit on the basis of a common platform upheld by the General Council. In Bakunin's view, however, there was a complete lack of pluralism in the International: instead, over time a monocratic structure increasingly emerged, to which Bakunin counterposed the idea of a federalist framework.[40]

According to Marx, Bakunin's 'conspiratorial' element presented all the characteristics of a secret sect, completely in disharmony with the public, non-secretive vocation of the International.[41] Moreover, the accusation that the International was 'authoritarian' seems questionable, not only because the General Council – the IWMA's executive – had no bureaucracy but rather 'submit[ted] its decisions to the judgment of the various federations which have to carry them out',[42] but also because the Bakuninists, the partisans of anti-authoritarianism, in reality used far more authoritarian methods – if not even dictatorial ones – than those employed by the leaders of the International. Indeed, the Alliance's non-public, secretive behaviour itself accentuated the presence within it of an arbitrary, unregulated authority.[43]

It was necessary to distinguish between authority and authoritarianism, and according to Marx and Engels the International could not be led in a purely spontaneist manner, even if it was not a political party: 'it is absurd to speak of the principle of authority as being absolutely evil, and of the principle of autonomy as being absolutely good. Authority and autonomy are relative things whose spheres vary with the various phases of the development of society'.[44] Bakuninist 'sects' moreover preached abstentionism, which was about as far as it was possible to get from the International's political position: 'The sects formed by these initiators are abstentionist by their very nature – i.e., alien to all real action, politics, strikes, coalitions, or, in a word, to any united movement'.[45] In order to understand the polemic between Marx and Bakunin, it is important always to bear in mind that what they were faced with was a

---

39 *MECW*, Vol. 23, p. 233.
40 See Eckhardt 2011, pp. 4 et sqq.
41 See also *MECW*, Vol. 23, p. 233.
42 *MECW*, Vol. 23, p. 255.
43 *MECW*, Vol. 23, p. 233.
44 *MECW*, Vol. 23, p. 424.
45 *MECW*, Vol. 23, p. 106.

struggle for hegemony within the International and the workers' movement, a struggle in which neither of them was without fault. It would be mistaken, therefore, to interpret these divisions in a solely theoretical manner without taking account of the fact that this was a political fight in which each rival also 'instrumentalised' his opponent's positions. That is not to say that there were not differences as well as points of substantial similarity, and not only in contingent matters.

First of all, Marx took a strongly critical stance with regard to Bakunin's total lack of economic analysis of the capitalist mode of production. Bakunin's conception was purely 'voluntaristic', without any underlying examination of the real conditions in which activity was inscribed. As Marx wrote in his 'Conspectus' on Bakunin's *Statism and Anarchy*: 'He understands absolutely nothing of social revolution, only its political rhetoric. Its economic conditions simply do not exist for him'.[46] As well as the absence of any social and economic analysis – or perhaps precisely to fill in this gap – Bakunin relied on an irrational, mystical and nationalist exaltation of the uniqueness of the Russian people: 'our people holds in its memory and as its ideal one precious element which the Western people do not possess, that is, *a free economic community*. In our people's life and thought there are two principles, two facts on which we can build: frequent riots and a free economic community. There is a third principle, a third fact, this is the Cossacks and the world of brigands and thieves which includes both protest against oppression by the state and by the patriarchal society and incorporates, so to say, the first two features'.[47]

We discussed the matter of the rural commune [*obshchina*] at length in our second chapter, focusing on the very great range of positions on this question in Russia and Marx's interest in it, also insofar as he attempted to understand whether it would be possible to pass from the *obshchina* to communism without fully having to suffer the 'labour pains' of capitalism. Beyond the reference to revolts – in whose social base, according to Bakunin, brigands and thieves play a conspicuous role – at the root of the disagreement (but also partial consensus) between Marx and Bakunin stood the question of the state and the working class's relation to it. Indeed, Marx reproached Bakunin for his absolute critique of the state, which was possible precisely because his lack of any articulated analysis of the socio-economic plane produced an undifferentiated vision of it: 'Thus it is not the Bonapartist State, the Prussian or Russian State that has to be overthrown, but an abstract State, the State as such, a State that

---

46   *MECW*, Vol. 24, p. 518.
47   Bakunin 1993, p. 18.

nowhere exists'.[48] Bakunin's declination of this problem thus displayed its generic character, since it presupposed that the state existed by itself: Marx's (and Engels's) reasoning, conversely, was based on a logic of specific determinations that rejected absolute assumptions decoupled from the conjuncture in which they were inscribed. So precisely because Bakunin lacked any genuine examination of the capitalist system, he interpreted capital as a sort of product of the state: 'Bakunin maintains that it is the *state* which has created capital, that the capitalist has his capital *only by the grace of the state*'.[49] As a consequence, the anarchists said 'that the Proletarian revolution has to begin by abolishing the political organisation of the State'.[50]

If Bakunin studied the state only abstractly, then his conception of the destruction of the state was outlined in similarly simplistic terms: 'Let us see, however, just what the consequences of the anarchist gospel are; let us suppose the state has been abolished by decree ... merely decreeing the abolition of the state is far from sufficient to accomplish all these fine promises'.[51] It is too easy to say that the state can be eliminated by decree. Marx criticised Bakunin's idea of a '*coup de main*' that would *ipso facto* destroy the state. This sense of immediacy also emerged from Bakunin's way of conceiving of the general strike: 'In the Bakuninist programme a general strike is the lever employed by which the social revolution is started. One fine morning all the workers in all the industries of a country, or even of the whole world, stop work, thus forcing the propertied classes either humbly to submit within four weeks at the most ...'[52] In this context, the question of politics was of central importance:

> The members of the Alliance ... had been preaching for years that no part should be taken in a revolution that did not have as its aim the immediate and complete emancipation of the working class, that political action of any kind implied recognition of the State, which was the root of all evil, and that therefore participation in any form of elections was a crime worthy of death[53]

The Bakuninists were opposed to any kind of political action, because this latter would always to some degree implicitly presuppose the presence and the

48   *MECW*, Vol. 23, p. 466.
49   *MECW*, Vol. 44, p. 307.
50   *MECW*, Vol. 47, p. 10.
51   *MECW*, Vol. 23, p. 468.
52   *MECW*, Vol. 23, p. 584.
53   *MECW*, Vol. 23, p. 582.

intervention of the state. Conversely, Bakunin was constant in his critique of Marx's statism, even defining him as a sort of Bismarckian socialist.[54] Another correlated question was the relationship between politics and trade unions: Marx tended to differentiate between these two levels, thus seeing politics as distinct from trade-union activity and closely connecting it to the dimension of class. Though he did recognise the importance of trade unions and strikes, he also made clear that the political struggle could not be identified with this. Trade-union initiatives did play the role of regulating the norms of exploitation, which was itself significant, but they did not eliminate exploitation or change the relations of production.

In reality, there were important points of contact between Marx and Bakunin on certain questions. It is true that Marx rejected the *coup de main*, and thus the immediate destruction of the state, but it is also true that his goal was the overcoming of the state and the constitution of a free association of equal human beings – that is, not a state. In this regard Marx even 'positively' employed the word 'anarchy'.[55] Moreover, the entire of Marx's itinerary was distinguished by his critique of the state-form, from his first texts (think of how the question of the abolition of the state is posed in the *Critique of Hegel's Doctrine of the State*, and the discussion of human emancipation – even beyond political emancipation – in *On the Jewish Question*) up until his last ('the free association of producers' in *Capital* Volume I, and the 'realm of freedom' in Volume III). The point that divided them was not, in fact, any difference in their evaluation of the state, with a 'statist' Marx counterposed to an 'anti-statist' Bakunin, but rather in the function each man assigned (or did not assign) to the state before the establishment of a society of freedom and equality. That is, whereas for Marx there had to be a transition, Bakunin completely rejected this idea, in the name of a new order being formed immediately after the revolutionary act. Even if the question of transition in Marx bristles with difficulties, to reject it entirely, as does Bakunin, is a rather simplistic way of solving the problem. The status of politics in Marx is rather unstable in that he does not only endorse 'another' politics, a proletarian politics different to the 'present state of things'. Sometimes it seems that his critique of the state sphere also concerns 'the political', interpreting politics as intrinsically characterised by a logic of domination. This thus poses the question of whether communism stands beyond politics as well as beyond the state. Whereas up until this point we have examined the polemic

---

54   Bakunin wrote numerous passages in this vein: see the collection Bakunin 2011, Vol. 2, for example pp. 826 et sqq. on the revolution against the state, and p. 920 for a critique of Marxism as a statist politics.

55   *MECW*, Vol. 23, p. 121.

between Marx and Bakunin with regard to their critiques of the state, it is now necessary to look into the other 'pole' of this discourse, represented by Lassalle's statism.

With the passing of time the relations between Marx and Lassalle deteriorated, even beyond their personal antipathies, on account of the great differences between their political positions and the strategies for working-class organisation that they sought to pursue.[56] It is worth remembering, indeed, that in 1869 a 'Marxist' party was founded in Eisenach thanks to militants like Liebknecht and Bebel. Even though Marx and Engels played a decisive role in the foundation of the Social-Democratic Workers' Party [*Sozial-Demokratische Arbeiterpartei*], the Lassalleans dominated the young German workers' movement in the 1860s. Lassalle had himself created a General Workers' Association [*Allgemeiner Arbeiterverein*]. In fact, Marx's theoretical distance from Lassalle would prove impossible to bridge, indeed much more markedly so than in the case of his engagement-confrontation with Bakunin.[57] Lassalle, who was not strictly speaking an economist, but had attentively studied Marx's texts, did not set himself the perspective of destroying classical political economy, and on the political plane he was by no means a proponent of proletarian revolution.

His economic outlook was socialist to the extent that it sought improvement in the workers' conditions and took a polemical stance against Schulze-Delitzsch's liberalism, but it was not compatible with Marx's critique of political economy. A decisive element of Lassalle's discourse – and the object of Marx's sarcasm – was the so-called 'iron law of wages'. In large measure Lassalle reprised Ricardo's argument according to which wages were determined in terms of the necessary means for a worker's existence. As such, the law of supply and demand would make sure that there was never any lasting gap between wages and a subsistence level:

> The iron law of wages, which determines the wages for labour in the present conditions on the basis of the rule of the supply and demand of labour, is as follows: the average wage is always reduced to the necessary

---

56 On the Marx-Lassalle relationship, see the detailed analysis in Ramm 2004, pp. 267–319, which reconstructs the principal aspects of this question across its various phases. Among others, Löwy 2003 emphasises the importance of Marx's critique of Lassalle, as does the more recent Petrucciani 2009, pp. 224–5.

57 See Perfahl 1982, in particular pp. 30–62, which rightly highlights the fact that Lassalle did not represent any real break with classical political economy.

means of subsistence that are fundamental for a population that wants to prolong its customary existence and produce children.[58]

It was thus almost a sort of natural law, which could not be changed by social factors like trade-union struggle, for example. In fact, this 'iron law of wages' was far from standing in disharmony with the doctrines of the bourgeois economists of the time, as Lassalle himself was ready to admit. But from this 'law' he drew social conclusions different from those of other economists. In particular, when he stated that the ultimate result of his reflection was the understanding that the workers could not save money even if they wanted to, he identified Schulze-Delitzsch as his polemical reference point. Lassalle's end goal was to arrive at a society that was still bourgeois but in which the workers' condition was ameliorated: and the means to obtain this outcome was universal suffrage. In this context, it is clear that there was no space either for class struggle, or for a radical trade-union struggle that was not directly political, in the Marxian sense. That is, Lassalle rejected any extra-parliamentary practice. Across his entire reflection, the state dimension played a crucial role, this being ascribed the function of implementing social reforms. However, it ought to be emphasised that Lassalle cannot be considered a theorist in the strict sense – also because, on the economic as well as the philosophical terrain (think of his interpretation of Hegel) the weakness of his argumentation was striking. He should, instead, be appraised in terms of his impact within the workers' movement. In this regard, he was of very great influence, leading the creation of an autonomous socialist party of the working class. Here the idea of a 'statist' root to socialism grew within Lassalle, to the point that he entertained an ambiguous relationship with – if not outright support for – Bismarck. The 'Bismarckism' for which Bakunin reproached Marx in reality constituted a distinctive trait of Lassalle's reflection (and political practice).

The enormous gap separating Lassalle from Marx is obvious. While their divergences were many, the disagreement between Marx and Lassalle was particularly profound with regard to three particular questions. The first concerned Lassalle's 'reformism', which he did not conceive in dialectical relation to Marxism's revolutionary dimension, but rather on the basis of a complete rejection of revolution and its *conatus* toward the abolition of the state. On the contrary, in Lassalle there emerged a sort of statolatry, as is clearly apparent from his relationship with Bismarck. Thus we arrive at the second point of their sharp divergence: the fact that Lassalle's approach was a nationalist one. It is

---

58   Lassalle 1893, p. 421.

worth emphasising that Marx's horizon was internationalist in character, thus being posed in terms critical of the principle of nationality. At the same time, given that in this epoch states the world over were taking the form of nation-states, there were no simple solutions to this problem: Marx and Engels gave political support to national demands that could in some way play a propulsive role in serving an overall revolutionary outcome. To return to Lassalle, a third limitation – in some senses linked to the rigidity of his position regarding the 'iron law of wages' – consisted in the fact that he undervalued working-class struggle and its organisation. For Marx, conversely, it was necessary to destroy the state, and he sought to articulate a proletarian politics irreducible to the state and its mechanisms of domination.

A Marxian text of absolutely decisive importance in this sense was his *Critique of the Gotha Programme*, in which he heavily criticised Lassalle's position. The entire outlook of this work was irredeemably contrary to the Gotha social-democratic programme, as it tore up the roots of the 'work ethic' and mocked the idea that labour was 'the source of all wealth and all culture'.[59] Any analysis of this question had to take account of the fact that labour was here being discussed not in an abstract sense, but in terms of the exploitation of labour-power by capital: namely, the distinctive trait of the capitalist mode of production:

> The bourgeois have very good grounds for ascribing supernatural creative power to labour; since precisely from the fact that labour is determined by nature, it follows that the man who possesses no other property than his labour power must, in all conditions of society and culture, be the slave of other men who have made themselves the owners of the material conditions of labour. He can work only with their permission, hence live only with their permission.[60]

In the *Critique of the Gotha Programme* Marx tore apart all of the categories of bourgeois society, including – in some senses surprisingly, given traditional preconceptions about Marx – that of equality. After all, this notion, or better, equality in the bourgeois sense, supposes that we use an equal measure for subjects who in reality are not equals at all, since they are bound by determinate class conditions. As Marx remarks in *Capital*, individuals are configured as personifications of determinate economic – that is, class – interests, and thus are not all in the same position. The bourgeois concept of equality thus entails a

---

59   *MECW*, Vol. 24, p. 81.
60   Ibid.

mystification. That is not to say that in addressing this question Marx put forward a total critique of equality: his goal was to bring about the society of free and equal individuals, communism, through the destruction of the 'present state of things'. This ambivalent attitude toward equality, which even took the form of depicting an 'unequal right',[61] also shows us that Marx's perspective was not one of 'dour' uniformity and the 'flattening down' of all individuals to one same level. On the contrary, in going beyond the bourgeois juridical horizon communism gives life to the realisation of singularities, in their differentiation and non-seriality.[62]

This theoretical and political articulation appears wholly incompatible with Lassalle's position. Moreover, Marx devoted several pages of his *Critique of the Gotha Programme* to a robust polemic against Lassalle. The 'Marat of Berlin', 'not at all displeasing to Mr. Bismarck',[63] had completely misunderstood the *Communist Manifesto*, failing to capture the workers' movement's international dimension and instead conceiving it 'from the narrowest national standpoint': 'its class struggle is national, not in substance, but, as the *Communist Manifesto* says, "in form"'. But the "framework of the present-day national state", for instance, the German Empire, is itself in its turn economically "within the framework of the world market", politically "within the framework of the system of states"'.[64] Thus there was no trace of internationalism in the Social-Democratic Workers' Party: and such a position clashed with Marx's whole perspective, distinguished as it was by the assumption that capitalism was global in character and the attempt to bring about an adequate international platform for struggle.

It was within this context that Marx addressed the 'iron law of wages', a true and proper obsession of Lassalle's, though according to Marx all that this latter had contributed to this law was the word 'iron': it was a sort of reformulation of Malthus's population theory, and was fully compatible with the bourgeois economists' 'naturalist' approach. Also at the level of wages, Lassalle did not in the slightest capture an aspect of decisive importance to Marx's entire critique

---

61   'To avoid all these defects, right would have to be unequal rather than equal': MECW, Vol. 24, p. 87. See the considerations in this regard in Di Marco 2005, p. 59: 'Only in a higher form of communist society, with the disappearance of individuals' submission to the division of labour and the opposition of intellectual and manual labour ... could the narrow bourgeois criterion of the exchange of equivalents be overcome also in the single case of the communist form, not the average'.

62   See Basso 2008a.

63   MECW, Vol. 24, p. 88.

64   MECW, Vol. 24, pp. 89–90.

of political economy: unlike the classical political economists, Marx saw not a coincidence but rather a 'separation' between essence and appearance. The question of fetishism and the dimension of appearance underlying it – neither reality nor mere unreality – provided various significant considerations, in this regard. Lassalle's mistaken understanding of this question had an echo in his interpretation of wages:

> Since Lassalle's death there has asserted itself in our Party the scientific understanding that wages are not what they appear to be, namely the value, or price, of labour, but only a masked form for the value, or price, of labour power ... Lassalle did not know what wages were, but following in the wake of the bourgeois economists took the appearance for the essence of the matter.[65]

As well as this completely erroneous view of wages, there remained the fact that the key element of Lassalle's reflection was the state – an abstractly conceived state, its protective function and the co-operatives it managed – since he ruled out all extra-parliamentary strategies: 'It is worthy of Lassalle's imagination that with state loans one can build a new society just as well as a new railway!'[66] Moreover, Marx's critique of positions that focused on the question of social reforms is well known. As we emphasised in relation to the discussion of the 'right to work' in the *Class Struggles in France* as well as *Capital*'s analysis of the struggles to reduce the working day, this was not a matter of establishing an antithesis between reform and revolution, but nor did it mean setting the question of reforms at the centre of his reflection. The important thing was to link this question to a transformative perspective: in each of these cases there emerged a class practice, and this was the decisive consideration, though in Lassalle this was absent or at least not clearly defined.

Pursuing his argumentation in the *Critique of the Gotha Programme*, Marx polemicised against Lassalle's 'democratism'. Even beyond the fact that some of the programme's democratic demands had already been partly achieved, it is worth noting that even on the 'abstractly' political plane Lassalle had not even the courage to demand a 'democratic republic', but in some senses defended the existing situation under Bismarck's rule, 'nothing but a police-guarded military despotism, embellished with parliamentary forms, alloyed with a feudal admixture and at the same time already influenced by the bour-

---

65   *MECW*, Vol. 24, p. 91.
66   *MECW*, Vol. 24, p. 92.

geoisie'.[67] Moreover, Marx and Engels's 'Circular letter' to Bebel and others forcefully stressed the absolute incompatibility between their own conception and that of other 'pseudo-socialists' like the Lassalleans:

> At the founding of the International we expressly formulated the battle cry: The emancipation of the working class must be achieved by the working class itself. Hence we cannot co-operate with men who say openly that the workers are too uneducated to emancipate themselves, and must first be emancipated from above by philanthropic members of the upper and lower middle classes.[68]

They thus depicted Lassalle as a sort of apologist for 'socialism from above', articulating a position wholly incompatible with any perspective of emancipation. It would thus seem wholly senseless to place Marx side-by-side with Lassalle: in reality, however, the question must be posed in somewhat more complex terms. For example, we must not forget that with the passing of time Marx's awareness of the significance of the state sphere did grow, though not at the cost of losing sight of the international dimension of socialism. This was not Lassallean statism, but nor did he simply dismiss the question in the manner that Bakunin did. There can be no doubt that Lassalle's approach was incompatible with Marx's, but it is likewise true that Marx understood the significance of the specific role of the state in the development of the workers' movement, if not from the same point of view as Lassalle. The Social-Democratic Workers' Party, in whose foundation Marx and Engels had played a decisive role, was, however, at first dominated by the Lassalleans.

This discussion of the state made clear the importance of the question of transition, which was also present in the *Critique of the Gotha Programme*. The transition period would not see the disappearance of political structures or their respective juridical forms, as these were necessary for the 'disarming' of the bourgeoisie: 'these defects are inevitable in the first phase of communist society as it is when it has just emerged after prolonged birthpangs from capitalist society. Right can never be higher than the economic structure of society and its cultural development which this determines'.[69] It did not mean

---

67   *MECW*, Vol. 24, p. 96.
68   *MECW*, Vol. 45, p. 408. See Ragionieri 1968, p. 20: 'Marx and Engels intransigently rejected Lassalle's philosophical idealism and simplifications in the matter of economics, no less than his political strategy and tactics, in which they suspected more than a little concession to Bismarck, German Bonapartism and the "unification from above" of Germany'.
69   *MECW*, Vol. 24, p. 87.

the end of the state, since its 'disciplinary' apparatuses continued to exist.
Marx thus clearly had a point of disagreement with Bakunin, here, considering
impossible any *coup de main* that would *sic et simpliciter* abolish the state:
rather, it would have to be preserved for a certain period. However, it is also
important to add a further consideration: this transition period could not be
conceived in static terms as the simple maintenance of state structures. What
was necessary was to make a sort of 'counter-use' of right, bringing about a
'class' state – and this was far from the same thing as Lassalle's 'people's state'.
In order to understand this moment, which was not still the same thing as the
bourgeois state but did not yet constitute communism, it is necessary to refer
to the concept of the dictatorship of the proletariat:

> Between capitalist and communist society lies the period of the revolu-
> tionary transformation of the one into the other. Corresponding to this is
> also a political transition period in which the state can be nothing but the
> revolutionary dictatorship of the proletariat. Now the programme deals
> neither with this nor with the future state of communist society. Its polit-
> ical demands contain nothing beyond the old democratic litany familiar
> to all: universal suffrage, direct legislation, popular rights, a people's mili-
> tia, etc. They are a mere echo of the bourgeois People's Party ...[70]

Thus emerges Marx's distance from both Bakunin's wish to make the state disappear immediately through a *coup de main*, and the 'people's state' theorised
by Lassalle, in which terms there could be no talk of the dictatorship of the proletariat. Notwithstanding any 'oscillation' between these two thinkers, Marx's
thought entertained a closer relationship with Bakunin, since their common
goal was the abolition of the state. However, it ought to be specified that this
question cannot be interpreted once and for all time, since it constantly inter-
sected with the 'twists and turns' of practice, that is, with specific historical
and political conjunctures. Indeed, as our analysis of clashes within the International demonstrated, each of these thinkers was battling for hegemony. It is
on account of these circumstances that we sometimes get the impression that
Marx's position oscillated, seemingly drawing closer to Lassalle as he criticised
Bakunin, and vice versa.[71] It should not be forgotten that even though Marx
articulated an extremely robust polemic against the Gotha Programme, he did

---

70   *MECW*, Vol. 24, p. 95.

71   Balibar 1997, p. 231 explains that '[p]erhaps we should not be surprised that Marx and
      his loyal supporter Engels, those indefatigable polemicists, ultimately proved unable to
      write an "anti-Lassalle" or an "anti-Bakunin", which would have been far more important

not publish this *Critique* and it only came to press several years after his death, on the initiative of Engels.

We could pose the question of why Marx limited himself to circulating this text among a few socialist confidants of his and decided not to print it, notwithstanding the fact that the Social-Democratic Party was, ultimately, 'his' party, even if strictly speaking he was not its political guide. One of the reasons may have been his fear of creating divisions within the workers' movement, and of taking up a position that many militants would probably not have understood. This consideration can be interpreted as a weakness in Marx's reasoning, or, instead, as a sign of his 'strategic' consciousness of the difficulty of giving a full political explanation of the framework of his *Critique*, with its radical critique of all statism and any form of 'labourism'. Indeed, if we look at the development of the workers' movement in Germany, then is it clear that in fact it was substantially guided by the Lassallean agenda, very far indeed from the platform of Marx's subsequent *Critique of the Gotha Programme*.[72] However, what we can see is that Marx had not only different contingent tactics to Lassalle's, but also a different way of understanding politics, even if he reached this in a tortuous and complicated manner. In order to understand his perspective, particularly with regard to the workers' government and its relationship to the state, it is necessary to study an event of crucial importance: the Paris Commune.

The Paris Commune: A 'Working-Class Government'

The Paris Commune[73] posed the question of working-class government: seeking, that is, to articulate communism not only in its insurrectionary sense, the 'movement that abolishes the present state of things', but also in the capacity to produce a sedimentation of such struggles. Indeed, the Commune exercised an enormous influence on later Marxism, leading to a true and proper 'mythology' of the 1871 revolution. It is necessary to bear in mind not only the specific doubts that Marx had about the Commune, but also the fact that it constituted a con-

---

practically than *Anti-Dühring* or a renewed anti-Proudhon ... If they did not do so, it was because they could not'. In an 'always-moving' 'political game', the only possibility seemed to be 'alternatively identifying with one or the other side of this antithesis'.

72   See Steinberg 1979, pp. 188 et sqq.

73   A good part of Marx's writings on the Commune appear in *MEGA* Vol. I/22 (*MECW*: Vol. 22). Moreover, a sort of anthology of writings on the Commune has recently appeared, with a wide-ranging introduction by Daniel Bensaïd: Marx and Engels 2008.

stant point of reference in the final phase of his *oeuvre*. First of all, the Commune provided a sort of 'condensation' combining his reflections on the International and more generally on working-class political action. Moreover, Marx repeatedly expressed the link between the Commune and the International:

> Our Association is, in fact, nothing but the international bond between the most advanced working men in the various countries of the civilized world.
>
> Wherever, in whatever shape, and under whatever conditions the class struggle obtains any consistency, it is but natural that members of our association should stand in the foreground ... Working men's Paris, with its Commune, will be for ever celebrated as the glorious harbinger of a new society.[74]

It is clear that the International gave its support to the working class in all the situations where its struggles reached a certain intensity, producing earth-shattering effects. The Commune represented a new level of struggle: it was the first time since 1848 that there was a revolutionary explosion in France. Marx asserted the Commune's continuity with the 'gigantic broom of the French Revolution' that 'swept away all [the] relics of bygone times, thus clearing simultaneously the social soil of its last hindrances to the superstructure of the modern State'.[75] Here returned the idea – present throughout Marx's works – that the French Revolution was the 'mother' of all revolutions, the revolution *par excellence*. Though he never dedicated any specific work to this revolution, he returned to it constantly, in an almost obsessive manner.

The Commune, heir to the French Revolution, was posed in direct antithesis to the Empire: 'Imperialism is, at the same time, the most prostitute and the ultimate form of the State power which nascent middle-class society had commenced to elaborate as a means of its own emancipation from feudalism ... The direct antithesis of the Empire was the Commune'.[76] Indeed, despite its rhetoric about being rooted in the peasantry and the working class, the Bonapartist Empire in fact strengthened the mechanisms of the capitalist mode of production, on the basis of the specific characteristics of the French society of the time. In the *Civil War in France* we again find the distinctive traits of Marx's analysis of Bonapartism, according to which the bourgeoisie

---

74   *MECW*, Vol. 22, pp. 354–5. Recently, with a very interesting interpretation of the Commune as a laboratory of political invention: Ross 2015.

75   *MECW*, Vol. 22, p. 328. See Basso 2013.

76   *MECW*, Vol. 22, p. 330.

ceded political power to Bonapartism but, in exchange, fully maintained and in certain senses reinforced its economic power. In this context, there was a further consolidation of the state 'machine': 'The State power, apparently soaring high above society, was at the same time itself the greatest scandal of that society and the very hotbed of all its corruptions'.[77] The Commune was a political form directly counterposed to the state structure, meaning not just the particularly oppressive peculiarities it manifested in the Bonapartist era but also the 'centralised and organised force [Gewalt] of society' that characterised the state as such.[78] In this regard it is worth turning back to what Marx stated in his *Eighteenth Brumaire*: if up until that moment revolutions had strengthened the state machine, it was now, instead, time to smash it. Proletarian revolutions, with their radical critique and constant new breaches, went beyond the limits of bourgeois revolutions.[79] Therefore, 'the working class cannot simply lay hold of the ready-made State machinery, and wield it for its own purposes'.[80]

To return to the distinctive traits of the Commune, it is worth emphasising that:

> The Commune was formed of the municipal councillors, chosen by universal suffrage in the various wards of the town, responsible and revocable at short terms. The majority of its members were naturally working men, of acknowledged representatives of the working class. The Commune was to be a working, not a parliamentary, body, executive and legislative at the same time ... From the members of the Commune downwards, the public service had to be done at workmen's wages ... Not only municipal administration, but the whole initiative hitherto exercised by the State was laid into the hands of the Commune.[81]

In this political form, the separation between executive and legislative powers disappeared, as did the key role of representation. This was now replaced with binding mandates, thus allowing the continual possibility of recalling the Commune's members:

> the Communal Constitution brought the rural producers under the intellectual lead of the central towns of their districts, and there secured to

---

77 Ibid.
78 *MECW*, Vol. 35, p. 739.
79 See Kouvelakis 2003.
80 *MECW*, Vol. 22, p. 328.
81 *MECW*, Vol. 22, p. 331.

them, in the working men, the natural trustees of their interests. – The very existence of the Commune involved, as a matter of course, local municipal liberty, but no longer as a check upon the, now superseded, State power.[82]

This federal structure was not a different articulation of the state, but rather a true and proper 'dissolution' of the state and its apparatuses of discipline. Among other things, if we think back to our previous chapter's discussion of science and a possible 'counter-use' of it, it is interesting to note Marx's statement that under the Commune: 'not only was education made accessible to all, but science itself freed from the fetters which class prejudice and governmental force had imposed upon it'.[83] Despite the lack of any further investigation of this question, more precisely determining its distinctive traits, it is clear that there was here an attempt to articulate a modality of science different from that of the bourgeoisie.

Underlying Marx's whole reflection was the element of class, the reference to the proletariat and its 'explosive' character: 'the French working class is only the advanced guard of the modern proletariat'.[84] If we pick up the thread from the previous section concerning the relationship between 'working class' and 'proletariat' and the rare appearance of the term 'proletariat' in *Capital*, it is worth noting that this word is, conversely, frequently employed in *The Civil War in France*. One of the few places that it is used in *Capital* is in the 1873 'Afterword' to the second edition: that is, in a text heavily influenced by the 1871 Commune. After 1848, the Paris Commune was the event that more than any other 'injected' the element of subjectivity into Marx's framework. In the first draft of *The Civil War in France* Marx referred precisely to this working-class dimension, as he stressed that in the Commune public functions became 'real workmen's functions'.[85] It is, however, necessary to go further, shining a light on the nexus between class and class struggle and between class struggle and dictatorship of the proletariat. As regards the first aspect, it is evident that the Commune did not at all mean an end to the class struggle:

> The Commune does not [do] away with the class struggles, ... but it affords the rational medium in which that class struggle can run through its different phases in the most rational and humane way. It could start

82   *MECW*, Vol. 22, pp. 333–4.

83   *MECW*, Vol. 22, p. 332.

84   *MECW*, Vol. 22, p. 354.

85   *MECW*, Vol. 22, p. 490.

> violent reactions and as [sic] violent revolutions ... The working class
> know that they have to pass through different phases of class struggle.[86]

Thus emerges a political interpretation of the class struggle, one adequate to
various complex situations, even ones that require the use of violence, but
which cannot be reduced to the *coups de main* that the anarchists envisaged.
However, sometimes the term 'proletariat' does not appear by itself in Marx's
writings on the Commune and other matters in this period and afterward;
rather, it appears next to the word 'dictatorship'. Hence the very famous expression 'dictatorship of the proletariat', which has sparked so many polemics.[87] For
example, in Engels's 1891 introduction to *The Civil War* in France, he makes the
following incisive comment: 'Well and good, gentlemen, do you want to know
what this dictatorship looks like? Look at the Paris Commune. That was the
Dictatorship of the Proletariat'.[88]

There is no *consensus omnium* among Marx scholars, on this question:
rather, there is an extremely differentiated range of positions, and the dictatorship of the proletariat is a matter of great controversy. In particular, in recent
years there has been a rise in the tendency either to criticise Marx for the use
of this concept, or else to praise Marx but to 'underestimate' the importance
of the dictatorship of the proletariat. The perspective delineated in the present
work, conversely, tends to see this concept as playing a decisive function in the
late Marx's reflection. We have addressed this question here, in relation to the
Paris Commune, precisely because Marx understood the Commune to represent the dictatorship of the proletariat. However, before anything else we should
specify that the word 'dictatorship' – in Marx's time and in his use of it – had
a very different meaning from the one to which we are accustomed today, as
it substantially indicated the rule of one class over another. At all events, the
conceptual horizon of the nineteenth century recalled the exceptional, temporary character of the *dictator's* role in ancient Rome. Moreover, the element
of dictatorship, if it was associated with the proletariat, underwent a 'change
in meaning' from its bourgeois usage (for example, the dictatorship of Louis

---

86   *MECW*, Vol. 22, p. 491.

87   See Balibar 1976, which, interpreting a substantial continuity between Marx and Lenin's
      approaches in this regard, brings out the structural connection between the dictatorship
      of the proletariat and socialism, as distinct from communism. See, moreover, Draper 1987,
      which has a perspective different from that followed in this work, maintaining that Marx's
      understanding of the dictatorship of the proletariat was almost entirely linked to his
      polemic against the Blanquists.

88   *MECW*, Vol. 27, p. 191.

Bonaparte). There was, therefore, almost no comparison between the two: the dictatorship of the proletariat was not merely a matter of overturning the balance of forces, but of changing its whole coordinates. However, the dictatorship of the proletariat tended not to denote communism true and proper, but rather the transition period, as clearly emerges from the *Critique of the Gotha Programme*:

> Between capitalist and communist society lies the period of the revolutionary transformation of the one into the other. Corresponding to this is also a political transition period in which the state can be nothing but the revolutionary dictatorship of the proletariat ... Now the programme deals neither with this nor with the future state of communist society.[89]

Such reference to a transition characterised by the dictatorship of the working class had already emerged in the early 1850s. Indeed, it had appeared in very similar terms, for example, in the *Class Struggles in France* after the defeat of 1848: thus bearing further testimony to the connection between 1848 and 1871. The dictatorship of the proletariat characterised socialism, the transition period in which the state continued to exist, and not communism, in which the state and its respective class structure disappeared entirely. Here we see Marx's differentiation between socialism, which still bears the 'marks' of the state, and communism. This distinction must be studied in all its ambivalence: on the one hand, it indicates the irreducibility of communism to socialism, and thus sketches out a landscape profoundly different from the order established by twentieth-century 'actually-existing socialism' (not 'actually-existing communism', that is); on the other hand, as against the anarchist idea of immediately making the state disappear through a *coup de main*, it recognises the need for a period in which 'the centralised and organised force [*Gewalt*] of society' is used against the capitalist class.[90] It followed that socialism would not eliminate the state, but rather 'change its meaning', giving it a role different to that which it had previously played. Very significant in this regard was Engels's statement, already cited in our Introduction:

> since the state is merely a transitional institution of which use is made in the struggle, in the revolution, to keep down one's enemies by force, it is utter nonsense to speak of a free people's state; so long as the proletariat

---

89 *MECW*, Vol. 24, p. 95.
90 See Lenin 1932.

still *makes use* of the state, it makes use of it, not for the purpose of freedom, but of keeping down its enemies and, as soon as there can be any question of freedom, the state as such ceases to exist. We would therefore suggest that *Gemeinwesen* ['commonalty'] be universally substituted for *state*; it is a good old German word that can very well do service for the French 'Commune.'[91]

Here forcefully returns the rejection of Lassalle's 'free people's state'. However, a further element also emerges, here: though the transition period is not characterised by freedom, it is a sort of anticipation of the subsequent communism. Very interesting, in this regard, is the fact that Engels uses the term *Gemeinwesen* (homologous to the French *commune*) rather than the word *Staat* to denote this situation. We need not dwell once again on the extraordinarily significant role that this consideration plays throughout Marx's entire work, from his first writings to his last, on the basis of an extremely dense conceptual and political reflection. 'Being in common', *Gemeinwesen*, which is irreducible to the state-form, cannot be defined once and for all; rather, it must continually be articulated within each of the situations in which it is inserted. It is not configured in harmonious terms, but rather as a 'field of forces' that are not immediately compatible and are often even in tension with one another.

In any case, the 'revolutionary dictatorship of the proletariat' had nothing in common with the platform of the Gotha Programme, but rather was counterposed to it. If we assimilate the Commune to the dictatorship of the proletariat, then at first glance the reasons for this association may not seem immediately obvious. Indeed, in many ways the Commune defined itself in anti-centralist terms, on the basis of a sharp critique of bureaucracy and a high regard for autonomy, characterised by almost federalist traits.[92] Moreover, certain already-mentioned aspects of the Commune might lead us to believe that it was less a dictatorship than an expansive form of democracy, without any division between the people and those who exercise public powers. It was not a representative democracy, nor a constitutional democracy based on the division of powers: there was not representation but the imperative mandate, with the possibility of recalling those who did not act in line with the will of the people.[93] Engels observed, however, that even in a democratic republic the state represented a form of domination: 'the state is nothing but a machine for

---

91   *MECW*, Vol. 24, p. 71.
92   See Lefebvre 1965, p. 163.
93   Hobsbawm's analysis in this regard is very apt: 'Marx never used the term "dictatorship" to indicate a specific institutional form of government, but always and only to define

the oppression of one class by another, and indeed in the democratic republic no less than in the monarchy'.[94]

In his definition of the Commune, Marx did not employ the word 'democracy' (which he used in positive terms almost only in his very first writings, such as the *Critique of Hegel's Doctrine of the State*), but rather 'social republic',[95] a political form capable of sustaining the tendency toward emancipation. Marx's whole reflection sought to bring out the 'class' elements of the Commune, its configuration as a 'working-class government':

> it was a thoroughly expansive political form, while all previous forms of government had been emphatically repressive. Its true secret was this. It was essentially a working-class government, the produce of the struggle of the producing against the appropriating class, the political form at last discovered under which to work out the economical emancipation of Labour ... The political rule of the producer cannot coexist with the perpetuation of his social slavery ... With labour emancipated, every man becomes a working man, and productive labour ceases to be a class attribute.[96]

The distinctive trait of the Paris Commune was its expansiveness, its advance beyond existing limits: and such a political process could not be restricted to the French capital alone, but rather had to serve as a model, inspiring other 'Communes'.[97] In any case, here a 'class' dynamic was at work, this expansive-

---

its content ... The only regime that Engels defined as a "dictatorship of the proletariat" (Marx did not do so explicitly) was the Paris Commune, and its characteristics that he emphasised were far from dictatorial (in the literal sense of the term) ... the dictatorship of the proletariat had the task of implementing the mass, democratic transformation of political life at the same time as taking the necessary measures to prevent a counter-revolution by the defeated ruling class' (Hobsbawm 1978, pp. 256–7). See Ricciardi 2001, p. 152: 'The dictatorship of the proletariat, which Marx developed from the nineteenth-century radical-democratic concept of the "people's dictatorship", had to accompany a democratic constitutional process free of the formalism that is integral to modern constitutionalism'. See, moreover, with different approaches, Artous 1999, p. 251; Berger 2003, pp. 29–46; and Screpanti 2007, pp. 150–60, which stresses that this concept 'was intended as a stipulation that would clarify the *social* implications of a true democracy'; Ducange and Fayçal Touati 2010, particularly pp. 79–81.

94 *MECW*, Vol. 27, p. 190.

95 *MECW*, Vol. 22, p. 330.

96 *MECW*, Vol. 22, pp. 334–5.

97 *MECW*, Vol. 22, p. 332: 'The Paris Commune was, of course, to serve as a model to all the

ness taking the form of the dictatorship of the proletariat. At the basis of the Commune was the *conatus* toward emancipation: and we ought constantly to bear in mind that this latter was a 'red thread' throughout Marx's entire reflection, even from his very first texts. For example, 'emancipation' was a key term in his *On the Jewish Question*, where Marx operated a distinction between political emancipation – proper to modernity, in particular the French Revolution – and human emancipation. This latter indicated what he would later term 'communism', capable of transcending the current scenario – but starting from the basis that this present state of affairs had provided, and not by harking back to the past. Far from disappearing, this idea of emancipation continued to play a central role even in the last period of Marx's *oeuvre*, as he linked it to the question of class: that is, the emancipation of the working class, an emancipation that entered into the 'depths' of production. However, his approach in *On the Jewish Question* did not mean to say that human emancipation follows political emancipation in a mechanical series of stages. Rather, there is a continual exchange between the 'social' and the 'political': there is no social movement that is not also political, and vice versa. Marx's goal was to combine the political and economic dimensions (hence, the 'economic emancipation of labour'), unlike the anarchists, who focused on the 'political' but undervalued the 'economic'. He thus sought a political articulation of the workers' 'acting in common', starting from a definite material basis.

In this context, Marx explicitly posed the question of communism, of which the Commune constituted a sort of prefiguration:

> the Commune ... aimed at the expropriation of the expropriators. It wanted to make individual property a truth by transforming the means of production, land and capital, now chiefly the means of enslaving and exploiting labour, into mere instruments of free and associated labour. – But this is Communism, 'impossible' Communism! ... If co-operative production is not to remain a sham and a snare; if it is to supersede the Capitalist system; if united co-operative societies are to regulate national production upon a common plan, thus taking it under their own control, and putting an end to the constant anarchy and periodical convulsions which are the fatality of Capitalist production – what else, gentlemen, would it be but Communism, 'possible' Communism?[98]

---

great industrial centres of France ... the Commune was to be the political form of even the smallest country hamlet ... The rural communes of every district were to administer their common affairs by an assembly of delegates in the central town ...'

98   *MECW*, Vol. 22, p. 335.

Thus emerges the ambivalence, or even ambiguity, that we previously mentioned: on the one hand, as an example of the dictatorship of the proletariat the Commune constituted a 'socialist' phase that thus maintained the state apparatus; on the other hand, it itself incorporated the weakening of this disciplining structure, progressively losing the characteristics of this latter. Rather telling as an example of structures' 'change of meaning' is Marx's use, here, of the term 'co-operation', which in *Capital* is usually employed to refer to the general form of capitalist production. In this passage, conversely, it is conceived as the common terrain – as communism. There is no simple, mechanical succession of phases: rather, the dictatorship of the proletariat presents certain traits that anticipate communism.

To conclude: we cannot pass over in silence a difficult aspect of this question that it would be absurd not to address. Namely, the facts that the Commune lasted for only a short time, was not 'sedimented', and was followed by harsh repression. This does not mean to accept the history of the victors, but nor does the history of the vanquished suffice alone. The Commune played a significant role in Marx's reflection: in the last analysis, after 1848 it was the only concrete example of the dictatorship of the proletariat that Marx and Engels could draw on. At the same time, however, nor can the Commune be used as a sort of trans-historical mode of communism, as if it did not present its own internal problems and contradictions. Marx and Engels themselves in part identified this, commenting 'what a lack of critical attitude is needed to declare the Commune impeccable and infallible'.[99] The international conjuncture favoured such a negative outcome: we need only think of 'the presence of the Prussians in France and their position right before Paris'.[100] Moreover, examining the history of the Commune, it should not be forgotten – as Marx himself recognised – that it was not solely proletarian in character, in the strict sense, since it also made a particular appeal to the so-called middle-class: 'for the first time in history the petty and *moyenne* middle class has openly rallied round the workmen's Revolution, and proclaimed it as the only means of their own salvation and that of France! ... The principal measures taken by the Commune are taken for the salvation of the middle class'.[101] Very telling, in this regard, are Engels's comments on the composition of the Commune in his introduction to a later edition of the *Civil War in France*, written amidst profoundly changed circumstances:

---

99   *MECW*, Vol. 24, p. 18.
100   *MECW*, Vol. 44, p. 137.
101   *MEGA* I/22, p. 63.

> The members of the Commune were divided into a majority, the Blan-
> quists ... and a minority ... chiefly consisting of adherents of the Proud-
> hon school of socialism ... in the economic sphere much was left undone
> which, according to our view today, the Commune ought to have done.
> The hardest thing to understand is certainly the holy awe with which they
> remained standing respectfully outside the gates of the Bank of France[102]

Engels emphasised that, as often happens (and here returns the question of the
'gap' between theory and politics), in reality both the Blanquists and the Proudhonians had not really applied their own theoretical positions in the Commune, and had in many respects disregarded them. As concerns the Blanquists,
it is worth stressing that they conceived of the revolution as a true and proper
'*coup de main*', the fruit of conspiratorial manipulation on the part of revolutionaries, and not the proletariat as a whole. In Marx and Engels's view, such
means of action could not but lead to negative outcomes. Though the Blanquists were theoretically distant from the Bakuninists, they were united by this
positive appraisal of the '*coup de main*'. Moreover, it would be remiss of us not to
note that the Commune – as it came into being historically – presented various
Proudhonian features (for example, the definition of a decentralised structure
and the significant role of the 'artisanal' petty bourgeoisie), more so than Marx
and Engels were ready to admit, for obvious reasons.[103] More generally, beyond Marx's underestimation of the Proudhonians' role, a further problem in
his reading consists in the fact that he lacked any deep class analysis of the
reasons for the Communards' defeat.[104] Engels, in polemic with the anarchists'
total critique of authority, lucidly highlighted the limitations of the Commune:

> It seems to me that the phrases 'authority' and centralisation are much
> abused. I know of nothing more authoritarian than a revolution, and
> when one imposes one's will on others with bombs and rifle bullets, as
> in every revolution, it seems to me one performs an authoritarian act. It

---

102   *MECW*, Vol. 27, p. 187.

103   See Rougerie 1971 and Rougerie (ed.) 1964, rightly insisting on the Proudhonian parentage
      of various aspects of the Commune.

104   Althusser 2006, p. 50: 'Yet there is something in his analysis of the Commune that leaves
      us unsatisfied: his virtual silence when it comes to analysing the balance of class forces in
      France, and, especially, the forms and conditions of the *bourgeois class struggle*, hence
      the class conditions surrounding the Communards' defeat ... And how is it that Marx
      also made no attempt to understand what was happening on the *ideological plane in the
      Communards' case* ...?'

was the lack of centralisation and authority that cost the life of the Paris Commune[105]

Marx highlighted the 'decency' of the Commune's actions – not wanting to 'start the civil war' – and the Central Committee's hurry, through 'conscientious scruples' and 'honourable' conduct, too quickly to surrender its power in a mad rush to 'make way for the Commune'.[106]

> You may, perhaps, refer me to the Paris Commune but, aside from the fact that this was merely an uprising of one city in exceptional circumstances, the majority of the Commune was in no sense socialist, nor could it have been[107]

> There was much misunderstanding about the Commune. The Commune could not found a new form of class government. In destroying the existing conditions of oppression by transferring all the means of labor to the productive laborer, and thereby compelling every able-bodied individual to work for a living, the only base for class rule and oppression would be removed. But before such a change could be effected a proletarian dictatorship would become necessary, and the first condition of that was a proletarian army[108]

Looking back on the Commune, Marx and Engels's enthusiasm was supplemented by a series of considerations on its limitations and thus the factors that had contributed to its failure. This was not, therefore, a matter of either exalting the historical Commune in the strict sense (since they did not capture its substantially Proudhonian character), or conceiving it as a sort of *passe-partout* philosophical model. Rather, the Commune had to be 'worked with' politically, albeit starting from an analysis of the specific present situation. From Marx's analyses of the shortcomings of the Commune cited above, there emerge the

---

105   *MECW*, Vol. 44, p. 295.
106   *MECW*, Vol. 44, p. 132. See Barot 2011, p. 84.
107   *MECW*, Vol. 46, p. 66.
108   *MECW*, Vol. 22, p. 634. In certain respects Badiou 2003's reading of this question is problematic. Badiou's text has the notable merit of seeking to 'revive' theoretically the ambivalent experience of the Commune, not reducing it to a past event to be either rejected or exalted. But his idea of the Commune's radical otherness with respect to democracy and 'the Left' creates a series of difficulties, as should be clear from the above discussion.

outlines of a scenario that could only come into being in the twentieth century, after Marx and Engels's deaths: namely, a proletarian revolution based on the dictatorship of the proletariat, earth-shattering in character.[109] This brings out a consideration of very great importance, namely Marx's continual rectification (which is not to say self-critique) of his own perspective: politics had to be continually recalibrated, starting from the new conjuncture being defined at that particular moment.

The 'Metamorphous' Character of Politics: The Correction of the *Manifesto*

At work in Marx is a logic of specific determination, based on a sort of 'thinking in the conjuncture': it is impossible to hypostatise any theoretical schema that is valid for all cases and all circumstances, in isolation from the given historical and geographical context.[110] It is particularly interesting to compare the situation in 1848 and that of the 1860s and 1870s, thus examining the question of the legacy of the *Communist Manifesto*.[111] In the first place, it is necessary always to bear in mind that the *Manifesto* reflects an expansive phase in which it was imagined possible to establish a European – if not even worldwide – revolutionary platform. An emancipatory scenario seemed immediately possible, in opposition to the 'Holy Alliance' of capital. If the French Revolution had represented the 'mother' of all revolutions – but was in many senses 'only' a bourgeois revolution – then the task now at hand was to bring about history's first proletarian revolution, in which the proletariat would be the revolutionary subject. Indeed, *The Class Struggles in France* gave account of the presence, during Paris's June Days, of the first true and proper class struggle between the bourgeoisie and the proletariat. Unfortunately, however ('Woe to the June uprising!'), this did not lead to the much-awaited proletarian revolution. Thus Marx had to 're-elaborate' his considerations on the 1848

---

109   See Negri 1992, pp. 306–9.

110   See, on the status of politics, the approaches of Maguire 1978, who rightly underlines the 'non-systematic' character of Marx's thematisation: 'Marx did not produce a general theory of politics, any more than he produced a general theory of human history' (p. 221); Gilbert 1981, which, with particular reference to his 1840s writings, highlights the tensions internal to communist politics, in an anti-deterministic perspective; Barbier 1992, which insists in particular on the ambiguity in Marx's engagement with the question of the state; Texier 1998; Borrelli 2000; Mezzadra and Ricciardi 2002.

111   See Rossanda (ed.) 2000.

defeat, with particular reference to the country in which he had invested so many hopes, namely France. The repression and its consequences were extremely heavy: this was the onset of Bonapartism.

Marx's reflection did not pass over 'in silence' 1848 and the reconfiguration of Europe, particularly Bonapartism; on the contrary, all this compelled him to mount a substantial rearticulation of his political analysis, since certain considerations that had come to light in 1848 and been condensed in the *Manifesto* would have to be revisited. For example, the role of the state could no longer be reduced to that of the 'executive committee of the bourgeoisie'. The events that followed 1848 'complicated' the picture, making it ever more difficult to work through this problem solely in terms of the immediate derivation of the state from the interests of the bourgeois class. With Bonapartism there emerged the – at least partial – autonomy of the state with respect to the bourgeoisie.[112] With the passing of time, Marx sought to develop a more attentive analysis of the phenomenon of nationalism, which could not be dismissed as a sort of epiphenomenon of class dynamics. Moreover, as we saw in our discussion of *Capital*, though the state does serve in function of the interests of the capitalist class, it is also a terrain of struggle. After all, the English working class sought to reduce the length of the working day by obtaining state legislation to this effect. It is worth specifying that the new considerations here introduced do not deny the structural character of the link between the state and the capitalist class, but they do nonetheless complicate the question in various ways. Not least among them, the drum often beaten by certain Marxists (Gramsci, for example)[113] noting the centrality of the state: capital has a very great need for the state for the reproduction of its own system of exploitation. Finally, with regard to the French case, it must not be forgotten that the period of the French Empire was characterised by considerable capitalist development, bearing witness to the fact that the problematisation of the specific characteristics of the state did not put in question its capitalist valence.

It is necessary, however, to examine also the subjective side of this question, since the 1848 defeat led to a rearticulation of proletarian politics. The fact that the fate of the revolution became more uncertain did not in any sense mean that this question disappeared from view. Even in the *Eighteenth Brumaire*,

---

See Karatani 2003, pp. 142–51.

113   Gramsci 1971, pp. 159–60: 'since in actual reality civil society and State are one and the same, it must be made clear that *laissez-faire* too is a form of state "regulation", introduced and maintained by legislative and coercive means. It is a deliberate policy, conscious of its own ends, and not the spontaneous, automatic expression of economic facts'. See P. Thomas 2009, pp. 159–95.

marked though it was by Marx's awareness of the significance of the 1848 defeat and the subsequent advent of Bonapartism, revolution played a crucial role in his reflection:

> But the revolution is thorough. It is still journeying through purgatory. It does its work methodically. By December 2, 1851 it had completed one half of its preparatory work; it is now completing the other half. First it perfected the parliamentary power, in order to be able to overthrow it. Now that it has attained this, it perfects the executive power ... And when it has done this second half of its preliminary work, Europe will leap from its seat and exultantly exclaim: Well burrowed, old mole![114]

In the *Eighteenth Brumaire* Marx effected a differentiation between bourgeois revolutions, such as had played out up to that moment, and the possible proletarian revolution of the future. This latter would attempt to 'break' the state machine: the idea of the extinction of the state was inadequate, since it would not disappear all by itself, through the full playing out of the contradictions of capital. Rather, there had to be a political break. In this sense there emerged a point of close connection with the anarchists and their goal of destroying the state.

Another aspect in continuity with the *Manifesto* was the fact that Marx did not abandon the internationalist platform that had animated that earlier text. Rather, his discussion of the International brought to light his renewed awareness of the need for working-class political action to take to the international plane, without which there could be no talk of communism. This international dimension ought not be interpreted in counterposition to the national plane, since the working-class takes its first organisational step at the national level: the first manifestation of its political action. Moreover, Marx and Engels could not but take account of the concrete situation of the time, in particular in Germany, where significant nationwide working-class organisations had emerged. It ought not be forgotten that already in the *Manifesto* they had underlined the importance of the national dimension as the first terrain on which the working-class struggle emerges. In their texts on the International as elsewhere there were some near-word for word quotations from the *Manifesto*, bearing witness to the fact that Marx and Engels did not consider this text to be simply 'outmoded'.

---

114   *MECW*, Vol. 11, p. 185.

We can use the term 'rectification' to denote the relationship between the *Manifesto* and Marx's political reflection in his final phase, thus giving account of the complex continuity-discontinuity in his reasoning.[115] This was not purely a process of intellectual maturation: rather, it was the outcome of a close engagement with contingent political events and the shifting grounds on which they took place. Therefore, it was primarily history and politics, and not some abstract theoretical construction, which produced significant changes in Marx's perspective. In the series of prefaces to the *Manifesto* that Marx and Engels produced over the years, they made clear some of the limitations of this text – or rather, insisted on the fact that it ought not to be understood as rigid and immutable. The *Manifesto* was itself open to contestation, necessary to interpret anew in each scenario in accordance with the shifts in the international conjuncture and the corresponding political struggle. For example, in the preface to the 1872 German edition Marx and Engels emphasised that 'the gigantic strides of modern industry', as well as the 'practical experience' of the 'February revolution, and then, still more, in the Paris Commune' had shown that the programme contained in the *Manifesto* had 'in some details become antiquated'.[116] Of no little significance, with regard to the comment that the *Manifesto* had become somewhat dated, is the fact that in the passage just cited Marx and Engels evoked two crucial historical situations to which we have already referred, namely 1848 in France and the Paris Commune. Also of interest is another preface – in the second Russian edition – in which Marx emphasises that Russia and the United States were absent from this text. These were two countries that played a fundamental role in the global chess-game of the 1860s and 1870s, and were thus of some importance for understanding the dynamic of class subjectivity.

An awareness of the need to make alterations did not, however, mean questioning the fundamental coordinates of the *Manifesto*. This text ought not be hypostatised, but rather rearticulated politically on the basis of the new scenario coming into formation: in Marx there was a 'singular' logic, continually commensurate with the specific situation in its immanent development, but, at the same time, also in critical tension with it. Marx's 'thinking in the conjuncture', and thus the continual rectification of his political trajectory, did not mean toning down the revolutionary valence of his perspective. In his writings on the International as in those concerning the Commune (which represented a significant political 'investment' for the International) the theme of working-

---

115   Cf. Balibar 1974.
116   *MECW*, Vol. 23, p. 175.

class political action to 'abolish the present state of things' remained central. At the basis of his reflection was the search for working-class emancipation, its capacity to give rise to a new 'acting in common'. This political perspective could not be fulfilled by a clique, but rather had to be inscribed in working-class practice: 'the emancipation of the working classes must be conquered by the working classes themselves'.[117] In the last phase of Marx's (and Engels's) production, emphasis on emancipation was closely connected to the appraisal of proletarian politics as something heterogeneous from bourgeois politics.

There was a degree of ambivalence in Marx – which could lead to ambiguity – with respect to the status of politics.[118] Indeed, it often seems that he was making a total critique of politics, such as to outline a communist scenario in which there was no politics – thus suggesting that politics is structurally functional to the logic of one class ruling over another. Certainly such a perspective does exist in Marx; but it is also doubtless true that even though Marx wished to distinguish between bourgeois and proletarian politics, he does sometimes risk maintaining the fundamental 'grammar' of the former, albeit overturning its power relations. Moreover, sometimes it seems that even though Marx wanted to mark the distance between proletarian and bourgeois revolution, he surreptitiously used the bourgeois revolution *par excellence* – the French Revolution – as a model for proletarian revolution.[119] The ambivalence (or even ambiguity) of the political dimension could not be systematically solved by theory in the narrow sense, since it was continually subject to the 'twists and turns' of practice. That is, practice continually re-posed the link but also possible 'separation' between theory and politics, as politics could never be fully deduced from some all-embracing theoretical schema. Here we see again the oft-mentioned priority of the Machiavellian 'real truth of the matter' [*verità effettuale della cosa*] over thought.

Notwithstanding any such possible depreciation of politics, it is necessary to bear in mind that from the *Manifesto* onward Marx's critique was not directed against politics, but rather political domination – that is, the rule of one class over another, a specific element of the capitalist mode of production. To uphold such a position is not to say that it is impossible to identify 'another' politics. Proof of this is the fact that in Marx and Engels's polemic with the anarchists one of the most important elements of their elaboration is the value they ascribe to working-class political action: 'The ass [Bakunin] has not even seen

---

117   *MECW*, Vol. 21, p. 332.
118   See Balibar, Luporini and Tosel 1979.
119   See Krahl 1971, which rightly emphasises that for Marx the French Revolution was always a model for the future proletarian revolution, whether explicitly or implicitly.

that every class movement as a class movement, is necessarily and was always a political movement'.[120] Elsewhere, Engels argues:

> The workers' party already exists as a political party in most countries. It is not up to us to ruin it by preaching abstention ... Especially in the aftermath of the Paris Commune, which placed the political action of the proletariat on the agenda, abstention is quite impossible ... We seek the abolition of Classes. What is the means of achieving it? The political domination of the proletariat. And when everyone is agreed on that, we are asked not to get involved in politics! All abstentionists call themselves revolutionaries, even revolutionaries par excellence. But revolution is the supreme act of politics; whoever wants it must also want the means, political action, which prepares for it, which gives the workers the education for revolution ... But the politics which are needed are working class politics; the workers' party must be constituted not as the tail of some bourgeois party ...[121]

This reflection condensed various aspects of Marx and Engels's previous discussion of politics: the rejection of abstentionism, in favour of working-class political action; revolution as the supreme act of politics; and the non-homology of proletarian and bourgeois politics.[122] These issues had to be inserted within the question of the so-called transition phase, in which there emerged an unstable dialectic between political movement and political power:

> The political movement of the working class naturally has as its final object the conquest of political power for this class, and this requires, of course, a previous organisation of the working class ... which arises from the economic struggles themselves. But on the other hand, every movement in which the working class comes out as a class against the ruling classes and tries to coerce them by pressure from without is a political movement. For instance, the attempt in a particular factory, or even in a particular trade, to force a shorter working day out of the individual capitalists by strikes, etc., is a purely economic movement. The movement to force through an eight-hour law, etc., however, is a political movement. And in this way, out of the separate economic movements of

---

120   *MECW*, Vol. 43, p. 491.
121   *MECW*, Vol. 22, p. 417.
122   See Lefort 1978.

the workers there grows up everywhere a political movement, that is to say a movement of the class, with the object of achieving its interests in a general form, in a form possessing general, socially binding force.[123]

On the basis of a clear differentiation between the merely trade-union sphere and the political one (useful even for understanding the question of the reduction of the working day), Marx identified the intersection of the political and economic dimensions as a distinctive trait of working-class action. Its purpose was defined by its capacity to impose its own interests in a generalised manner: this was a more complex way of rearticulating the theme, already present in Marx's first texts, of the proletariat-as-'partial universal', directed toward a universal goal but on the basis of a determinate portion of society. Therefore, Marx's schema was class – class struggle – political movement – political party: in the last instance, class is not possible without class struggle, and this latter brings a political movement into being, leading to the recognition that a political party is necessary – an organisation capable of making struggles effective and preventing the dispersion of their efforts. However, it is necessary to bear in mind that there is always a 'remainder': these stages never follow in mechanical succession, whether because the political party is often unable to 'capture' the full radicalism of the political movement,[124] or because the political movement does not only belong to the working class in the strict sense but also to the multitudes – which are partly distinct from the working class, and which, however difficult they may find it to achieve organisational 'condensation', can nonetheless play an earth-shattering role.[125]

This reference to the question of political power, and thus to the continued existence of the state, brings us back to our earlier considerations regarding the dictatorship of the proletariat *qua* specific element of socialism, a constitutively ambiguous one. On the one hand emerges the 'concentrated and organised force of society', the state, with its class substratum; on the other,

---

123 *MECW*, Vol. 44, p. 258.

124 Cf. Sartre 1991. The *Critique of Dialectical Reason*'s theses on the relationship of group to party are well summarised in Sartre 1972b. I share in Sartre's stress on the incipient risk of the 'sclerotisation' of the party, namely its incapacity to keep alive the subjective vitality of the mass. At the same time, however, it is difficult to think this latter politically in the absence of an organisation.

125 Without here being able to delve into the complex theme of the relationship between the working class and the multitude, it is worth referring to Negri's works addressing this latter (in particular Negri 1992, and Hardt and Negri 2001 and 2010) as well as the partially different stance in Virno 2002.

it contains a sort of prefiguration of what will later become communism, since the relations among individuals begin to be configured differently to the manner in which they developed under the capitalist mode of production: it is a sort of 'non-state state'. The political change is practiced starting from the existing relations of force, from the already-operational institutions, but in critical tension with respect to them. Though we can agree in part with Marx's polemic against the anarchists' *coup de main* and the correlated idea of the immediate disappearance of the state, the question of the modalities of transition (if it is a transition) to communism presents certain difficulties.

Communism and the 'Totally Developed Individual': A Scenario Free of Fetishism?

At the end of this search, we can identify in Marx two different modalities of interpreting the question of communism. The first, to invoke the definition in the *German Ideology*, is that of the 'real movement which abolishes the present state of things': a practice of struggle capable of achieving a generalised valence. The second modality consists of understanding communism to mean communist society, the 'realm of freedom' (to take the expression used in *Capital* Volume III): so not only a movement, but also a political organisation. The first usage is fundamental, indicating the permanent tendency of the class struggle. This 'movementist' tension cannot be expunged from Marx's reflection: as he made clear already in the *Manifesto*, the struggle begins with the very existence of the proletariat. In the last instance, for Marx, it is in the class struggle that classes come into being: their movement is thus central, denoting an inexorable dynamism directed toward a radical challenge to the existing order. There is a continual 'exchange' between the social and political dimensions: there is no political movement without a social substratum, and conversely there is no purely social movement, since, from 1848 onward, all social movements had an immediately political connotation. Thus the task at hand was to bring about a proletarian revolution, taking this earth-shattering exchange between the 'social' and the 'political' to its full conclusion. In this scenario, the dictatorship of the proletariat would be crucial. But at this point, it is necessary to pose ourselves the question of how to go beyond this horizon: so as to say, how to 'establish' the *jacquerie*. In the terminology of the late Marx, the problem was the transition from socialism to communism.

We thus arrive at the second meaning of communism. First of all, it is worth bearing in mind our previous discussion of the ambivalence of socialism, a sort of 'non-state state': communism is not some absolute 'leap' with unfathomable origins. But even if communism does not appear out of the blue, it is however posed in terms of discontinuity with respect to the capitalist horizon that preceded it: communism (not socialism) is an alternative to capitalism.[126] It is, however, worth emphasising that however much Marx's *oeuvre* was continually traversed by the *conatus* toward communism, his references to communist society were rather sporadic. This is only apparently paradoxical, if we consider the fact that Marx did not want to 'write recipes for the cookbooks of the future': a detailed description of future communism would have risked outlining a scenario wholly decoupled from the actual material conditions. There is no question, here, of counterposing realism and utopianism, since the former is also ideological in character, and, as we saw in our discussion of fetishism, presupposes that what appears to be so is identical with the real, confusing appearance and essence. The 'separation' between these two planes is, indeed, a distinctive trait of Marx's critique of classical political economy. Moreover, certain considerations that are often defined as 'utopian' in fact play a significant role in Marx's reflection, when they are conceived as an inexorable tendency toward the realisation of human capacities and faculties beyond the productive sphere, on the basis of an anti-economistic vision.

Two passages of *Capital* are particularly significant with regard to Marx's communism, one in Volume I and the other in Volume III. In the first case, part of the section dedicated to fetishism, after referring to historical examples

---

126   In recent years, a far-reaching debate has developed on the 'idea of communism', based on the attempt to appraise communism beyond the terms of the historical experience of actually-existing socialism, thus encouraging a differentiation between communism and socialism. Very different positions have emerged on the basis of this apt common denominator: in our view, the most relevant are those of Negri and Hardt, centring around the constitutive power of the 'commonwealth', and on the other hand, those of Badiou and Žižek. Other significant, more eccentric readings include those of Rancière, based on a democratic *pathos*, and Nancy, with what is in some regards a 'theoreticist' framework. Without being able to delve into each and every articulation of this problem, we will limit ourselves to emphasising that the reasoning outlined in this chapter does not strike the same tone as Badiou's 'philosophical' and 'Platonist' approach, which is built around communism as an Idea, counterposed to the course of history. On the contrary, in a materialist perspective communism is posed not as an Idea, but as a movement and an organisation and institution, based on a specific historical and political practice taking place in determinate circumstances. See Douzinas and Žižek (eds.) 2011 (the outcome of a 2009 seminar in London); Badiou and Žižek (eds.) 2011 (the outcome of a 2010 seminar in Berlin); and AAVV 2010 (a monographic issue of the journal *Actuel Marx*). See moreover, with a perspective looking to appraise differentiated singularities, Balibar 2000.

of precapitalist forms and the capitalist mode of production, Marx comes to examine communism:

> Let us now picture to ourselves ... a community [*Verein*] of free individuals, carrying on their work with the means of production in common [*gemeinschaftlichen*], in which the labour power of all the different individuals is consciously applied as the combined labour power of the community ... Labour time would, in that case, play a double part. Its apportionment in accordance with a definite social plan maintains the proper proportion between the different kinds of work to be done and the various wants of the community. On the other hand, it also serves as a measure of the portion of the common labour borne by each individual ... The social relations of the individual producers, with regard both to their labour and to its products, are in this case perfectly simple and intelligible, and that with regard not only to production but also to distribution ... The life-process of society, which is based on the process of material production, does not strip off its mystical veil until it is treated as production by freely associated men, and is consciously regulated by them in accordance with a settled plan. This, however, demands for society a certain material ground-work or set of conditions of existence[127]

The reference to the 'community of free individuals' stands in continuity with Marx's previous work: think of the 'real community' of the *German Ideology* or the 'association' of the *Communist Manifesto*. He is outlining a sort of collective 'Robinson' whose determinations are not atomistic but social, a 'social' that is not conceived in opposition to the 'individual': even labour time reflects the mutual implication of the 'individual' and the 'social'. Communism cannot be understood either as individualism or organicism, but instead as the form capable of politically working through the connections among differentiated singularities. This means articulating the common with the singular not by way of subsumption (as in the capitalist mode of production) but on the basis of co-operation among individuals, thus empowering their individual faculties.

It is, however, necessary to highlight a difficulty that the above-cited passage poses, where it refers to simple and transparent social relations. The problematic aspect lies in the fact that it risks posing communism in terms of perfect transparency: communism thus sometimes appears as a site free of contradictions and conflicts. This approach can, in fact, lead us into a vicious circle.

---

127   *MECW*, Vol. 35, pp. 89–90.

SUBJECTIVITY AND CLASS: THE SPACE OF POLITICS

To pick up again on the theme addressed in the first chapter, sometimes it seems that communism is understood to mean non-fetishism, as if it were possible to remove all screens and barriers of any kind between individuals and things. This conception is not only unrealistic but also hardly desirable: a society without conflicts would mean a lack of dynamism and tension toward change. Marx's trajectory is not, however, reducible to this simplistic critique of capitalist fetishism, given that he also attempted to articulate politically the overcoming of the present situation. Communism is not in any way homologous to the capitalist system, and nor does it constitute a mechanically developing outcome of its contradictions. Moreover, the situation founded on the associated individuals' common control does not necessarily imply either bureaucratic 'ossification' or an elimination of conflicts, a 'pacifying' vision.

To complete this line of argument, *Capital* Volume III's thematisation of communism as the 'realm of freedom' appears to be of some significance:

> In fact, the realm of freedom actually begins only where labour which is determined by necessity and mundane considerations ceases; thus in the very nature of things it lies beyond the sphere of actual material production. Freedom in this field can only consist in socialised man, the associated producers, rationally regulating their interchange with Nature, bringing it under their common control, instead of being ruled by it as by the blind forces of Nature; and achieving this with the least expenditure of energy and under conditions most favourable to, and worthy of, their human nature. But it nonetheless still remains a realm of necessity. Beyond it begins that development of human energy which is an end in itself, the true realm of freedom, which, however, can blossom forth only with this realm of necessity as its basis. The shortening of the working day is its basic prerequisite.[128]

Certainly, here some of the problems noted in the course of the present work again return, in particular the delineation of an excessively linear scenario and the risk of a too-easy dialectical 'evolution' from the realm of necessity to the realm of freedom. But the passage goes further than such an approach, in that it poses the fundamental question of how to think the communist society of the future: it is in sharp discontinuity with respect to the capitalist present, but at the same time, it starts out from the material conditions in which it is inscribed, thus not in total isolation from the 'realm of necessity'. In this sense,

---

128   *MECW*, Vol. 37, p. 807.

there can be no one way of thinking communism that is valid for all historical epochs and geographical situations, and thus decoupled from the present conjuncture. To uphold such a position does not mean to say that we cannot think of determinate distinctive traits of communism as a radical alternative to capitalism; and certainly two among these are a full understanding of the global dimension of the struggle – and thus the challenge to the state-form and any communitarianism functional to it – and the critique of private property.

It is worth noting, however, that this destitution of private property over the means of production does not mean a negation of individual property, but rather presupposes a sharp differentiation between these two elements, as forcefully emerges from the conclusion to *Capital* Volume I. Underlying the passage cited above, and indeed Marx's entire production, is the tendency toward individual realisation, in counterposition to the estrangement entailed in the capitalist system. This means bringing about an 'association of free individuals', in which, as the *Manifesto* states, 'the free development of each is the condition for the free development of all'.[129] Moreover, the expression 'realm of freedom' appears in *Capital* precisely in order to indicate that this individual *conatus* is constitutive of communism. In the first volume of *Capital*, Marx emphasises that it is necessary 'to replace the detail-worker of to-day [*Teilindividuum*], crippled by life-long repetition of one and the same trivial operation, and thus reduced to the mere fragment of a man, by the fully developed individual [*das total entwickelte Individuum*], fit for a variety of labours, ready to face any change of production, and to whom the different social functions he performs, are but so many modes of giving free scope to his own natural and acquired powers'.[130] Even if Marx does run the risk of outlining a situation free of contradictions and characterised by total individual realisation, his reflection cannot be reduced to this framework only. Rather, it is also pervaded by the quest to fulfil individual workers' faculties, seeking to find a place for these within the realm of freedom, which stands in discontinuity with respect to the capitalist older, in which individuals are the 'other face' of the social power materialised in money. This leaves open the question of who the communists are in the present scenario, and what are the elements that will gather these subjectivities and adequate them to the 'movement as a whole'.

At the basis of Marx's perspective is the attempt to go beyond the capitalist mode of production, along with the fetishism (which does not mean unreality or mere mystification) characteristic of this system, and thus also the specific,

129 *MECW*, Vol. 6, p. 506.
130 *MECW*, Vol. 35, pp. 490–1.

historically determinate modality that is wage labour: communism is not distinguished by a generalisation and democratisation of this latter, but on the contrary represents its abolition. Even if we lack any detailed indications in this regard, the element that is not eliminated is *Gemeinwesen* – this no longer being the spectral *Gemeinwesen* of money, but a 'being in common' which consists in a sociality different to that which serves the dominion of capital. A proletarian politics, being a politics of transformation, is connected with the struggles waged in order to change working conditions, and the first 'traces' of communism already start to emerge in these struggles: but at the same time, it also goes beyond this horizon. Thus communism appears not as the necessary outcome of the historical process, nor as a dialectical 'negation of the negation', but rather as an open question for the future. It is an attempt to articulate new forms of social relations, combining the antagonistic character of the movement and awareness of the need for an order in which there do exist elements of authority, but not according to a static hierarchy, and in which the acting in common of workers' singularities can be 'condensed' politically in a manner adequate to their needs and capacities. In the fight for emancipation there emerges an anthropological dynamic: this is not connected to any sort of abstract study of human nature, but rather concerns the determinate 'corporeality, or the living person' of the worker.

Conclusion

This study has brought out the centrality of the question of the common in Marx's reflection, from *Capital* to his last texts. In some aspects, this line of inquiry develops the landscape that we depicted in the first book, also appearing in Brill's *Historical Materialism* series, entitled *Marx and Singularity. From the Early Writings to the 'Grundrisse'*. This does not mean that *Marx and the Common* is strictly dependent on the previous text; rather, it is a stand-alone work. In any case, the element of continuity between the two books has a chronological dimension as well as a more properly theoretical one. From the chronological point of view, while the first book went up to the *Grundrisse*, the present study begins from the 1860s: the two works thus together 'cover' the whole of Marx's trajectory. But to note the unitary character of Marx's discourse, arguing that we cannot speak of 'two Marxes' (the 'young' Marx and the 'mature' Marx) does not mean denying that within Marx's trajectory there were not just rearticulations of his positions but also a series of internal fractures. These latter are not reducible to a sort of intellectual reconsideration, since they were continually traversed by the 'twists and turns' of practice. With this consideration, we have already passed from the chronological plane to a theoretical-political one. If *Marx and Singularity* presented singularity as a key concept, conceiving communism as the attempt to allow individual realisation, then *Marx and the Common* is based precisely on the need to capture what it is that associates these singularities and thus produces subjectivities, starting from a dynamic vision that is rooted in the sphere of action.

This theme can be inserted within the present-day debate on the common (or commonwealth) and on the commons (without identifying the two), though Marx's case is both specific and complex in its articulation. Indeed, the question of the common plays out on various planes: and these planes must be not only borne in mind but also considered in distinction from one another, to avoid both conceptual and political confusion. Across Marx's whole work, but particularly in his last period, we find various different usages of 'common': think, for example, of elements such as community, the rural commune, and the (Paris) Commune. In general, it is worth avoiding a conflation among these concepts, or making them immediately overlap with communism: the present work does, however, interpret the common starting from this latter. In the first place, communism does not coincide with the community of the present, which is bound up with the state-form, and thus necessarily means the physical and metaphorical delimitation of a territory based on determinate disciplining mechanisms. Marx's position in this regard presents a series of difficulties, as is clear if we look at the question of the so-called transition period between capitalism and communism, through the proletariat assuming the functions of state power. The anarchists emphasised this problem, particularly Bakunin (among others), who forcefully polemicised against Marx's 'statism'. In reality, despite Marx's complex and never resolved relationship with the state sphere (many people over the years have maintained that there was no true and proper theory of the state in Marx), it seems to us that there is no doubt that for Marx, communism meant going beyond the state. Moreover, communism is distinguished from socialism precisely on account of the fact that it does not bear the marks of statehood, and thus cannot be interpreted in terms of 'community', given that the present community is functional to the state-form. It is worth noting that after the *German Ideology*, Marx no longer employed the term 'community' [*Gemeinschaft*] to denote communism, instead using the term 'association' [*Verein*] allowing him to give greater account of a non-'holistic' means of articulating political discourse. The whole priority that he gave to the individual dimension, as studied in *Marx and Singularity*, pointed precisely in this direction. Significant in this regard, albeit in a different conceptual and political context, is Sartre's expression 'the universal singular'. In any case, when it comes to the 'grammar' of the common, the reference to the other elements mentioned above, in particular the rural commune and the Paris Commune, presents very complex characteristics and is wholly irreducible to an abstract vision decoupled from an engagement with history and politics.

As for the rural commune [*Gemeinde*], the 'late' Marx went beyond the level of his previous analysis, for example the section on 'Precapitalist forms' in the *Grundrisse*, but also, in some regards, the analysis in *Capital*. Or better, Marx stuck by an element that characterised the whole of his work, namely his refusal to idealise pre-modern structures like communal property that had been eroded by the capitalist mode of production. In this sense, communism cannot be understood as being the restoration of a past precapitalist order, this latter being static and hierarchical. But the picture is still more complicated. Indeed, the 'final' Marx, in which extracts on the natural sciences played a significant role, in particular (as regards the themes addressed in the present work) his so-called *Ethnological Notebooks*, problematised his previous studies of the relationship between precapitalist forms and capitalism, avoiding the idea of a linear historical succession based on a too-simplistic critique of the communities of the past, interpreted *sic et simpliciter* as being 'backward'. But, still further, he represented the capitalist mode of production in a more complex manner, as it is not entirely solid or 'monolithic' in character; on the contrary, internally it is extremely articulated. Indeed, capitalism has not developed everywhere in the same way, and thus there are differentiated – if not centrifugal – situations within the 'world system', which mark out a complex landscape. The schema of *Capital*, which is substantially 'tailored' to the English model (even if there are very telling references to extra-European situations, particularly in the notes), has to be reconsidered, even going beyond Marx, on the basis of this articulation. Moreover, in the last phase of Marx's production his interest for extra-European situations grew, or in any case those outside of Western Europe. Particularly important, in this regard, is his reference to the Russian commune and the possibility that it afforded of passing directly to communism without having to undergo the 'labour pains' of capitalism. The task at hand is not so much to provide an answer to this question (moreover, Marx's position is rather uncertain and indeterminate), as much as to rearticulate the theme – of great current relevance – of the relationship between capitalism and communism within a global perspective, and not a horizon limited to Western Europe. Moreover, it should not be forgotten that this problem cannot be addressed on an abstractly theoretical plane, since it is directly political in character.

Again, here, emerges the question of politics *sans phrases*, which is not simply derived from some pre-determined theory. Instead, it is based on an intersection but also a possible tension among these planes. And thus we arrive at another, immediately political dimension of the 'common': the Paris Commune. After showing initial scepticism, Marx 'invested' a great deal in the Commune, a 'possible communism', the only concrete historical example of the dictatorship of the proletariat and first attempt to bring about a working-class government. Here he rearticulates the schema of revolution delineated in the *Manifesto of the Communist Party*. In any case, the 'late Marx' neither considered the Commune as a new model, endowed with a trans-historical character, nor rejected it as eccentric with respect to the scenario prefigured in the *Manifesto*, but rather set 'rectification' of the *Manifesto* as his theoretical-political procedure: 'rectification' meaning neither auto-critique nor the mechanical reproposition of an immutable schema. As became clear also in my previous work *Marx and Singularity*, here we have a sort of 'thinking in the conjuncture' starting from political practice in its singularity and irreducibility to any all-embracing approach.

But the other 'face' of Marx's reflection, in addition to the 'conjunctural' dimension, is his recognition of the need for a scientific articulation. Without the element of abstraction, it is impossible to develop a critique of political economy, since this is inevitably of general significance and stands above the multiplicity of specific situations emerging amidst continual historical and geographical variations. Moreover, the critique of political economy proved asymmetrical with respect to classical political economy on account of the fact that it grasped the non-coincidence of essence and appearance: all Marx's analysis of fetishism (in many regards, a reformulation and a 'complication' of the question of ideology) brings into relief the opacity of the capitalist mode of production. In any case, the two 'poles' of Marx's discourse are represented by politics and the critique of political economy, dimensions that are connected but also in possible reciprocal tension, each of them marked by a constitutive ambivalence. Indeed, the critique of political economy has a political character, since it is conducted from the standpoint of the proletariat: labour-power, *qua* the set of physical and intellectual dispositions that exist in the corporeality of the individual worker and are thus impossible to separate from this corporeality, potentially constitutes a form of resistance to the 'dead mechanism' of capital. At the same time, precisely because of its general character, Marx's critique is partly autonomous from politics, being a conceptual mechanism. And while politics is, on the one hand, connected to the critique of political economy and not purely voluntaristic, on the other hand it cannot immediately be deduced from this critique. This complex relationship between the critique of political economy and politics, as well as the wider relationship between theory and practice, is of central importance to examining the question of the common – which is never resolved once and for all – and its relationship with the aforementioned Paris Commune, rural commune, and the community linked to the state-form.

At root, Marx was attempting to articulate communism politically, on the basis of an intersection between movement and organisation. On the one hand, this meant the 'real movement which abolishes the present state of things' (as the *German Ideology* puts it) with its explosive implications: in Mephistophelian terms, 'all that exists deserves to perish'. On the other hand, over the years the need for political organisation became ever more clear in Marx's works, with the scope of preventing struggles from dispersing without the conquests that they had achieved being 'sedimented': that is to say, 'establishing' the *jacquerie* and constructing a radically new scenario. But the relationship between movement and organisation (or, in more articulated terms, between working class, political movement, political power, and communist society) must be interpreted not in the sense of a succession of stages, from a first purely 'destructive' phase to a second, 'constructive' one. On the contrary, there was a continual interweaving of these elements, in the sense that if the movement is political in character then it must already contain an organisational dimension, a line of march, a horizon towards which it moves. And for Marx the organisation cannot be configured as a negation of the 'movementist' impulse, but rather must try to keep open an 'expansive' dynamic starting from a transformative practice.

At the centre of the political perspective delineated in this book is the singularity–common plexus, based on the attempt to go beyond the specific modality with which the relationship between the individual and collective subjects has been effected within the capitalist order. In this latter order, starting from an individualist presupposition we arrive at the subjection of individuals to the social power of money and capital. Yet the delineation of a scenario different from the 'present state of things' and the articulation of the common must escape any form of 'naturalism': the common is not already given, is not rooted in the structure of things, and does not refer back to some hypostatised past order.

Moreover, it is configured as a movement that is critical of the 'present state of things' and thus cannot be identified with a specific existing community, this latter inevitably being connected to the state-form. But such a theoretical and political tension must not approximate to any sort of ahistorical model, defined once for all time, irrespective of the distinctive traits of the present conjuncture. *Capital* itself ought not be interpreted in a 'theoreticist' manner, since it is continually traversed by the historical dimension: in particular, the central chapters of Volume I on co-operation, manufacture and big industry outline a history of capital, and at the same time a history of the class struggle in its 'metamorphic' character and variation across time and place. The common, which is very much historically rooted, does not constitute an abstract backdrop, yet at the same time it is not reducible to a purely artificial element. Rather, it is based on the concrete manner in which individuals relate to one another. Crucial, for grasping this element (and difficult to translate into other languages), is the term *Gemeinwesen*, 'common being', which as Engels also remarked in a letter cited at the beginning of my Introduction: 'We would therefore suggest that *Gemeinwesen* ['commonalty'] be universally substituted for *state*: it is a good old German word that can very well do service for the French "Commune".'[1] Thus the basis of the discourse developed in the present work is the dimension of the common: and this, in turn, is connected to the attempt to bring about a reciprocal interaction of the 'movementist' dynamic and the formation of an institution where that which unites singularities, their needs, capacities, and daily life, can achieve political articulation.

---

1 Cf. Introduction, p. 1.

References

AAVV 1972, 'Sul marxismo e le scienze', *Critica marxista*, 6.

———— 2002, *Beiträge zur Marx-Engels Forschung, Neue Folge 2002*, Berlin: Argument.

———— 2006, *Beiträge zur Marx-Engels Forschung, Neue Folge 2006, Karl Marx und die Naturwissenschaft im 19. Jahrhundert*, Berlin: Argument.

———— 2010, 'Communisme?', *Actuel Marx*, 48: 10–103.

Adorno, Theodor and Max Horkheimer 1999, *Dialectic of Enlightenment*, London: Verso.

Althusser, Louis 1969, *For Marx*, New York: Pantheon.

———— 1970, *Reading Capital*, London: NLB.

———— 2006, 'Marx in his limits', in *Philosophy of the Encounter: Later Writings 1978–1987*, London: Verso.

Anderson, Kevin 2010, *Marx at the Margins*, Chicago: University of Chicago Press.

Apter, Emily S. and William Pietz (eds.) 1993, *Fetishism as Cultural Discourse*, Ithaca, NY: Cornell University Press.

Arrighi, Giovanni 2007, *Adam Smith in Beijing. Lineages of the Twenty-First Century*, London: Verso.

Arthur, Christopher J. 2002, *The New Dialectic and Marx's 'Capital'*, Leiden: Brill.

Artous, Antoine 1999, *Marx, L'État et la politique*, Paris: Syllepse.

———— 2006, *Le fétichisme chez Marx. Le marxisme comme théorie critique*, Paris: Syllepse.

Assoun, Paul-Laurent 2002, *Le fétichisme*, Paris: PUF.

Axelos, Kostas 1965, *Marx penseur de la technique*, Paris: Minuit.

Backhaus, Hans Georg 1997, *Dialektik der Wertform*, Freiburg: Ça ira.

Badaloni, Nicola 1980, *Dialettica del capitale*, Rome: Editori Riuniti.

Badiou, Alain 1992, 'Philosophie et politique', in *Conditions*, Paris: Seuil.

———— 1998, *Abrégé de métapolitique*, Paris: Seuil.

———— 2003, *La Commune de Paris: Une déclaration politique sur la politique*, Paris: Les Conférences du Rouge-Gorge.

———— 2009, *L'hypothèse communiste*, Paris: Lignes.

Badiou, Alain and Slavoj Žižek (eds.) 2011, *L'idée du communisme, II*, Fécamp: Lignes.

Bakunin, Mikhail 1993, *Bakunin on Violence*, New York: Anarchist Switchboard.

———— 2007, *Ausgewählte Schriften, Konflikt mit Marx Teil 1*, edited by Wolfgang Eckhardt, Berlin: Kramer.

———— 2011, *Ausgewählte Schriften, Konflikt mit Marx Teil 2*, edited by Wolfgang Eckhardt, Berlin: Kramer.

Balibar, Étienne 1974, *Cinq études de materialisme historique*, Paris: Maspero.

———— 1976, *Sur la dictature du proletariat*, Paris: Maspero.

———— 1995, *The Philosophy of Marx*, London: Verso.

———— 1997, *La crainte des masses*, Paris: Galilée.

———— 2000, 'Quel communisme après le communisme'? in *Marx 2000*, edited by Stathis Kouvelakis, Paris: PUF.

———— 2001, 'Gewalt', in *Historisch-kritisches Wörterbuch des Marxismus, Band 5, Gegenöffentlichkeit bis Hegemonialapparat*, edited by Wolfgang Fritz Haug, Hamburg: Argument.

———— 2010, *Violence et civilité*, Paris: Galilée.

Balibar, Étienne and Toni Negri 2010, 'On the Common, Universality, and Communism', *Rethinking Marxism*, 22, 3.

Balibar, Étienne and Immanuel Wallerstein 1988, *Race nation classe. Les identités ambiguës*, Paris: La Découverte.

Balibar, Étienne, Cesare Luporini and André Tosel 1979, *Marx et sa critique de la politique*, Paris: Maspero.

Ball, Terence 1979, 'Marx and Darwin: A Reconsideration', *Political Theory*, 4: 469–83.

Banaji, Jairus 2010, *Theory as History. Essays on Modes of Production and Exploitation*, Leiden: Brill.

Barbier, Maurice 1992, *La pensée politique de Marx*, Paris: L'Harmattan.

Barker, Jeffrey H. 1986, *Individualism and Community. The State in Marx and Early Anarchism*, Westport, CT: Greenwood Press.

Barot, Emmanuel 2011, *Marx au pays des Soviets ou les deux visages du communisme*, Montreuil: La Ville Brûle.

Basso, Luca 2001, 'Critica dell'individualismo moderno e realizzazione del singolo nell'*Ideologia tedesca*', *Filosofia politica*, 2: 233–56.

———— 2008a, *Socialità e isolamento: la singolarità in Marx*, Rome: Carocci.

———— 2008b, 'Tra forme precapitalistiche e capitalism: il problema della società nei *Grundrisse*', in *La lunga accumulazione originaria. Politica e lavoro nel mercato mondiale*, edited by Devi Sacchetto and Massimiliano Tomba, Verona: ombre corte.

———— 2008/9, 'Marx: quale libertà', *Quaderni materialisti*, 7/8: 69–87.

———— 2009a, 'The ambivalence of "Gewalt" in Marx and Engels: On Balibar's Interpretation', *Historical Materialism*, 17, 2: 215–36.

———— 2009b, 'Feticismo e costituzione della soggettività nel *Capitale*', *Fenomenologia e società*, 4, 112–27.

———— 2009c, 'Politica e contingenza in Marx: il 1848' in *Verità, ideologia e politica*, edited by Fabio Frosini and Adriano Vinale, Naples: Cronopio.

———— 2010, 'Mercato mondiale e "movimento assoluto del divenire" nei "Grundrisse"', *Fenomenologia e società*, 3: 40–52.

———— 2012, *Marx and Singularity: From the Early Writings to the "Grundrisse"*, Leiden: Brill.

———— 2013, 'Rivoluzione francese e temporalità del soggetto collettivo: tra Sieyès e Marx', in *"Tempora multa". Il governo del tempo*, Milan/Udine: Mimesis.

Bellofiore, Riccardo, Guido Starosta and Peter D. Thomas (eds.) 2013, *In Marx's Laboratory. Critical Interpretations of the "Grundrisse"*, Leiden: Brill.

Bellue, Françoise 1989, 'La critique du fétichisme, point d'articulation du gnoseologique et de l'anthropologique dans *Le Capital*', in *Antropologia, prassi, emancipazione. Problemi del marxismo*, edited by Georges Labica, Domenico Losurdo and Jacques Texier, Urbino: Quattroventi.

Benot, Yves 2003, *La modernité de l'esclavage. Essai sur la servitude au coeur du capitalisme*, Paris: La Découverte.

Bensaïd Daniel 1995, *Marx l'intempestif. Grandeurs et misères d'une aventure critique*, Paris: Fayard.

Bensussan, Gérard 2007, *Marx le sortant. Un pensée en excès*, Paris: Hermann.

Berger, Denis 2003, 'Marx et la révolution' in *Marx contemporain*, Paris: Syllepse.

Bhabha, Homi 1994, *The Location of Culture*, London: Routledge.

Bidet, Jacques 1985, *Que faire du "Capital"? Matériaux pour un refoundation*, Paris: Klincksieck.

Biral, Alessandro 1987, 'Hobbes: la società senza governo', in *Il contratto sociale nella filosofia politica moderna*, edited by Giuseppe Duso, Bologna: Il Mulino.

Blackburn, Robin 1997, *The Making of New World Slavery. From Baroque to the Modern 1492–1800*, London: Verso.

Bobbio, Norberto 1976, *Quale socialismo? Discussione di un'alternativa*, Turin: Einaudi.

———— 1997, *Né con Marx né senza Marx*, Rome: Riuniti.

Bohlender, Matthias 2010, 'Herrschaft der Gedanken. Über Funktionsweise, Effekt und die Produktionsbedingungen von Ideologie', in Karl Marx and Friedrich Engels, *Die deutsche Ideologie*, Berlin: Akademie Verlag.

Bologna, Sergio 1973, 'Moneta e crisi: Marx corrispondente per la "New York Daily Tribune"', *Primo maggio*, 1: 1–14.

Bonefeld, Werner 2001, 'The Permanence of Primitive Accumulation: Commodity Fetishism and Social Constitution', *The Commoner*, 2.

Bongiovanni, Bruno 1989, *Le repliche della storia. Karl Marx fra la rivoluzione francese e la critica della politica*, Turin: Bollati Boringhieri.

Borkenau, Franz 1980, *Der Übergang vom feudalen zum bürgerlichen Weltbild*, Darmstadt: Wissenschaftliche Buchgesellschaft.

Borrelli, Gianfranco 2000, 'Marx e la critica della politica dal "Manifesto" al "Capitale"', *Diritto e cultura*, 10: 81–100.

Brosses, Charles de 1988 [1760], *Du culte des dieux fétiches, ou Parallèle de l'ancienne réligion de l'Egypte avec la réligion actuelle de Nigritie*, Paris: Fayard.

Brown, Heather A. 2012, *Marx on Gender and the Family: A Critical Study*, Leiden: Brill.

Burgio, Alberto 2000, *Strutture e catastrofi. Kant Hegel Marx*, Rome: Editori Riuniti.

Capograssi Colognesi, Luigi 2009, 'Presentazione' in Karl Marx, *Quaderni antropologici*, Milan: Unicopli.

Carandini, Andrea 1979, *L'anatomia della scimmia. La formazione economica della società prima del capitale*, Turin: Einaudi.

Castoriadis, Cornelius 1975, *L'institution imaginaire de la société*, Paris: Seuil.

Certeau, Michel de 1998, *The Capture of Speech and Other Political Writings*, Minnesota: University of Minnesota Press.

Chakrabarty, Dipesh 2000, *Provincialising Europe. Postcolonial Thought and Historical Difference*, Princeton: Princeton University Press.

Chignola, Sandro 2004, *Fragile cristallo. Per la storia del concetto di società*, Naples: Editoriale Scientifica.

————— 2014, *Foucault oltre Foucault. Una politica della filosofia*, Roma:DeriveApprodi.

Cohen, Gerald A. 1978, *Marx's Theory of History. A Defence*, Oxford: Clarendon.

Cole, George D.H. 1954, *A History of Socialist Thought*, II, London: Macmillan.

Colletti, Luciano 1973, *Il marxismo e Hegel*, Bari: Laterza.

————— 2011, *Il paradosso del "Capitale"*, Rome: liberal edizioni.

Cotten, Jean-Pierre 1982, 'La notion d'individu social', *La Pensée*, 228: 73–82.

————— 1993, 'Le statut des techniques dans l'oeuvre de Marx', *Philosophique*, 29–65.

Cowling, Mark and James Martin (eds.) 2002, *Marx's "Eighteenth Brumaire". (Post)modern Interpretations*, London: Pluto.

Curcio, Anna and Ceren Özselçuk (eds.) 2010 'The Common and the Forms of the Commune', *Rethinking Marxism*, 22, 3.

Dardot, Pierre and Christian Laval 2012, *Marx, prénom: Karl*, Paris: Gallimard.

————— 2014, *Commun. Essai sur la révolution au XXIe siècle*, Paris: La Découverte.

Debord, Guy 1979, *La société du spectacle*, Paris: Buchet/Chastel.

Deleuze, Gilles and Félix Guattari 1972, *L'anti-Oedipe*, Paris: de Minuit.

De Palma, Armando 1971, *Le macchine e l'industria da Smith a Marx*, Turin: Einaudi.

Della Volpe, Galvano 1964, *Rousseau e Marx e altri saggi di critica materialistica*, Rome: Editori Riuniti.

Di Marco, Giuseppe Antonio 1984, *Marx Nietzsche Weber*, Naples: Guida.

————— 2005, *Dalla soggezione all'emancipazione umana. Proletariato, individuo sociale, libera individualità in Karl Marx*, Soveria Mannelli: Rubbettino.

Dimoulis, Dimitri and John Milios 2004, 'Commodity Fetishism vs. Capital Fetishism. Marxist Interpretation vis-à-vis Marx's Analyses in "Capital"', *Historical Materialism*, 13, 3: 3–42.

Dörig, Johann Anton (ed.) 1960, *Marx contra Rußland*, Tübingen: Seewald Verlag.

Douzinas, Costas and Slavoj Žižek (eds.) 2011, *The Idea of Communism*, London: Verso.

Draper, Hal 1987, *The 'Dictatorship of the Proletariat' from Marx to Lenin*, New York: Monthly Review Press.

Ducange, Jean-Numa and Mohamed Fayçal Touati 2010, *Marx, l'histoire et les revolutions*, Lassay-les-Châteaux: La Ville Brûle.

Duso, Giuseppe 1988, *La rappresentanza. Un problema di filosofia politica*, Milan: Franco Angeli.

———— 1999, *La logica del potere. Storia concettuale come filosofia politica*, Bari: Laterza.

Dussel, Enrique 2009, *El último Marx (1863–1882) y la liberación latinoamericana*, Mexico City: Siglo XXI.

Eckhardt, Wolfgang 2011, 'Einleitung' in Bakunin 2011.

Elster, Jon 1985, *Making Sense of Marx*, Cambridge: Cambridge University Press.

Erckenbrecht, Ulrich 1976, *Das Geheimnis des Fetichismus*, Frankfurt: Europäische Verlagsanstalt.

Faber, Karl-Georg, Karl-Heinz Ilting and Christian Meier 1972–90, 'Macht-Gewalt' in *Geschichtliche Grundbegriffe. Historisches Lexicon zur politisch-sozialen Sprache in Deutschland, Band 3*, Stuttgart: Klett-Cotta.

Fanon, Frantz 1963, *The Wretched of the Earth*, New York: Grove Press.

———— 1967, *Black Skin, White Masks*, New York: Grove Press.

Federici, Silvia 2004, *Caliban and the Witch*, New York: Autonomedia.

Ferrari Bravo, Luciano 2001 [1975], 'Vecchie e nuove questioni nella teoria dell'imperialismo', in *Dal fordismo alla globalizzazione*, Rome: manifestolibri.

Fiaschi, Giovanni 2014, *Il desiderio del Leviatano. Immaginazione e potere in Thomas Hobbes*, Soveria Mannelli: Rubbettino.

Finelli, Roberto 1987, *Astrazione e dialettica dal Romanticismo al capitalismo*, Rome: Bulzoni.

———— 2014, *Un parricidio compiuto. Il confronto finale di Marx con Hegel*, Milan: Jaca Book.

Fischbach, Franck 2009a, *Sans objet. Capitalisme, subjectivité, aliénation*, Paris: Vrin.

———— 2009b, *Comment le capital capture le temps*, in Franck Fischbach (ed.) *Marx. Relire "Le Capital"*, Paris, PUF.

Fogel, Robert W. 1989, *Without Consent or Contract. The Rise and Fall of American Slavery*, London: W.W. Norton.

Foraboschi, Politta 2009, 'Introduzione' in Karl Marx, *Quaderni antropologici*, Milan: Unicopli.

Foucault, Michel 2003, *Society Must be Defended*, New York: Picador.

Frosini, Fabio 2009, *Da Gramsci a Marx. Ideologia, verità e politica*, Rome: DeriveApprodi.

Fumagalli, Andrea and Sandro Mezzadra (eds.) 2009, *Crisi dell'economia globale. Mercati finanziari, lotte sociali e Nuovi scenari politici*, Verona: ombre corte.

Gambino, Ferruccio 2003, *Migranti nella tempesta*, Verona: ombre corte.

Garo, Isabelle 2000a, *Marx, une critique de la philosophie*, Paris: Seuil.

———— 2000b, 'Le fétichisme de la marchandise chez Marx entre réligion, philosophie et économie politique', in *Marx 2000*, edited by Stathis Kouvelakis, Paris: PUF.

———— 2012, *Marx et l'invention historique*, Paris: Syllepse.

Geierhos, Wolfgang 1977, *Vera Zasulič und die russische revolutionäre Bewegung*, Munich: Oldenbourg.

Geras, Norman 1971, 'Essence and Appearance: Aspects of Fetishism in Marx's "Capital"', *New Left Review* I/65: 69–85.

Gilbert, Alan 1981, *Marx's Politics. Communists and Citizens*, New Brunswick, NJ: Rutger University Press.

Gitermann, Valentin 1945, *Geschichte Rußlands*, Vol. 2, Zürich: Büchergilde Gutenberg.

Godelier, Maurice 1973, *Horizon, trajets marxistes en anthropologie*, Paris: Maspero.

———— 1975, *Rapports de production, mythes, société*, Paris: Maspero.

Godelier, Maurice and Lucien Sève 1970, *Marixsmo e strutturalismo. Un dibattito a due voci sui fondamenti delle scienze sociali*, Turin: Einaudi.

Goldmann, Lucien 1970, *Marxisme et sciences humaines*, Paris: Gallimard.

Goux, Jean-Joseph 1973, *Freud, Marx: économie et symbolique*, Paris: Seuil.

Graham, Keith 1992, *Karl Marx: Our Contemporary. Social Theory for a Post-Leninist World*, New York: Harvester Wheatsheaf.

Gramsci, Antonio 1971, *Selections from the Prison Notebooks*, New York: International Publishers.

Griese, Anneliese 2006, 'Die geologischen, mineralogischen und agrochemischen Exzerpte von Marx im Vergleich mit seinen chemischen Manuskripten. Ein Beitrag zu ihrer wissenschaftshistorischen Einordnung', in AAVV 2006.

Griese, Anneliese and Hans Jörg Sandkühler (eds.) 1997, *Karl Marx. Zwischen Philosophie und Naturwissenschaften*, Frankfurt: Peter Lang.

Guerraggio, Angelo 1982, 'Lo strumento matematico in Marx' in Angelo Guerraggio and Ferdinando Vidoni, *Nel laboratorio di Marx: scienze naturali e matematica*, Milan: FrancoAngeli.

Guha, Ranajit and Gayatri Chakravorty Spivak 1988, *Selected Subaltern Studies*, Oxford: Oxford University Press.

Haber, Stéphane 2007, *L'aliénation*, Paris: PUF.

———— 2008, 'Quelques remarques sur la critique de l'argent au début du livre I du "Capital" de Marx', in *Marx – l'image*, Annales Littéraires de l'Université de Franche-Comté, Philosophique 2008, Besançon: Presses Universitaries de Franche-Comté.

Hardt, Michael and Antonio Negri 2001, *Empire*, Cambridge, MA: Harvard University Press.

———— 2010, *Commonwealth*, Cambridge, MA: Harvard University Press.

Harvey, David 2003, *The New Imperialism*, Oxford: Oxford University Press.

———— 2010a, *The Enigma of Capital and the Crises of Capitalism*, Oxford: Oxford University Press.

———— 2010b, *A Companion to Marx's Capital*, London: Verso.

Hatem, Jad 2006, *Marx, philosophe du mal*, Paris: L'Harmattan.

Heinrich, Michael 2004, *Kritik der politischen Ökonomie. Eine Einführung*, Stuttgart: Schmetterling Verlag.

———— 2008, *Wie das Marxsche "Kapital" lesen?*, Stuttgart: Schmetterling Verlag.

Heyer, Paul 1982, *Nature, Human Nature, and Society. Marx, Darwin, Biology and the Human Sciences*, Westport, CT: Greenwood Press.

Hindess, Barry and Paul Hirst 1977, *Mode of Production and Social Formation. An Auto-Critique of "Pre-Capitalist Modes of Production"*, Atlantic Highlands, NJ: Humanities Press.

Hobbes, Thomas 1996, *Leviathan*, edited by Crawford B. Macpherson, Harmondsworth: Penguin Books.

———— 2011, *Leviathan*, revised edition, Buffalo, NY: Broadview.

Hobsbawm, Eric J. 1965, 'Introduction', in Karl Marx, *Pre-capitalist Economic Formations*, London: Lawrence and Wishart.

———— 1978, 'Gli aspetti politici della transizione dal capitalismo al socialismo', in *Storia del marxismo*, Vol. I, Turin: Einaudi.

Hobsbawm, Eric J. and Terence Ranger 1983, *The Invention of Tradition*, Turin: Einaudi.

Honneth, Axel 2005, *Verdinglichung*, Frankfurt: Suhrkamp.

Iacono, Alfonso Maurizio 1982, *Il Borghese e il selvaggio. L'immagine dell'uomo isolato nei paradigmi di Defoe, Turgot e Adam Smith*, Milan: Franco Angeli.

———— 1985, *Teorie del feticismo: il problema filosofico e storico di un "immense malinteso"*, Milan: Giuffré.

———— 2009, 'Postfazione' in Karl Marx, *Quaderni antropologici*, Milan: Unicopli.

Ilyenkov, Evald 1982, 'The Dialectics of the Abstract and Concrete in Marx's Capital', Moscow: Progress.

Jäckel, Peter 1997, 'Aktualisierte Übersicht über die naturwissenschaftlichen Exzerpte von Karl Marx (1846 bis 1882)', in Griese and Sandkühler (eds.) 1997.

Jaffe, Hosea 2007, *Davanti al colonialismo: Engels, Marx e il marxismo*, Milan: Jaca Book.

Jameson, Fredric 2014, *Representing Capital: A Commentary on the Volume One*, London: Verso.

Jánoska, Judith (ed.) 1994, *Des 'Methodenkapitel' von Karl Marx. Ein historischer und systematischer Kommentar*, Basel: Schwabe & Co.

Karatani, Kojin 2003, *Transcritique. On Kant and Marx*, Cambridge-London: The MIT Press.

Kofman, Sarah 1998, *Camera Obscura of Ideology*, Ithaca, NY: Cornell University Press.

Koselleck, Reinhart 1979, *Vergangene Zukunft*, Frankfurt: Suhrkamp.

Kouvelakis, Stathis 2003, *Philosophy and Revolution*, London: Verso.

Krader, Lawrence 1966, *Anthropology and the Early Law*, London: Basic Books.

———— 1972, 'Introduction', in Marx 1972.

———— 1976, *Ethnologie und Anthropologie bei Marx*, Frankfurt: Ullstein.

———— 1978, 'Evoluzione, rivoluzione e Stato: Marx e il pensiero ethnologico', in AAVV *Storia del marxismo*, Vol. 1, Turin: Einaudi.

Krätke, Michael 2003, ' "Hier bricht das Manuskript ab" (Engels). Hat das "Kapital" einen Schluß?' in AAVV 2002.

Krahl, Hans-Jürgen 1971, *Konstitution und Klassenkämpfe*, Frankfurt: Verlag Neue Kritik.

Krüger, Peter 2006, 'Vor-Lesen und Nach-Schreiben: Zur Methode der Marxschen Rezeption geologischer Literatur', in AAVV 2006.

Labica, Georges 2008, *Théorie de la violence*, Paris: Vrin.

Lacan, Jacques 1975, *Séminaire. Livre XX. Encore 1972–1973*, Paris: Seuil.

Laclau, Ernesto and Chantal Mouffe 1989, *Hegemony and Socialist Strategy*, London: Verso.

Lassalle, Ferdinand 1893, *Reden und Schriften*, Berlin: Vorwärts.

Lebowitz, Michael A. 2003 [1993], *Beyond "Capital". Marx's Political Economy of the Working Class*, Basingstoke: Palgrave Macmillan.

Lecourt, Domnique 1992, 'Marx in the Sieve of Darwin', *Rethinking Marxism*, 5, 4: 6–28.

Lefebvre, Henri 1965, *La proclamation de la Commune: 26 mars 1871*, Paris: Gallimard.

———— 1976, *De l'État. 2. Théorie marxiste de l'État de Hegel à Mao*, Paris: Union Générale d'Éditions.

———— 1980, *Une pensée devenue monde. Faut-il abandonner Marx?*, Paris: Fayard.

———— 2002, *The Critique of Everyday Life*, Volume II, London: Verso.

Lefort, Claude 1978, *Les forms de l'histoire. Essais d'anthropologie politique*, Paris: Gallimard.

Lenin, Vladimir 1932, *State and Revolution*, New York: International Publishers.

———— 1956, *The Development of Capitalism in Russia*, Moscow: Progress.

———— 1969, *What is to be Done?*, New York: International Publishers.

Lévi-Strauss, Claude 1960, *Tristes tropiques*, Paris: Plon.

———— 1963–76, *Structural Anthropology*, New York: Basic Books.

Lichtheim, George 1988 [1963], 'Marx and the "Asiatic Mode of Production" ', in *Interpretations of Marx*, edited by Tom Bottomore, Oxford: Blackwell.

Linden, Marcel van der 2005, 'Plädoyer für eine historische Neubestimmung der Weltarbeiterklasse', *Sozialgeschichte*, 20: 7–28.

Löwy, Michael 2003 [1970], *The Theory of Revolution in the Young Marx*, Leiden: Brill.

Lohmann, Georg 1991, *Indifferenz und Gesellschaft. Eine kritische Auseinandersetzung mit Marx*, Frankfurt: Suhrkamp.

Lucas, Erhard 1964, 'Marx' und Engels' Auseinandersetzung mit Darwin', *International Review of Social History*: 433–69.

Lukács, György 1971, *History and Class Consciousness*, Cambridge, MA: MIT Press.

Lukes, Steven 1985, *Marxism and Morality*, Oxford: Clarendon.

Luxemburg, Rosa 2003, *The Accumulation of Capital*, London: Routledge.

Macherey, Pierre 1965, 'À propos du processus d'exposition du "Capital"', in *Lire le "Capital"*, Vol. 1, Paris: Maspero.

———— 2014, *Le sujet des normes*, Paris: Editions Amsterdam.

Macpherson, Crawford B. 1962, *The Political Theory of Possessive Individualism*, Oxford: Clarendon.

Maffi, Bruno 2008, 'Prefazione', in Karl Marx, *India, China, Russia*, Milan: Il Saggiatore.

Maguire, John M. 1978, *Marx's Theory of Politics*, Cambridge: Cambridge University Press.

Maihofer, Andrea 1992, *Das Recht bei Marx*, Baden-Baden: Nomos-Verlag.

Maine, Henry Sumner 1931, *Ancient Law: Its Connection with the Early History of Society and Its Relation to Modern Ideas*, London: Oxford University Press.

Marx, Karl 1968, *Matematiceskie rukopisi*, Moscow: Izd. Nauka.

———— 1972, *The Ethnological Notebooks of Karl Marx*, edited by Lawrence Krader, Assen: Van Gorcum.

———— 1981, *Die technologisch-historischen Exzerpte*, edited by Hans-Peter Müller, Frankfurt: Ullstein.

———— 1999, *Naturwissenschaftliche Exzerpte und Notizen*, in MEGA, IV, 31.

———— 2011, *Exzerpte und Notizen sur Geologie, Mineralogie und Agrikulturchemie*, in MEGA, IV, 26.

Marx, Karl and Friedrich Engels 2008, *Inventer l'inconnu. Textes et correspondances autour de la Commune*, Paris: La Fabrique.

Matarrese, Francesco 1975, 'Introduzione' in Karl Marx, *Manoscritti matematici*, Bari: Dedalo.

McCarthy, George E. 1990, *Marx and the Ancients. Classical Ethics, Social Justice and Nineteenth Century Political Economy*, London: Rowman and Littlefield.

Meikle, Scott 1985, *Essentialism in the Thought of Karl Marx*, London: Duckworth.

Meillassoux, Claude 1975, *L'economia della savana*, Milan: Feltrinelli.

Mészáros, István 1970, *Marx's Theory of Alienation*, London: Merlin.

Mezzadra, Sandro 2001, *Diritto di fuga. Migrazioni, cittadinanza, globalizzazione*, Verona: ombre corte.

———— 2008a, *La condizione postcoloniale*, Verona: ombre corte.

———— 2008b, 'La "cosiddetta" accumulazione originaria', in AAVV, *Lessico marxiano*, Rome: manifestolibri.

———— 2014, *Nei cantieri marxiani. Il soggetto e la sua produzione*, Rome: manifestolibri.

Mezzadra, Sandro and Maurizio Ricciardi 2002, 'Introduzione' in *Marx. Antologia degli scritti politici*, Rome: Carocci.

Michaud, Jean-Claude 1960, *Teoria e storia nel "Capitale" di Marx*, Milan: Feltrinelli.

Micocci, Andrea 2009, *The Metaphysics of Capitalism*, Lanham, MD: Lexington.

Morgan, Lewis Henry 1877, *Ancient Society*, London: Macmillan.

Moulier Boutang, Yann 1998, *De l'esclavage au salariat*, Paris: PUF.

Müller, Hans-Peter 1981, 'Materialismus und Technologie bei Karl Marx', in Marx 1981.

Nancy, Jean-Luc 1996, *Être singulier pluriel*, Paris: Galilée.

———— 2008, *Vérité de la démocratie*, Paris: Galilée.

Natalizi, Marco 2006, *Il caso Cernysevskij*, Milan: Bruno Mondadori.

Negri, Antonio 1970, *Descartes politico o della ragionevole ideologia*, Milan: Feltrinelli.

———— 1991, *Marx beyond Marx*, London: Pluto Press.

———— 1992, *Il potere costituente*, Carnago: SugarCo.

———— 2006, *Il libri del rogo*, Rome: DeriveApprodi.

Nimtz, August 2003, *Marx, Tocqueville and Race in America*, Lanham, MD: Lexington.

Ollmann, Bertell 1971, *Alienation. Marx's Conception of Man in Capitalist Society*, Cambridge: Cambridge University Press.

Panzieri, Raniero 1961, 'Sull'uso capitalistico delle macchine nel neocapitalismo', *Quaderni Rossi*, 1: 53–72.

Pappenheim, Fritz 1959, *The Alienation of Modern Man*, New York: Monthly Review Press.

Pashukanis, Evgenii 1978, *Law and Marxism: A General Theory*, London: Ink Links.

Patterson, Thomas Carl 2009, *Karl Marx, Anthropologist*, Oxford: Berg.

Perfahl, Brigitte 1982, *Marx oder Lassalle? Zur ideologischen Position der österreichischen Arbeiterbewegung 1869–1889*, Vienna: Europaverlag.

Petrucciani, Stefano 2009, *Marx*, Rome: Carocci.

Piccinini, Mario 1999, 'Potere comune e rappresentanza in Thomas Hobbes' in *Il potere. Per la storia della filosofia politica moderna*, edited by Giuseppe Duso, Rome: Carocci.

———— 2003, *Tra legge e contratto: una lettura di "Ancient Law" di Henry S. Maine*, Milan: Giuffré.

Pike, Jonathan E. 1999, *From Aristotle to Marx*, Aldershot: Ashgate.

Poggio, Pier Paolo 1978, *Comune contadina e rivoluzione in Russia. L'obščina*, Milan: Jaca Book.

Ponzio, Augusto 1975, 'Introduzione' in Karl Marx, *Manoscritti matematici*, Bari: Dedalo.

Postone, Moishe 1993, *Time, Labor and Social Domination: a Reinterpretation of Marx's Critical Theory*, Cambridge: Cambridge University Press.

Ragionieri, Ernesto 1968, *Il marxismo e l'Internazionale*, Rome: Riuniti.

Raimondi, Fabio 2004 'L'impensabile politica di Althusser', in Louis Althusser, *Marx nei suoi limiti*, edited by Fabio Raimondi, Milan: Mimesis.

———— 2011, *Il custode del vuoto. Contingenza e ideologia nel materialismo radicale di Louis Althusser*, Verona: ombre corte.

Raimondi, Fabio and Maurizio Ricciardi (eds.) 2004, *Lavoro migrante. Esperienza e prospettiva*, Rome: DeriveApprodi.

Ramm, Thilo 2004, *Ferdinand Lassalle. Der Revolutionär und das Recht*, Berlin: Berliner Wissenschafts-Verlag.

Rancière, Jacques 1965, 'Le concept de critique et la critique de l'économie politique des "Manuscrits de 1844" au "Capital"', in *Lire le "Capital"*, Vol. 1, Paris: Maspero.

———— 1995a, *La mésentente*, Paris: Galilée.

———— 1995b, *On the Shores of Politics*, London: Verso.

Read, Jason 2003, *The Micro-Politics of Capital. Marx and the Prehistory of the Present*, Albany, NY: SUNY.

Reichelt, Helmut 1970, *Zur logischen Struktur des Kapitalbegriffs bei Karl Marx*, Frankfurt: Europäische Verlag.

———— 2008, *Die Marx-Neue-Lektüre*, Hamburg: VSA Verlag.

Renault, Emmanuel 1995, *Marx et l'idée de critique*, Paris: PUF.

———— 2008, *Souffrances sociales. Philosophie, psychologie et politique*, Paris: La Découverte.

Ricciardi, Maurizio 2001, *Rivoluzione*, Bologna: Il Mulino.

———— 2010, *La società come ordine*, Macerata: Eum.

Roemer, John (ed.) 1986, *Analytical Marxism*, Cambridge: Cambridge University Press.

Rosdolsky, Roman 1992, *The Making of Marx's Capital*, London: Pluto.

Roseberry, William 1997, 'Marx and Anthropology', *Annual Review of Anthropology*, 26: 25–46.

Ross, Kristin 2015, *Communal Luxury: The Political Immaginary of the Paris Commune*, London: Verso.

Rossanda, Rossana (ed.) 2000, *Il Manifesto del Partito Comunista 150 anni dopo*, Rome: manifestolibri.

Roth, Karl Heinz 1974, *Die 'andere' Arbeiterbewegung und die Entwicklung der kapitalistischen Repression von 1880 bis zur Gegenwart*, Munich: Trikont.

Rougerie, Jacques (ed.) 1964, *Procès des communards*, Paris: Julliard.

———— 1971, *Paris libre 1871*, Paris: Seuil.

Rovatti, Pier Aldo 1973, *Critica e scientificità in Marx*, Milan: Feltrinelli.

Sacchetto, Devi 2004, *Il Nordest e il suo Oriente*, Verona: ombre corte.

Sacchetto, Devi and Massimiliano Tomba (eds.) 2008, *La lunga accumulazione originaria*, Verona: ombre corte.

Said, Edward 1978, *Orientalism*, London: Routledge.

Sanyal, Kalyan 2007, *Rethinking Capitalist Development*, London: Routledge.

Sartre, Jean-Paul 1972a, 'L'anthropologie', in *Situations IX – Mélanges*, Paris: Gallimard.

———— 1972b, 'Masses, spontanéité, parti', in *Situations IX - Mélanges*, Paris: Gallimard.

———— 1991, *Critique of Dialectical Reason*, London: Verso.

Sayers, Sean 2011, *Marx and Alienation. Essays on Hegelian Themes*, Houndmills, Basingstoke: Palgrave Macmillan.

Schiera, Pierangelo 1987, *Il laboratorio borghese: scienza e politica nella Germania dell'Ottocento*, Bologna: Il Mulino.

Schmidt, Alfred 1962, *Der Begriff der Natur in der Lehre von Marx*, Frankfurt: Europäische Verlag.

Schwartz, Nancy L. 1979, 'Distinction between Public and Private Life. Marx on the "zoon politikon"', *Political Theory*, 2: 245–66.

Schwarz, Winfried 1978, *Vom "Rohentwurf" zum "Kapital". Die Strukturgeschichte des Marxschen Hauptwerkes*, Berlin: Verlag das Europäische Buch.

Screpanti, Ernesto 2007, *Comunismo libertario. Marx, Engels e l'economia politica della liberazione*, Rome: manifestolibri.

Sereni, Paul 2007, *Marx: la personne et la chose*, Paris: L'Harmattan.

————— 2010a, *La communauté en question. Tome 1, Chose publique et bien commun chez Marx*, Paris: L'Harmattan.

————— 2010b, *La communauté en question. Tome 2, Marx, l'association et la liberté*, Paris: L'Harmattan.

Sève, Lucien 1969, *Marxisme et théorie de la personnalité*, Paris: Éditions Sociales.

Shanin, Teodor (ed.) 1983, *Late Marx and the Russian Road. Marx and the Peripheries of Capitalism*, London: Routledge.

Smith, Adam 1976, *An Inquiry into the Nature and Causes of the Wealth of Nations*, in *The Glasgow Edition of the Works and Correspondence of Adam Smith*, Vol. 2, Oxford: Clarendon.

Sofri, Gianni 1969, *Il modo di produzione asiatico. Storia di una controversia marxista*, Turin: Einaudi.

Spivak, Gayatri Chakravorty 1999, *A Critique of Post-Colonial Reason*, Cambridge, MA: Harvard University Press.

Steinberg, Hans-Joseph 1979, 'Il partito e la formazione dell'ortodossia marxista', in *Storia del marxismo*, Vol. II, Turin: Einaudi.

Sylvers, Malcolm 2004 'Marx, Engels und die USA – Ein Forschungsprojekt über ein wenig beachtetes Thema', *Marx-Engels Jahrbuch*, 2004: 31–53.

Terray, Emmanuel 1969, *Le marxisme devant les sociétés primitives: deux études*, Paris: Maspero.

Texier, Jacques 1998, 'Révolution et démocratie chez Marx et Engels', in *Actuel Marx*, Paris: PUF.

Thomas, Josef G. 1987, *Sache und Bestimmung der Marx'schen Wissenschaft. Hobbes-Hegel-Marx*, Frankfurt: Peter Lang.

Thomas, Peter 2009, *The Gramscian Moment. Philosophy, Hegemony and Marxism*, Leiden: Brill.

Thompson, Edward P. 1963, *The Making of the English Working Class*, Harmondsworth: Penguin.

Thorner, Daniel 1966, 'Marx on India and the Asiatic Mode of Production', *Contributions to Indian Sociology*, 9: 33–66.

Tomba, Massimiliano 2010, 'Tempi storici della crisi nel mercato mondiale a partire dalla "Marx renaissance"', *Fenomenologia e società*, 2: 53–71.

———— 2011, *Strati di tempo. Karl Marx materialista storico*, Milan: Jaca Book.

Tomich, Dale 2004, *Through the Prism of Slavery. Labor, Capital and World Economy*, London: Rowman and Littlefield.

Tort, Patrick 2006, *Marx et le problème de l'idéologie*, Paris: L'Harmattan.

Toscano, Alberto 2007, 'Marxism Expatriated. Alain Badiou's Turn', in *Critical Companion to Contemporary Marxism*, edited by Jacques Bidet and Stathis Kouvelakis, Leiden: Brill.

Tosel, André 1995, 'Marx et le rationalisme politique', *La Pensée*, 303: 35–45.

———— 1996, *Études sur Marx (et Engels). Vers un communisme de la finitude*, Paris: Kimé.

Touboul, Hervé 2004, *Marx, Engels et la question de l'individu*, Paris: PUF.

———— 2010, *Chemins de Marx*, Paris: Les Presses du réel.

Tronti, Mario 1980 [1966], *Operai e capitale*, Turin: Einaudi.

———— 2008, 'Classe', in *Lessico marxiano*, Rome: manifestolibri.

Tvardovskaja, Valentina A. 1975, *Il populismo russo: da "Zemlja i volja" a "Narodnaja volja"*, Rome: Editori Riuniti.

Vadée, Michel 1992, *Marx penseur du possible*, Paris: Klincksieck.

Vanzulli, Marco 2008, 'Presentazione' in Karl Marx and Friedrich Engels, *Opere*, Vol. XXII, Naples: Città del Sole.

———— 2009, 'Marx e la politica dell'Internazionale alla Conferenza di Londra del 1871', in *Marx e la storia*, edited by Carlo Antonio Barberini, Milan: Unicopli.

Venturi, Franco 1972, *Il populismo russo*, Turin: Einaudi.

Vidoni, Ferdinando 1982, 'Ruolo delle scienze naturali nel pensiero marxiano', in *Nel laboratorio di Marx: scienze naturali e matematica*, Milan: Franco Angeli.

———— 1985, *Natura e storia. Marx e Engels interpreti del darwinismo*, Bari: Dedalo.

Vilar, Pierre 1978, 'Marx e la storia', in *Storia del marxismo*, Vol. I, Turin: Einaudi.

Vincent, Jean-Marie 1973, *Fétichisme et société*, Paris: Anthropos.

Vinci, Paolo 2011, *La forma filosofia in Marx. Dalla critica dell'ideologia alla critica dell'economia politica*, Rome: manifestolibri.

Virno, Paolo 2002, *Grammatica della moltitudine. Per un'analisi delle forme di vita contemporanee*, Rome: DeriveApprodi.

———— 2015 [1999], *Déja Vu and the End of History*, London: Verso.

———— 2008, 'Cooperazione', in *Lessico marxiano*, Roma: manifestolibri.

Visentin, Stefano 2009, 'Verità e visibilità della politica in Rancière et Badiou', in *Verità ideologia politica*, edited by Fabio Frosini and Adriano Vinale, Naples: Cronopio.

Vygotsky, Vitaly 1965, *Istoria odnogo velikogo otkrytiya Karla Marxa*, Moscow: Mysl.

Walicki, Andrzej 1969, *The Controversy over Capitalism: Studies in the Social Philosophy of the Russian Populists*, Oxford: Clarendon.

Weiner, Robert 1982, *Das Amerikabild von Karl Marx*, Bonn: Bouvier.

Wendling, Amy E. 2009, *Karl Marx on Technology and Alienation*, Houndsmills, Basingstoke: Palgrave Macmillan.

Winch, Donald 1978, *Adam Smith's Politics. An Essay in Historiographic Revision*, Cambridge: Cambridge University Press.

Wood, Allen W. 1986, 'Marx and Equality', in Roemer (ed.) 1986.

Wolf, Frieder Otto 2009, *Radikale Philosophie. Aufklärung und Befreiung in der neuen Zeit*, Münster: Westfälisches Dampfboot.

Young, Robert C. 2001, *Postcolonialism: An Historical Introduction*, Oxford: Blackwell.

Zanini, Adelino 1997, *Adam Smith. Economia morale diritto*, Milan: Mondadori.

Žižek, Slavoj 2004, *Revolution at the Gates*, London: Verso.

——— 2008, *In Defence of Lost Causes*, London: Verso.

Index